ethnic dress

Executive Art Editor	**Larraine Shamwana**
Project Manager	**Mary Lambert**
Art Editor	**Geoff Fennell**
Copy Editor	**Chris Morley**
Production	**Christine Campbell**
Map Illustrations	**Kevin Hart**
Picture Research	**Anna Smith, Emily Hedges and Julia Ruxton**
Design Director	**Jacqui Small**
Executive Editor	**Judith More**

First published in Great Britain in 1994 by Mitchell Beazley,
an imprint of Reed Consumer Books Limited

Facts On File, Inc.
460 Park Avenue South
New York NY 10016

Library of Congress Cataloging-in-Publication Data
Kennett, Frances.
    Ethnic dress / Frances Kennett
       p. cm
    Includes bibliographical references and index.
    ISBN 0-8160-3136-3 (acid-free paper)
    1. Costume.   I. Title.
GT511.K46 1995
391--dc20   94-37638
                                                 CIP

_ _ 10 9 8 7 6 5 4 3 2 1

This book is printed on acid-free paper.

Typeset in Caslon 540 Roman 10/13pt and Caslon 3 italic 8/11
Colour reproduction and printing by Mandarin Offset (Singapore)
Printed and bound in China

ethnic dress

Frances Kennett

with

Caroline MacDonald-Haig

Facts On File®

AN INFOBASE HOLDINGS COMPANY

Contents

INTRODUCTION

ABOVE: A girl of the Palaung people, Burma, one of many hill tribes living in inaccessible regions. They maintain a virtually intact traditional way of life, including making by hand their textiles and clothes.

ABOVE: Quechua Indians living in Peru. Although Catholic by faith, they attend a Sun Festival with roots in Inca beliefs. Local culture can be kept alive in ritual and dress even after conquest and colonization.

ABOVE: Women's finery in many societies indicates dowry expectations when single, and displays status and prosperity after marriage, as with this Rajput mother, decked in gold, in North India.

This book celebrates the dress of people who do not adhere to the trends of westernized fashion. It is intended to be a source of inspiration, to point to general themes and principles, and to be illustrative rather than definitive.

A significant social change at the end of the 20th century is the worldwide concern with identity. It leads to nationalism at worst, global cooperation at best. Clothing plays its part. It is not just a matter of protection or convenience, but is full of value and meaning. This fragile but brilliant aspect of culture reinforces social ties and reflects beliefs. As one American scholar, Gail Altermann, has observed, cloth is a cultural document. In dress, you can read the history of a people, their conquests and defeats, their religious beliefs, their values, and their trade.

There is a widespread need for community among all peoples. Sharing in celebration is one of the key ways that different social groups, ethnic minorities, or the emerging nations keep a sense of who they are.

It can take three forms. Firstly, dressing up is part of any festive occasion. In eastern Europe, for example, folk dress is undergoing a much-studied revival at numerous cultural events. Secondly, national dress provides a way for many countries of the world to find out who they were, so as to know what they might become. Ukrainian emigrés return to their homeland from America with a rich store of conserved information about their regional dress and customs that would otherwise have been lost. Thirdly, older nation-states such as Japan and Korea are beginning to reappraise and appreciate their traditional costume, instead of pursuing a policy of "westernization" without a backward glance.

There is a growing realization that people do not flourish without the "regulation" that traditional life once offered. Regulation can be positive, a means of validating life. While keeping customs, such as dress codes, members of society are given scope to express individuality *within certain precise confines*. The overriding concern is to have respect for, and affirm the cumulative experience of, generations: to show that you are a part of a continuum. The renowned costume historian Angela Bradshaw writes on dress:

"The importance of decoration in costume cannot be overemphasized, for it reveals with freedom and natural charm many aspects of the life and customs of a country and its people."

Definitions of ethnic, traditional, or folk – even dress or costume – can be contentious and are the proper concern of academics. Margaret Mead provides a useful explanation of the term "culture:" "It consists of ideas, rather than things."

In general this book looks at dress that is worn everyday, and for festivals and holidays.

craft jewelry is a significant part of enriching identity. Is it fashion or ethnic dress?

It used to appear as if fashionable, westernized clothing would eventually spread throughout the world. There are signs that this may not happen. Fashion can become a leveler rather than a means to express individuality, when we "consume" it, rather than clothe ourselves with it. When "fashion" is followed regardless of body shape, social situation, suitability of color or cloth, the mass production of westernized fashion makes us uniform, not unified.

tourists relieve or exacerbate the predicament of indigenous people?

The fleeting image of an African tribesman is unforgettable: a marginalized nomad, he wears grease and ocher paste on his skin and a loincloth, but he sleeps on a headrest to protect his elaborate, clay-molded hairstyle with its macramé feather holder set on top. With minimal goods he expresses the dignity of who he is.

Christian Feest has written on the native arts of North America: "Forms of decorations of ethnic art tend to be a mixture of

ABOVE: *The Ainu are one of the oldest indigenous people of Japan. Their culture is attracting much attention in a highly developed country that is re-evaluating and conserving its own traditions in a unique way.*

ABOVE: *Certain techniques such as silk making, cotton spinning,* ikat *weaving, batik dyeing, and embroidery, occur widely in ethnic dress. These men are wearing* chapans, ikat *men's robes, in Tashkent, Uzbekistan.*

ABOVE: *In contrast to the highly skilled peoples in the world, there are nomadic groups who employ primitive technology like the Masai of Kenya. They keep complex rules for hairstyles, body decoration and jewelry.*

Religious dress is generally excluded, but there are exceptions, such as the clothing worn in the sacred kingdom of Bhutan.

Elsewhere in the world, "ethnic roots" are being reinvented. In the Bahamas the Junkanoo street festival has been imported from the Caribbean. Although it is not part of the island's own history it gives young people some locally valid means of expression: a chance to design, paint, sing, and come together constructively. This can help balance the general dissatisfaction young people feel with their lives, which compares unfavorably with prosperous foreign visitors.

Carnival costume is another focus of culture in the West Indies. In Trinidad, a reinterpretation of the indigenous motifs in clothing, tie-dye, or in painted textiles and

There are wonderful exceptions to westernized dress. This book looks at the surviving minorities where old traditions, once deemed primitive, have never been lost – and which are now being accorded a new respect. Anthropologist Walter Fairservis wrote in 1971: "As western man tries to develop what he labels 'undeveloped' or 'emerging,' he slaughters native cultures by the dozens."

In the 1990's, minority groups are, in theory, better protected, but there is the question of tourism, which poses various threats. Minorities all over the world are persecuted while their very cultures are appropriated and exploited for national symbolism and tourism. Ethnic artefacts are the primary sources of the "local color" that travelers throughout the world enjoy, but do

native traditions and foreign expectations, sufficiently native to be recognized as exotic and sufficiently foreign to be acceptable to the buyer." There are many forms of "ethnic dress" on display worldwide that are the sartorial equivalent of such art.

Adaptation of costume is not a new phenomenon. Ethnic dress is continually evolving. North American Indians gave up doing time-consuming quillwork when the Portuguese traders brought them beautiful glass beads. Yet no one would consider the Native American beadwork inauthentic. Madeleine Ginsburg, a costume expert, formerly of the Victoria and Albert Museum in London, helpfully encouraged us with the reminder that all around the world, traditional dress "is constantly reinventing itself."

NORTH AMERICA

Throughout North America a large number of people wear the traditional costume of their family's country of origin for holidays. Many of these costumes are replicas of clothing brought from the Old World. The festive dress of, say, a New York Ukrainian community will, therefore, stand close comparison to its native counterpart (see pages 112–121). Among Native Americans, too, traditional costume is generally reserved for special occasions, although some groups find theirs practical for activities such as hunting, for example. Only a small minority of Americans, notably the Amish, habitually wear, almost unaltered, their traditional dress.

Not included in this chapter, for lack of space, is the way in which the process of maintaining an identity continues among modern refugees and the immigrants to North America. Textile manufacturers from Cambodia, for example, have continued their tradition of silk weaving to supply the needs of their own small communities, generating interest from museum curators and other craft experts.

The origins of the first inhabitants of the Americas go back more than 15,000 years. There are even signs of habitation dated by some experts as early as 45,000 BC. The original settlers came across the Bering Strait to Alaska from Asia, and from there spread downward through what is now Canada and the United States, and then into Central and Latin America.

The Arctic peoples – the Inuit and the Aleut – are related but distinct. The Aleut are considered to be a true Mongoloid people, whereas the Inuits and Native Americans are of Asian or mixed origin.

ABOVE: **A Navajo Indian woman wearing silver and turquoise jewelry, wrapped in a colored geometric-patterned blanket.**

OPPOSITE: **The arrival of the horse caused a dramatic change in Indian lifestyles. Costumes were adapted from long robes to short tunics, vests and leggings.**

Some Indian tribes – the Ahtena, Chipewyan, Ingalik, and Montagnais – settled in the Arctic region. The Northwest Coast is the home of the Tlingit and Chilkat, among others.

One of the most iconic images to emerge from native Indians of the Southwest is the feather-bonneted warrior galloping across an endless plain teeming with buffalo. However, this character represents only a small part of a huge range of native groupings in this area. The Plains Indians were originally nomadic people living in numerous distinct and scattered groups, with quite different culture patterns, customs, and languages. The arrival of the horse in this region in the late 17th century, brought by the Spanish conquistadores, unified their lifestyles and created new confederacies. Some of the offspring of Spanish cavalry and pack animals ran wild, spreading rapidly across the Plains area. It took only 75 years after Cortés landed in Mexico in 1519, for the South Plains Indians to become knowledgeable horse breeders. There were also technical adaptations: bows and arrows were shortened for use from the saddle, and dress was made for riding.

Indian costume at its peak was divided into three general types, elements of which are still apparent in the clothing worn by American Indians today. These are everyday clothing, war attire, and ceremonial dress, in which the ornamentation is more elaborate and symbolic.

Form and designs were handed down through generations. It is interesting how the common origin of indigenous North and South Americans is revealed in elements of their dress. For example, the featherwork of Southwest Indians is not far removed from the artifacts of the pre-Columbian Indians of Mexico and Peru. Similarly, there is the same lineage in the turkey-feather mantles of the American Southwest peoples and the mosaic featherwork of Mayan Indians.

There are other enduring links: Southwest Indians always traded with distant cultures for unusual items to use in their costumes. Europeans' goods (such as glass beads from Venice and Prague) were acceptable to them because they had a well-established and sophisticated taste for the colorful and unusual.

Inuits and Aleuts

Although western-style clothing is worn by most Arctic peoples for everyday wear, many prefer traditional clothes for cold-weather hunting because they are better for keeping the wearer warm and dry. Down and quilting are not as warm as a caribou parka and trousers, or fur-lined boots and gloves. The technique of manufacture, as old as the hunt itself, shows how people have made good use of natural resources in these extreme conditions. For example, boots are made of caribou or bearded seal-skin, called *ugurulik* by the Inuits. The soles are made of the waterproof hide of bearded seal. The hair is removed and the skin softened in water so that it can be bent up and crimped to caribou-skin uppers. The uppers themselves are made from the caribou leg skin: one boot would traditionally require the skin from all four legs of a caribou. Sewing is now done with nylon dental floss, but braided sinew would have been used in the old days, and is still used on the finest custom-made pairs. For inland hunting another kind of boot, called a *tuttulik*, is worn; this has soles made from caribou skin. In both cases, the boots are treated with seal oil to make them waterproof.

The parka, or traditional *atigi*, is worn by both sexes and by children. It too is made of caribou fur, worn with the hair inside and skin outside. The trim around the hood is always wolverine, because it sheds frost easily and does not get clogged with snow when the wind is up. When hunting, Inuits wear a cloth cover over the hood to protect the skin and particularly the seams; it is usually white for camouflage. Sometimes a chin protector, made of strips of caribou

RIGHT: **This Inuit hunter in Greenland wears the style of clothing that is found throughout the Arctic Circle and which is perfectly adapted, by long years of use, to the traditional hunting life. The parka, or** atigi, **is worn by both sexes and children, and is traditionally made of caribou fur. The trim around the hood is usually wolverine, because it sheds frost readily. The hunter is also wearing hide leggings, though these are nowadays often replaced by army-surplus pants with woolen leggings underneath. The hunter will also have fur mittens and a cloth cover, to protect the seam stitching of his parka.**

OPPOSITE BELOW: **These Inuit children dress in traditional fur clothing at an outpost camp on Baffin Island, N.W.T, Canada. Their parkas are scaled-down versions of adult clothing. In the towns they would be more likely to wear westernized clothing. Many other craft traditions of the Inuit have disappeared – among them the netted fabric women made for carrying game, a decorative form of netted beadwork used for clothing, and, among the Athapascas of the western subarctic region, a technique of woven quillwork.**

hide is also tied over the hood, while home-made knitted headbands or caps are worn inside it. At one time gloves and other accessories would be hand-embroidered with caribou hair, sinew, and wool in special motifs thought to bring luck to the hunt and protect the hunter from harm or evil spirits. In earlier times, bird-skin parkas could be found – cormorant being popular because it was very waterproof – but these too are no longer worn. Nowadays, a rope or cloth belt is slipped over a parka to keep in body warmth, and as a place to keep the hunting knife.

The manufacture of all Arctic hunting clothes draws on an exact knowledge of the qualities of different furs. All fur dries much quicker than any other material. Sealskin and polar bear skin are waterproof and are used for the long mittens worn when setting traps: the fur can be used to brush snow over the trap and conceal it. In emergencies the mittens can be used as extra

ABOVE: **An Inuit mother with her child in a fur hood at Baffin Island, Canada. Nowadays, hides are imported to the Arctic to supplement the local supply of materials. These include alpaca and sheepskin from South America and reindeer hide from Siberia.**

socks to prevent frostbite. Wristlets are also made of sealskin or polar bear fur to cover the gap between the glove and sleeve.

Trade has made other types of hide available. Rubber boots are used in the fishing and whaling industry and for daily wear, but not for hunting.

Women's clothing follows much the same lines as men's, except that they traditionally wore a long jumper, rather than trousers. Trousers have now been adopted because of practicality. Younger girls wear western-style slacks and jeans with parkas in the towns and settlements because it is cheaper and more fashionable. Some western-style clothing is better adapted for local use; among these are the quilted *amautik* parkas of the Inuit, which are commercially made with a large baby carrier to be worn on a parent's back, and with a passing resemblance in the stitched braid trimming to the hand-made embroidered ribbons of the past.

Indians of the Southwest

When looking at Native American costume, the focus is inevitably on the Southwest – Arizona, New Mexico, and south Colorado – because that is where the largest concentration of handicrafts and traditional dress is to be found. About 10 percent of all the 1.5 million American Indians in the United States live in the state of Arizona. Cultural differences between native groups, such as the Navajo, Hopi, Apache, Pueblo, and Yaqui, still exist. Clothing in southwest America has developed more than in other regions because its tribes were first to adopt new clothing materials in preference to traditional bark and plant fibers (such as yucca), and native hides of deer and antelope. In the 16th century the Spaniards gave sheep (not looms, as is generally believed) to the Pueblo people, who in turn introduced them to the Navajo. From there the art of weaving wool spread to other tribes. In fact, the Pueblo had used small, horizontal looms to weave cotton fiber since the 12th century. Comparatively isolated from the westward progress of the Europeans, the indigenous people of the Southwest were able to incorporate certain elements of Hispanic and other European cultures without their own being over-

BELOW: Inter-tribal gatherings, powwows, are an important means of reinforcing tribal identity for contemporary Indians. This dance group at a gathering in New Mexico displays every aspect of Indian decorative art: beadwork for headbands and belts; featherwork for headdresses; hide work for leggings. The ketoh *or wrist bowguard is now purely decorative.*

whelmed as happened in the Eastern states.

The history of weaving and of the Navajo blanket has been the subject of much academic discussion. It appears that weaving was originally a male activity among the Pueblo, but was then taken up by Navajo and Zuñi women. From 1650 to 1868, the classic Navajo period, cotton was replaced by wool, and the most accomplished work was achieved. The Navajo sold their products to other tribes and to the Spanish. The Navajo took to weaving rectangular *serapes*, or cloaks, as well as their traditional clothing and during the 19th century they made textiles for their own use (called "chief's blankets"), as well as other designs for trade.

In the work of the late 19th century, a poorer quality of wool is found, although the Navajo blanket still remained the leading textile product for much of southwestern North America.

At the turn of the century, the influence of white traders and the outside market was considerable, with all kinds of innovative techniques and "inauthentic" designs were incorporated into the work. This development is a subject of debate among purists,

but, as in other countries, "traditional dress" and artifacts are never static, but open to change – in fact, such adaptations are necessary for the survival of indigenous people.

Today, standard dress for the Navajo man is a cotton check shirt and straight-leg jeans, accompanied by a turquoise-stone necktie and a Stetson hat.

Traditional female dress was the *bil*, or blanket dress, made of two oblong handwoven pieces tied at one shoulder, and held in place with a belt. Today, women wear long skirts, stitched in three gathered tiers, and a blouse with tucks on the front, long cuffed sleeves, and a leather or handwoven belt. Women keep their hair long and tie it back with white yarn skeins. The crowning feature of the Navajo costume is jewelry: heavy silver pieces, encrusted with stones, predominately turquoise, in many traditional designs. Ancient turquoise mines are found all over the Southwest and in Mexico.

The Navajo learned silversmithing from the Spanish, and since the 1920s Navajo silver has been famous. The craft has developed rapidly since the 1970s, with the increasing interest in ethnic design.

Festivals and inter-tribal ceremonies – such as the buffalo dance – are the places to see the finest displays of costume and dancing. The buffalo dance traditionally assured good fortune in the hunt and is still performed today on Christmas Day among the Pueblo in New Mexico. Old elements of dress are revitalized with new embellishments in dance costumes.

In the crown dance of the San Carlos Apaches, for example, a participant has been recorded as wearing a Venus war motif painted on his chest. Two different styles of eagles, were applied to his elaborate, fanshaped, light-wood headdress, and he also wore a fringed wrap skirt that was made from hide.

Navajo men attending such events wear knee bands and moccasins in place of western-style boots. Dancers may wear a vestige of past times: the *ketoh*, or bow guard, which is a wide leather strap worn as a wrist cover, but now purely decorative. Belts, worn by both sexes, are called *concha* (meaning shell), derived from the horse trappings of the Spanish. A *concha* consists of silver ornaments mounted onto a leather

strap, with fetishistic motifs, such as clan animals, bears and eagles, engraved on them. Navajo *concha* are separated by studded butterfly shapes. Women often wear such belts for display over their handwoven sashes.

Next to the *concha*, the most coveted piece of jewelry of a Navajo woman is the "squash blossom" necklace, traditionally a sign of fertility. The motif was adopted from the Spanish, who in turn borrowed it from Islamic tradition. Young women may wear western clothing normally, but they add these distinctive accessories and reserve traditional finery for special days.

"Pueblo" was the name given by the Spaniards to the flat-roofed dwellings of the people of the Southwest. The original clothing of the Pueblo people bore a technical resemblance to the *huipil* of the Indians of Guatemala, which consisted of a piece of fabric folded in two in order to make the front and back of a tunic, without shoulder seams and with a slit neck.

Pueblo women have worn their traditional garment, the *manta*, for 400 years. It is made from three strips of fabric dyed in natural brown, black, or blue colors and stitched together in horizontal seams, selvage to selvage, to form a piece long enough to reach from shoulder to mid-calf. After contact with Europeans, Pueblo women adopted an under-dress as a concession to the standards of "decency" that were required by the puritanical newcomers.

For special ceremonies the *manta* is worn on its own as originally intended, or more commonly over store-bought blouses and skirts, but tied in the traditional manner over the right shoulder. During these occasions, male dancers wear an older costume: a kilt, sometimes fastened with large turquoise or silver pins, worn with no more than strings of beads on the torso. Stylized motifs on the kilt symbolize rain, clouds, or growing crops in red, black, and white.

Apache people live in small groups in Arizona, New Mexico, and Oklahoma. The Spaniards called them Apache – a variation of the Zuñi word for enemy. Originally wearers of skin garments, they were among the first people to abandon these because the demands of constant warfare precluded hunting and the time-consuming preparations of the skins. Traded cloth and the styles of European pioneers were adopted instead. Apache women wear a loose, yoked top decorated with rickrack and other braids

BELOW: A Pueblo woman dressed for the traditional basket dance wears a manta, one of the few remaining indigenous clothing shapes. Now it is used only for ceremonials, and store-bought fabric pieces with red or green for the borders are commonly used.

ABOVE: A dancer at a powwow in Sqylax, British Columbia, Canada, wears a vest of plastic beading reviving the style of the authentic quillwork that has long been abandoned because of the time and effort it took to make.

over a tiered skirt. Skin painting was, and is, still reserved for ceremonial purposes.

The Seminole Indians of Florida were once part of the Creek Confederacy, known in the early records of the United States government as the "Five Civilized Tribes": Cherokee, Choctaw, Creek, Chickasaw, and Seminole. In 1859 they formed a federation and were given territory to the west of the Mississippi, present-day Oklahoma. Many of them resisted the move, however, and retreated into swampland, now the site of the Florida reservations.

The development of Seminole clothing follows the same pattern observed above: originally they wove Spanish moss, then later adopted skins for tunics. Distinct from other indigenous groups, the Seminole began to work with fabric scraps in the 1830s, during the Seminole wars, to make patchwork clothing – a matter of necessity at a time of deprivation.

In common with peoples of the East Coast and Great Lakes area, who came into contact with the British and French forces, the Seminoles adopted a coat shape based on the European soldiers' greatcoat and, in preference to a feathered headdress they wore a turban with a small crest of feathers. Later additions of European inspiration

were the ruffles added to the coat collar and the use of epaulettes. Modern ruffled and yoked Seminole men's shirts also show their European origin, but unlike other North American Indian costumes, the Seminoles' has changed markedly this century and is still evolving. Women wear a loose robe gathered onto a round, narrow neck yoke, with long sleeves, over a long ample skirt. Satin is the preferred fabric.

The Iroquois League was a group of native peoples, the Onondaga, Mohawk, Oneida, Cayuga, Seneca, and Tuscaroa, who lived in New York State, forming a protective alliance in 1570. They sided with the British in the Revolutionary War and on their defeat many were exiled to Canada, where some descendants live. Originally, the women wore a wraparound deerskin skirt and quillwork top, but this was superseded by tradecloth and beadwork.

In the 19th century the Iroquois adopted pioneer-style dress, with an unusual feature of a drape effect at the back, in imitation of a British official's coat. Until recently, this style had largely been abandoned, the Iroquois people assuming the dress of the predominant Plains Indians for ceremonial occasions. But the original dress is now beginning to return.

BELOW: A Seminole Indian man of Florida wears the distinctive jacket with yoke (and sometimes added epaulettes) derived from the shapes of European military coats of the 18th century. A simple cloth is also worn as a headcovering.

Indians of the Plains and the Northwest

The Plains Indians occupied a v-shaped chunk of the United States and Canada that started in the provinces of Saskatchewan and Alberta and went down to Montana, across to Minnesota and south to Colorado, Kansas, Oklahoma, and Texas.

The dress style of the Plains Indians is what is generally regarded as typical of the Native American. The basic garment is the skin dress or robe, which in common with all nomadic, hunting societies, makes the maximum use of the skin available. This outfit incorporates a wide yoke shape that forms a drape sleeve and has a loose fit in the body. Sleeves were cut differently to distinguish individual groups. The decoration around the hem also varied, from cowrie shells to embroidery and beadwork.

Robes were worn by both men and women, but they had different designs with the men favoring the "black bonnet" motif of concentric, feather-shaped circles. Fur-less hides were worn in summer. Buffalo robes lined with fur were worn by men both as a practical garment and as a visual record of their hunting and warrior exploits, details of which were painted on the skin.

Men also wore a short shirt or a vest (argued by some as the first European shape to be adopted by the Native American) decorated with native quillwork. Leggings, breechcloth, and moccasins then completed the outfit.

Religious practice was important to Indian peoples. For example, the Sioux of the Great Plains had seven major rites, the most

important of which was the Sun Dance, which is still performed by them today. Special garments decorated with mystical motifs have always been made for specifically ritual purposes.

During the late 19th century, a great reawakening of Plains culture took place, and the Ghost Dance was created. During this dance, participants would go into a trance state, communicate with their ancestors, and later recount their experiences. A unique garment, the ghost dress, came into being, with many of the ritual motifs from other objects, such as hide war shields, painted on it by men. Women did not make or touch certain ritual objects, as this was believed to reduce their potency. These dresses are highly prized collectors' pieces and important artifacts of Native American culture. Many other accessories, including rawhide containers, leggings, mittens, caps, and bags, were richly decorated with painting, beading, or fringing.

Face painting has always been part of the Great Plains Indians' customs. Mineral pigments are mixed with water and grease and applied with fingers, twigs, or feathers. Face painting has various significance and is applied for rituals, as an expression of mood, for the recording of a ceremonial event, or as a protective measure.

Blanket robes were worn widely among the Plains Indians, again painted with the deeds of the wearer. The blanket robe has a "language" akin to that of the fan. There is meaning in how it is worn and who is invited to sit and warm themselves under it, and it can indicate status, among other things.

Plains Indians, in common with other groups, also wore a separate war costume. In general, when an Indian went to fight, he donned no more than his breechcloth, leggings, moccasins, and body paint. The war shirt was worn after battle by those in positions of authority and honor, and by chiefs and elder warriors. It was heavily fringed, beaded, embroidered, or painted and was considered to have great "medicine" and to offer protection to the wearer.

Featherwork has always been an art form of immense variety among all the Indian peoples. It was used for many headdresses besides the famous swept-back bonnet of the Plains Indians: for dancing masks and bustles, for trimming drums and spears, and in making *kachina* or ancestor dolls.

New designs are created for the numerous dance festivals and other congresses that take place all over North America – growing inventiveness mirroring how strongly the Native Americans not only preserve but also pursue their own values.

What is now thought of as the classic feather bonnet belonged firstly to the Sioux and other peoples. However, many tribes did not wear feathers as flamboyantly as the Great Plains people: a single feather might have sufficed as an acknowledgment of an Indian's bravery.

On the northwest coast of Canada, a broad-brimmed basket hat gave better protection from the rain, while woodland

ABOVE: **A Crow Indian wears a typical Great Plains war costume: breechcloth, leggings, moccasins, and beads.**

BELOW: **A Blackfoot chief participates in a congress at Edmonton, Canada. The quillwork of his vest is a revival of the styles once common to many Indian groups. Trade beads were admired by native craftsmen and soon replaced quills, as they were varied, colorful, and quick to work.**

tribesmen of British Columbia wore fur caps, sometimes decorated with feathers. One style incorporated a tube of bone, in which a single upright feather rotated as the wearer walked.

Today, the use of feathers is in dispute, because the traditional styles put endangered species of birds at risk. However, a limited amount of high-quality featherwork is still allowed to be made.

In Canada, the northwest coastal tribespeople are most noted for their woodcarving skill. Their traditional garments were minimal, and were woven from cedar-bark fiber. The Salish have a long tradition of twining (fine basketry), and produced a textile-like material that was a mixture of vegetal fibers and goat or dog hair. The Salish are still making textiles, but they now also use commercial yarns.

The Chilkat Indians also made a blanket that consisted of woven bark and mountain sheep wool, which they then supplied to other peoples.

The Europeans also brought trade blankets with them, and these were readily adopted in the Northwest. The finest examples from this region are called "button blankets," after the mother-of-pearl decoration that was added to them. Appliqué borders in red flannel are also a feature of Northwest blankets.

A wool blanket coat, or *capote*, is also typical of north Californian and Columbian groups; trade blankets supplied by the Hudson's Bay Company were cut up and made into a sleeved jacket with hood. Other types of blankets, which were imported into the country, found particular favor among the Navajo Indians.

Moccasins have persisted as a potent symbol of the Native American. Hand-sewn moccasins were cut and decorated in different styles to show the wearer's tribe (in warfare a warrior might wear another tribe's moccasins to confuse his trackers).

Underlining the traditional symbolic significance of Native American clothing, Marz and Nono Minor write in *The American Craft Book* that: "It was believed that moccasins must be made beautiful, because the foot should be as lovely as the flowers and grasses it walked upon. The earth must see that the Indian was not unmindful of her."

The Amish

ABOVE: *The rules governing dress in Amish communities also extend to the children. The 18th-century-style bonnets are worn by all females, young and old, and solid-color fabrics in subdued shades are preferred. Older women may wear brighter aprons and lighter, white lawn bonnets.*

LEFT AND ABOVE: *A Mennonite man and some Amish boys, both wearing essentially the same clothing: wool trousers, fastened with buttons and held up with braces, and waistcoats and jackets that are secured with hooks and eyes. Straw or felt hats are always worn when outside the house.*

Amish communities are found primarily in Pennsylvania, Ohio, and Indiana, although there are smaller groups scattered around from Delaware to Missouri, in Oregon, and Ontario, Canada. These people are descended from the Swiss Amish, a group of dissenters from the Anabaptist movement. Both the Amish and the related Mennonite sects follow the idea of an utterly plain form of dress and living environment.

The sect migrated to North America from the German Palatinate over the period from 1727 to 1850. The Amish are unique in that they wear a costume that is frozen in time, whereas even the most isolated forms of communities are open to change and adaptation. Amish costume is unlikely to disappear because it is worn as an expression of faith and as a boundary between the Amish and outsiders, whom they term "the English." It evolved up to the Civil War period, but since then has remained virtually the same.

The Amish are divided into two groups, the Old Order being stricter than the ordinary Amish. The women wear long dresses with matching aprons and face-covering, 18th-century style bonnets, with black stockings and shoes. No patterned fabric or jewelry is allowed.

Men wear black broadfall trousers (buttoned rather than zipped), short jackets fastened with hooks and eyes (buttons, along with lapels, are considered ornamental), white or solid-colored shirts, and straw or felt hats. Traditionally, colors are subdued, although in this century vivid pinks, purples, and blues have now crept into the permitted range. Men are forbidden to grow mustaches, but are required to grow a beard after marriage.

It is in their household embroidery and quiltmaking that Amish women give expression to a love of color and design. Quilts made before the 1940s are now highly prized by American folk-art museums.

Motifs on the quilts illustrate different aspects of their faith: the star (symbolizing Christ's birth); the diamond (representing Christ the rock or diamond), and sunshine and shadow (the night of sin and guilt, the bright, shining light of Grace).

North America Map

There are interesting paradoxes in the costume of North American peoples. On the one hand, the costume of the indigenous Indian people was originally made from plant fibers, notably yucca, cedar bark, limited amounts of yarn from elk, dog, and other indigenous species, some cotton, and many hides. Farther north, furs formed the basis of clothing for Arctic hunting communities, such as the Inuit. Clothing consisted of simple unshaped long tunics and cloaks. In certain areas, rawhide was used more commonly. The arrival of the Spanish and other Europeans subsequently brought great technological change. The introduction and breeding of the horse led to a change of costume, with shorter tunics and leggings in place of robes. The introduction of sheep and the treadle loom to the Pueblo Indians by the Spanish brought woven blankets and other forms of dress to the various tribes, fanning out from the Southeast. Quillwork was native to the Americas; beadwork and in some areas ribbon appliqué developed with materials brought in by Europeans. *Wampum*, meaning string of white beads, was made from shells until the traders introduced glass. Native American clothing had three functions: work, war, and ritual.

The ritualistic or symbolic function is the only one of these still thriving today. It can be seen at intertribal gatherings or powwows. Originally an Algonquin word meaning medicine man, "powwow" was later applied to ceremonies invoking divine aid through incantations and dancing. Modern powwows celebrate Native American culture at its finest, vividly conveying its love of the land and often including superb displays of horsemanship.

The horse is also central to the abiding European immigrant costume – that of the western cowboy. His dress has many features that are similar to the Latin American *gaucho* or *huaso*: leather chaps, boots, belt, metal or silver spurs, and a Stetson hat. The Indian and the cowboy also wear check shirts and jackets whose patterns were in turn inspired by early Indian blanket weaves. Whereas the Latin American cowboy wears wide trousers, the North American one wears jeans.

An Inuit whaler wearing fur clothing in the Northwest Territories in Canada.

A Zuñi Indian girl at a ceremony held in Gallup, New Mexico.

A Crow Indian boy at a powwow in New Mexico.

ABOVE: *A Picuris Pueblo Indian performs in the Basket Dance for a tribal ceremony in New Mexico. He is dressed in a skirt wrap and moccasins.*

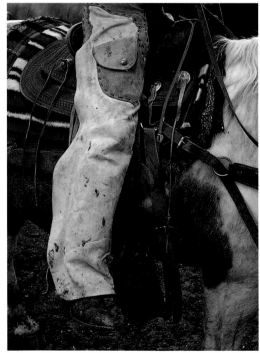

ABOVE: *A cowboy in a stockyard, Texas, wears standard western gear: jeans, chaps, and high-heeled boots. Spurs are also normal accessories.*

Key

Area covered by permanent ice

3,000 plus m (9,000 plus ft)

1,000–4,000m (3,000–12,000ft)

200–1,000m (600–3,000ft)

0–200m (0–600ft)

Sea, lakes and rivers

Note: peoples are shown in italics eg: *Picuris*

ARCTIC CIRCLE

ALASKA

Yupiks

Koyu

Inga

GREENLAND

Inuit

Inuit

Aleut

Inuit

upiat

hapascan

Tanana

Kutchin

itena

Tlingit

Haida

BRITISH
COLUMBIA

Bella Bella

Nootka

Salish

NORTH WEST TERRITORIES

Dene

Inuit

BAFFIN ISLAND

Inuit

Inuit

Inuit

CANADA

ALBERTA

Chipeywan

SASKATCHEWAN

Hudson
Bay

Inuit

Aleut

Chilkat
Salish
Montagnais

QUÉBEC

Bannouck

Ojibibwa

ONTARIO

Cree

Yahima

Nez Perce

OREGON

Bannock

MONTANA

Shoshone
Crow

UNITED STATES

MINNESOTA

Great Lakes

NEW
YORK

MASSACHUSETTS

Iroquois

PENNSYLVANIA

Amish

DELAWARE

CALIFORNIA

Ute

Zuñi

Hopi

Navajo

Yaqui

ARIZONA

Pueblo

Paiute

Cheyenne

Arapaho

COLORADO

Omaha

Pawnee

KANSAS

Picuris
Pueblo

NEW
MEXICO

Crow

Comanche

Apache

TEXAS

OKLAHOMA

Amish

INDIANA

OHIO

Mississippi

MISSOURI

Chickasaw
Creek
Choctaw

Natches

FLORIDA

Seminole

MEXICO

*An Inuit trapper of Canada
dressed in a fur-lined parka.*

*An Amish woman of
Massachusetts wearing a
regulation lace cap.*

*A Zuñi jewelry maker of
New Mexico.*

*A rodeo rider from Texas in
a typical cowboy outfit.*

21

NATIVE AMERICAN CRAFTS

TOP ROW, FROM LEFT TO RIGHT:

Zuñi rings and bracelets, including popular turquoise and other semi precious gemstones.

Canadian Indian wearing American eagle and Canadian maple leaf symbols in couched beadwork on a ceremonial costume.

San Juan Indian in New Mexico wearing beaded fringe and face paint.

Inuit woman of Pond Inlet, Baffin Island, Canada, wearing a garment of felt with cut appliqué work incorporating new and traditional motifs (beadwork copied from Arctic Indians).

A Buffalo dancer's woven waist sash decorated with a bird symbol and some feather decoration.

MIDDLE ROW, FROM LEFT TO RIGHT:

Cherokee Indian chief wearing a classic Plains Indian bonnet shape.

Navajo Indian of New Mexico, with a turquoise and garnet necklace.

Alaskan Inuit's dancing robe adorned with an appliqué of a couched beaded bear motif.

Zuñi jewelry including the popular "conch" motif on a leather belt.

Cherokee Indian boy with animal hair plume, beading, and face paint.

BOTTOM ROW, FROM LEFT TO RIGHT:

Beaded buckskin moccasins worn by a Kiowa chief's wife.

Zuñi woman carrying pot and and wearing traditional silver rings.

Indian in red flannel shirt and turquoise beads, at Gallup Ceremonial.

Indian woman of New Mexico at Gallup Ceremonial in satin blouse, with turquoise jewelry, carrying traditional pot.

San Juan Indian buffalo dancer's skirt pattern, with floating cloud motif on its border.

23

LATIN AMERICA

There are two principal layers of influence on the peoples of Latin America. First, the indigenous Indian cultures, ranging from the Maya of Central America to the Inca of Peru, and second, the influences of the colonizers (the Portuguese in Brazil and the Spanish in the rest of Central and South America) who began their incursions in the 16th century. Later waves of immigrants were of many nationalities: British, German, Italian, African, Asian-Indian, Japanese, and Middle Eastern. In some areas of Latin America, the native population was wiped out, initially by warfare and disease and later by genocide. It is estimated that since the colonization by the Europeans in South America, more than 20 million Indians have died. Whole tribes are still vanishing.

In *Arts of the Indian Americas*, Jamake Highwater estimates the total Indian population of North and South America to be somewhere in the region of 25 to 30 million. Only 1 million live in the United States and Canada, 3 million in Central America, and 10 million in the jungles of Bolivia and Peru. One million are spread through Brazil, Paraguay, Chile, Argentina, and Uruguay, while over 10 million pure- and mixed-blood Indians live in Mexico.

In comparison with the Indians of North America, the indigenous Latin Americans have had far less control over their own destiny. Even in those areas where ethnological organizations have tried to preserve cultural traditions, much of the effort comes from non-natives and foreigners. As Highwater notes: "The traveller in South America soon realizes that despite all the touristical pride in Indian heritage which bombards visitors, the Indians themselves are curiously,

ABOVE: This Kayapo man, from the Xingu region, Brazil, wears a macaw headdress, a famed Amerindian item.

OPPOSITE: Andean clothing mixes indigenous and western elements, as seen on this market seller, La Paz, Bolivia.

perhaps tragically, silent....The Indians who live in the major cities, such as Lima and Bogotá, are wretched and entirely demoralized." Jamake cites in particular the northwest coastal nations as the main strongholds of a "silent, native culture."

Mexico's record is better. The native people are Nahautl, Maya, and Zapotec and make up over eight percent of the population. Concerning Guatemala, where the Mayan Indians constitute approximately a third of the population, *The World Directory of Minorities 1991* comments: "In 1982, 10,000 Indians were killed in a massive counter-insurgency and 200,000 Mayan Indians fled the country. Ethnic discrimination is very basic: Indians are often equated with animals or subhumans and this state of affairs is made more insidious by state

proclamations of equality and concern for its Indian citizens. Maya culture is appropriated and exploited for national symbolism and tourism."

Sadly, Mayan Indians are still under threat, even though their colorful costumes and textiles are a major attraction for visitors to Guatemala. For Mayans to retain their ethnic dress in the face of economic and cultural discrimination can be seen as a gesture of defiance and survival.

A largely pre-Hispanic style of dressing persists among all the Indians, with many regional variations. In Central America, clothing is defined as pre-Columbian if it is made on the indigenous, narrow-width back-strap loom, and Spanish if made on the treadle loom, introduced by the Spaniards in the 16th century.

Many countries of Central America have both European and largely assimilated *mestizo* (people of mixed Indian and European parentage) populations. They now wear mainly western-style clothing that has a Spanish or Portuguese influence. Traditional costumes are likely to be colonial-style, and are worn only during festivals and special days. The people of Belize, Honduras, El Salvador, Nicaragua, and Panama fall into this category, as their indigenous peoples have either been wiped out or assimilated into the population.

Similarly, in the Caribbean islands of Cuba, Puerto Rico, and Hispaniola (Dominican Republic and Haiti), traditional dress is now rarely seen, with the exception of colonial-style Spanish or French costumes, which are worn for parties, carnivals, independence-day celebrations, and similar festive occasions.

Mexico and Central America

As has been noted elsewhere in this book, landscape is a great delineator of dress. In Mexico, the landscape varies from the high plateau or *altiplano* of Mexico City, site of the ancient Aztec capital Tenochtitlán, to the rugged rural highlands of the northern Sierra Madre del Sur. It also includes the deep valleys and tropical forests of the Chiapas to the southeast and the Yucatán peninsula, where descendants of the Maya live. Consequently, there are numerous regional differences in the dress.

Not only are there great distinctions between the lifestyles and costumes of rural and city populations, but differences can exist between villages separated by a single mountain range. More uniform costume is

worn by the very isolated Huichol people who live in the northwest mountain area, or the Tarahumara of the southeast Chiapas. Whatever the costume or region, it is in the

superior quality of workmanship, hand-spun yarn, ribbons and other trimmings, and the richness of costume design that women distinguish themselves – even if for the group there is a uniform "look." The use of traditional motifs is another way of identifying different groups or communities, and also represents a special link with the ancestors. (See page 33 for the Mayan symbolism notes under Guatemala.)

MEXICO

For Mexican men, the oldest form of costume was the loincloth, or *tagora*. Although it is fast disappearing today, it can be seen occasionally in remote areas. It is still found among the Tarahumara, who also decorate their face and body with white spots for

ABOVE MIDDLE: **Mexico's largely Indian population has continued a rich tradition of weaving and embroidery that reaches back to pre-Columbian times. These Masawas women wear vivid** quechquemitls, *an indigenous top garment originally worn without a blouse (which was introduced by the Spanish).* Quechquemitls *are woven on a narrow backstrap loom, and there are numerous ways of folding the strip cloth to make the neck opening.*

LEFT: **In an interesting parallel with male Muslim practice in the Middle and Far East, the wearing of pure white clothing among indigenous Indian peoples, such as these Mexicans in the Yucatán peninsula, is widespread in Latin America. Clean attire is seen as a religious observance, possibly attributable to the influence of the Catholic church in this region The symbolism of white worldwide is worth further study.**

festivities, and make feathered headdresses. Today, the Mexican Indian generally wears western clothing, such as jeans, shirts, and shorts, if he travels to town or farther afield for work, although Huichol men persist in wearing their white trousers and shirts even to visit Mexico City. However, Mexican Indians will revert to their traditional clothing in their home village.

The garment that supplanted the *tagora* was the European pair of trousers, called *calzoncillo*, which indicates its Spanish origin. The *calzoncillo* was traditionally homespun, but factory made cloth called *manta* is now widely used.

Trouser style varies from region to region. They may be cut with an insert at the crotch, wide and straight-legged, or full to the knee (Zacatepec men's trousers are short and embroidered with drawn thread work). Trousers may also be full and gathered in at the ankle, with a drawstring at the

ABOVE: *Tarahumara Indians formally dressed outside a church, Mexico, wearing long rectangular cloaks which are a vestige of the pre-Columbian drape. The Indian word for cloak among another group, the Otomi, is* tilmatli, *indicating its pre-Spanish origin. Tarahumaras wear theirs like the Navajo of North America, draped blanket-fashion. Their headbands are also a pre-Columbian detail.*

waist, or, more commonly, folded over and held by a broad sash. Handwoven sashes, sometimes wrapped twice, or one on top of another, as used by the Huichol, are then worn over the waist.

The top garment is the *cotón*, or shirt, and it has as many variations as the trousers. It may be handwoven, cut from a single piece of cloth the full loom-width, folded at the shoulder line, and cut at the center for a neck opening. Often the sides are left unstitched. This construction is exactly the same as that of the *huipil*, a pre-Columbian form of clothing (see also Guatemala on

page 31). Shirts with rectangular sleeves are added to this basic shape and are worn by many Tzotzil and Tzeltal groups. Sometimes two loom-widths are sewn together, so that the head opening falls on the central seam. Sleeves are embellished with embroidery at the cuffs. Sometimes the fold is made unevenly so that the back section is longer and forms a "tail." In southwest Mexico Oaxaca men wear handwoven, long-sleeved shirts with deep pleats at each front side, covered with fine drawn thread work and then embroidery using animal motifs.

There are some groups, such as the Lacandon of Naja, in which the men still wear the original longer *huipil* without trousers (this garment was formerly woven of bark cloth, but this has now been replaced by the store-bought *manta* cotton that is readily available).

Sometimes a front-opening, sleeveless wool vest, or *cotorina*, is worn. A cotton vest called a *colera* is worn by the men of Zinacantán. It is open at the front and made of two widths of red-and-white striped fabric with embroidery and fringed lower edges. However, in general the wool *serape* is still the accepted outer garment. Today, many are commercially made in factories, but the most coveted are still homemade on a treadle blanket loom. Designs indicate a person's region or village, but as always the picture is confused by skilled weavers who use the ideas of other craftsmen – particularly if there is a commercial or foreign tourist market for their goods.

In Chiapas state, southern Mexico, *serapes*, or cloaks, go by the name *chamarros*. Among the Maya people, traditional costume has largely disappeared, although their ring-woven blankets are some of the finest in Mexico and have become collectors' items. The blankets are made by winding warp threads around four vertical sticks for weaving, producing a complete circle of cloth, which when cut has two fringed ends. Tarahumara blankets are worn in the same fashion as among the North American Navajo – wrapped around the shoulders. Otomí men prefer a rectangular cloak, or *tilmatli*, which is a pre-Columbian garment.

It is common everywhere for men to carry the handwoven shoulder bags, or *morrales*. Many are still woven from vegetable-dyed yarns, and beautifully embroidered. A man

may have adopted western clothing, but will still wear his bag, which will identify his group and place of origin. Trimmings, pom-poms, ribbons, squirrels' tails, leaves, and flowers are all used to identify a particular group. Other identifiers are the Indian's adherence to thonged sandals (the *mestizo* has adopted the shoe) and the sombrero or straw hat. An Indian always covers his head outside his home, out of a sense of propriety.

In general, Mexican Indian women go barefoot, though occasionally they wear leather thonged or modern plastic sandals. There are two basic elements in women's clothing that are pre-Columbian. The first item is the *huipil*, a type of long blouse, found predominantly in southeast Mexico, and also among the Maya of Yucatán. The

older style of *huipil* tends to be very wide, using as many as four loom-widths of cloth, and has a central head-hole on a shoulder-line fold. Three widths are now the most common, as found in the Chiapas region. Length varies too. A *huipil* may be folded up for use as a headcover.

A strange variation is the *huipil grande* worn by the Zapotec women: the neck and lower edges are trimmed with lace flounces, and the women place the garment so that the lace neck opening frames the face, one sleeve falling to the front, the other behind. Other headcoverings, from triangular scarves to turban towels, show endless ingenuity and are still changing, as is noted in detail by Chloë Sayer in her book *Mexican Costume*.

The other pre-Columbian women's garment is the *quechquemitl*, a top garment worn in many parts of the north. The *quechquemitl* is a triangular folded garment for the upper body, the shape of which is defined by the narrow fabric of a backstrap loom. There are numerous ways of folding the long strip of cloth to make a hole for the head, with the triangle points falling over the chest and back and the fold lines forming the shoulders. It gives the impression of a closed or stitched shawl, and is usually made of the finest handwoven cloth and is decorated with a variety of embroidery and fringing. Women used to wear nothing under the *quechquemitl*, but now have adopted blouses.

ABOVE MIDDLE: **Tzotzil Indians of San Pedro Chamalho, Mexico, wear handwoven skirtwraps, shawls, and hats with ribbons. Each Indian group wears variations on this dress that identify their particular village.**

RIGHT: **A charro, or Mexican rodeo, is the place to see Spanish-colonial costume. Trousers were introduced at the conquest and became widespread in the Latin American flatlands with the introduction of the horse. Even in the mountains, European costume was compulsory.**

LEFT: **These Mexican Tarahumara Indians still live a remote, traditional existence in the southeast Chiapas region, painting their bodies with white chalk spots and wearing the oldest form of indigenous male attire, the loincloth, or** tagora. **It is interesting to note the parallels in forms of decoration between these people and various tribal groups of West Africa, where white chalk dots are also common decoration.**

Some women tend to wear blouses every day of the week with the wrap skirts, or *enredos*, and add the *quechquemitl* only for special occasions.

For their skirts, the Otomí people weave dark blue or black cloth to a wide measure, seam it into a tube, and gather it, to give three thicknesses at the back and deep pleats on the left hip. But it is more usual to find two or three loom widths seamed horizontally to give the required length, then stitched as a tube or wrapped with a loose fringed edge at the side front.

The sashes worn with these skirts are essential and have become a focus for considerable expression of skill and decorative prowess. In Oaxaca, women wear huge sashes with a *soyate*, or palm tube, inside, to form a deep roll around the waist. Alternatively, very long sashes are worn, wrapped around twice. Having a back support is believed important for a woman's health, especially in pregnancy.

Western-style skirts, or *enaguas*, gathered and stitched to a waistband, are being adopted by younger women, but generally meet with disapproval from the older ones. Skirts often bear cruder machine-made trimming, rickrack, or lace. However, the Tarahumara and Mazahua women have a unique way of wearing these modern skirts – they put several together in contrasting layers. Another western introduction to the

costume, seen only in the 20th century, is an apron, which is more a part of the traditional Spanish dress.

The principal Spanish element of all Mexican women's dress is the blouse. As with a man's shirt, this has been adapted by the use of embroidery on the yoke, below a typically square neckline. Embroidery is usually taken over the sleeves, which are invariably short or just an extension of the yoke. The blouse, introduced to add modesty to the indigenous *quechquemitl*, is now more likely to erode the wearing of the *huipil*, which is perceived by some younger women as being "backward" and cumbersome.

Of all the covering garments, the shawl, or *rebozo*, which was introduced by the Spanish, has become the most widespread.

Factory-made versions of the item will in time prevail. However, in the Chiapas highlands, rectangular-shaped capes that may hark back to Mayan dress are still found, while in the Oaxaca highlands women of certain groups, such as the Trique, wear blankets as extra cover.

There is one aspect of an Indian woman's appearance that has remained unchanged across the centuries: her hair. It is almost always kept long and braided with ribbons, wool, pompoms, and also tassels. The most impressive style is the pre-Columbian *rodete* style of the Zapotec women of Yalalag, in which thick twisted skeins of black yarn are entwined around the head like the brim of a hat. The hair is then smoothed back over this "brim" to create a halo of hair. Indian women usually wear an impressive display of jewelry, mostly made of cheap plastic and glass beads, though gold and silver pieces are still seen, particularly in Yucatán.

GUATEMALA

Situated south of Mexico and at the center of Mayan culture, Guatemala was established around 2500 B.C. Most of the Indian people of Guatemala live on the high plain (*altiplano*) or mountainsides (*mesetas*), particularly around Lake Atitán, in a cool, clear climate. Many men leave the region in the hot and humid season to find work on coffee or other cash-crop plantations. Unlike many of its Latin American neighbors,

ABOVE MIDDLE: A Mexican Indian woman works at her backstrap loom. This narrow weaving technique existed in Latin America before the conquest; the Spanish introduced the treadle loom in the 16th century. The fabric produced by the narrow loom is seamed in strips to produce the other indigenous garment form besides the quechquemitl: the huipil. *Older examples of this simple tunic can be very wide, using four widths, but nowadays three widths is the most common construction.*

LEFT: Mayan men of San Antonio Palopo in Guatemala wear handwoven wrap skirts, shirts, and cloaks, all beautifully handwoven by the women of their family. It is remarkable that the males still do wear their traditional attire, for in many societies the men turn to westernized dress before their womenfolk do. In Mexico and Guatemala, however, costume is often seen as a political statement in itself among some of the more oppressed groups.

Guatemala has, in the south, a strong Indian majority that is made up of many distinct groups. Huehuetenango, which is a beautiful region of Guatemala, is home to six different ethno-linguistic groups and is the oldest known dispersal point from which Mayan culture spread out.

Guatemalan dress is entirely handwoven on the pre-Columbian backstrap loom which produces narrow strips, as in Mexico, which are handsewn together and embroidered. It has become a symbol of Indian culture to maintain the costume. The 1940s and 50s enriched the clothing, as colored polished cotton and metallic lustrous threads began to be imported in bulk for embroidery and weaving work.

The *huipil* described in the section on Mexico is worn here by women as a tunic top without a collar or set-in sleeves. It is stitched in two grades: one for kitchen or everyday use, which is made of two widths; and a festive version, made from three widths and more elaborately decorated. Handwoven sashes are worn over the long wraparound skirts. All the old Mayan drawings depict exactly the same costume. The women wear long ribbons, 6 ½ to 9 yards (6 to 8 meters) long, braided or twisted around their heads. These are knitted or woven in

ABOVE: Guatemalan women make long ribbons, knitted or woven with red patterns, and wear them tied to the forehead with a fringed topknot and trailing ends. In modern weaving, current fashions are more evident.

strong reds with different patterns, and are tied on the forehead with a fringed topknot, with the ends trailing right down the back in two long tails.

Guatemalan men's costume also follows the styling described in the Central America and Mexico section on pages 29–31: a collarless tunic shirt; wide, loose trousers with a gusset and drawstring waist; a sash, or *banda*, (usually woven in red); and a *tzute*, or square piece of cloth worn either as a cloak, rolled up as a neckscarf, or tied over one shoulder. A machine-embroidered coat of

black wool with false sleeves, called a *capixaij*, is also worn. For special occasions, men wear Mayan headpieces, consisting of a narrow strip of cloth wrapped around the head 13 times and sewn with Mayan motifs, which are then repeated 13 times. Men, women, and children all carry the handwoven bag, and the children wear round, bell-shaped caps that are gathered up in the center of the crown.

In Guatemala the *huipil* is imbued with symbolic significance. Traditionally, the wearer's origin or village was identified by a pattern in the weave – such as a bird, an animal, a geometric motif, or particular combination of colors. For example, the Kanjobals of Soloma, San Juan Ixcoy, and Santa Eulalia wear silk and satin *huipils*, decorated by machine with appliqué, lace, rickrack, and ribbons in a wide band around the neckline. The women weavers get their ideas from their dreams. They tell of saints who appear to them and instruct them on which traditional motifs to reintroduce. Zoomorphic figures such as frogs, serpents, birds, and ducks abound. Vivid floral embroidery, punchwork, and crocheted necklines are other features.

Nowadays, as clothes-making is a living, not formalized activity, fashion and individ-

RIGHT: The Guatemalan man traditionally wore a plain white costume: trousers and shirt, with a shawl or tzute, *worn either as a cloak or rolled up as here and tied over one shoulder. Nowadays, men wear more colorful costumes for festive occasions, and new elements like the decorated shirt front and the straw hat with trim, as seen with this man here, are found.*

LEFT: Women's costume in Guatemala is entirely handwoven, and the narrow strips of fabric are joined with beautiful handstitching or decorative embroidery. The huipil, *handwoven sash, wraparound skirt, and cloak are all features of costume that can be seen in old Mayan drawings and are still unchanged.*

ual taste play a much larger part in the designing of *huipils* and so the old identity system no longer holds such sway.

A special weaving technique called brocading is a feature of Guatemalan textiles. More warp than weft threads are used, so that the warps cover the wefts totally or partially, making striped designs that are seen in reverse on the other side. A principal "floating" warp design produced is that of the *samayaak*, or hourglass shape. The ground weave is made of cotton, wool, or a mixture of cotton and acrylic. Brocading and embroidery are worked in cotton, acrylic, or *sedaline*, a fine, twisted lustrous yarn that was first imported in the 1940s. For appliqué work, velveteen, poplin, or dacron fabrics are used. *Ikat* weave is widespread, as is *jaspé* or *tejido jaspedo*, with designs in negative – white on a black or dark blue ground – weave.

Color symbolism is an ancient and sophisticated tradition. Warm colors stand for the

ABOVE: Guatemala used to export cochineal and indigo dyes until the introduction of chemical alternatives in the 1940s and 1950s. These natural substances explain the traditional predominance of purples, pinks, reds, and blues in the indigenous dress. Every color and motif also bears a symbolic meaning.

emotions: red, yellow, and orange for excitement; blue or violet for more passive feelings. Green stands between colors for tonality and to denote transitions. Blue is the color of the sky, spirit, and thought; red stands for blood and passion; yellow, for light and intuition. These colors also correspond to values, attributes of the gods, or aspects of nature. For instance, jade can signify water, peace, preciousness, or maize, depending on the context.

Such connections echo the oldest Mayan symbols. Even geometric shapes can be interpreted in this way. Rhomboids symbolize the sky and earth in unity; curves relate to the earth, fertility, and vegetation. The frog is a symbol of the fertility of the earth,

while the serpents lead people down to the underworld, according to Mayan legend.

The symbolism of the loom is linked to the symbol of a woman's hair, which in turn relates to her own fertility. Among many groups women do not braid their hair or make nets when they are pregnant, as it is considered to bring them bad luck. The basic notion of hair as a symbol of the life force is illustrated by a Mexican custom in which women dance with their hair hanging loose, so that the tassels of maize grown should grow as abundantly as their tresses.

In Guatemala and Mexico, as elsewhere, hair, serpents, and rain are connected in their symbolism. As described in Southeast Asia on page 126 of this book, a society needs to have created a small surplus in its economy, while not abandoning the traditional lifestyle, before women can take the time out from agriculture to weave. In this way, weaving comes to represent prosperity, fertility, and social well being.

The Andean Countries

RIGHT: The string of San Blas islands is situated near the border between Panama and Colombia. Here the Cuna Indians make the most beautiful reverse appliqué panels for their blouses, and wear a finely balanced mixture of woven patterns, jewelry, and other details of adornment. The leg wraps are similar to the styles worn by tribes in Southeast Asia.

The Andes extend down almost the whole length of South America – just under 5,000 miles (8,000 kilometers). In the north they run through Colombia, which is the fourth largest country of Latin America, and extend through Ecuador, Peru, Bolivia, Chile, and Argentina, the largest country in the southerly region of South America. This section covers the Andean Indian cultures.

Near the border between Colombia and Panama are the San Blas islands, where the Cuna Indians live. All their clothing is very colorful and distinctive. Cuna women make eyecatching *molas*, which are reverse appliqué panels in semi-abstract designs for their blouses.

COLOMBIA

This country is split into distinct physical regions, which are also ethnically divided. However, the majority of the population is *mestizo*. Some of Colombia's Indians, like the Pijoa, resisted the 16th-century Spanish conquest so fiercely that they became extinct; while many other tribes have been lost through assimilation. The purely native Indian population has retreated into the central mountain region of Cauca. The Paéz and Guambino people retained their culture because they were isolated in the highlands. They still speak their ancient Chibcha language, as well as Spanish. Other groups, such as the Cuna and Embera, have land reservations, but according to *The World Directory of Minorities 1991*, the Wayuu (Guajino) have had their land leased to mining and tourist enterprises, which jeopardizes their traditional way of life and could lead to their assimilation or disappearance.

Guambino males wear the classic Indian attire: blue cotton shirt, white woolen trousers, and white poncho, which is worn under a darker poncho – a *ruana*. In some communities the males wear a traditional wraparound skirt over trousers – a vestige of the pre-Columbian form of dress. The women wear short-sleeved blouses, blue cloaks (the same color as the men's shirts), and pleated wraparound skirts, woven with colored stripes on a black background. Both sexes wear the warm, thick felt hats found throughout the Andes.

Guambino women wear strands of glass beads to form a deep collar, and, as in many groups, the amount of jewelry indicates a person's status and wealth.

Another small group, the Amahuaca, wear long knee-length ponchos over *calzoncillos* (see Mexico, page 29) and knitted head-hugging caps. The women wear unusual tunics, each one open at one side, so when two are worn together the body is enclosed.

Many groups of Indians, such as the Yagua, inhabit the Amazonian headwaters of Colombia. The clothing of these numerous small groups is pre-Columbian in style: women weave fabric from the fibers of the chamba palm, or from cotton, to make skirt or body wraps. Men wear breechcloths or bark fiber penis belts, seed necklaces, and amulets. They protect their skin from insect bites with oils and herbal repellents. One repellent is made with two fruits, bright red-orange *achiote* and purple-black *huito,* which are then mixed with liquified fat from a tapir or spider monkey. The Amahuaca, living on the borders of the Peruvian *montaña* region, make cylindrical "top hats" from layers of bamboo and strips of woven cloth, which are soaked in *achiote,* then fringed and stitched with seeds and monkey teeth.

ECUADOR

There are now 10 listed minority groups of people in Ecuador, numbering 3 million people, most of whom have retreated into the inaccessible tropical forests, deep between the mountains of the central sierras. The climate varies, according to altitude, from the hot and fertile coastal region at sea level, home of 50 percent of the *mestizo* population, to the cooler Andean sierras and the jungle forests or *oriente* in the east.

Whereas the Indians living in neighboring Colombia are in retreat, those in Ecuador, by virtue of the impenetrability of their rugged terrain, have retained their traditional lifestyles. The Otavalo Indians of the sierra have always resisted conquest; the Inca

army of Peru waged war in this region and conquered all Ecuadorean tribes, one by one, but it took 17 years to subdue these people. The Spanish introduced a system of serfdom called *huasipungo* in which laborers received small plots of land in return for unpaid labor on the colonists' *haciendas* – a system that remained legal until land reform

acts in 1964. The Salasaca Indians were equally resistant. They were all originally transported from Bolivia to Ecuador as *mitimaes,* or forced laborers, and in spite of extensive missionary work in the 1940s, they maintain their own customs. They still insist that outsiders marrying into the tribe must learn Quechua and adopt traditional dress.

The collective name for Indians in Ecuador is *chimborazo.* They are seen in sierra market towns, where they descend from remote villages to sell their wares. Ambato and Riobamba are sites of the most colorful and abundant craft displays in the country. The Otavalo have become so successful at marketing their woven goods that they now own most of the land of their ancestral territory. Otavalo sales agents now travel to Europe and America to sell their textiles to specific outlets.

Jamake Highwater, the American Indian scholar and author of *Arts of the Americas,* describes an Otavalo market as popular with tourists and lovers of craftwork alike: "The dress is authentic, the crafts are excellent and relatively inexpensive, the people are exceptionally friendly and there is in the atmosphere . . . a pride and dignity and welcome to strangers."

The backstrap weaving of the Otavalo, in ponchos, belts, and blankets, is particularly

ABOVE: A Quechua Indian of Ecuador, whose ancestors formed part of the vast Inca Empire, wears his traditional clothing: a homespun poncho, typical tall hat and staff of office (he is mayor of his Andean village). The Quechua people are also found throughout Bolivia and Peru.

LEFT: A Colombian Guambino Indian family wear their traditional blue and white clothing. The man is wearing a dark, short poncho, or ruana, over a westernized market-bought shirt. The woman wears a more homogenous outfit, including the classic deep-pleated wraparound skirt and glass trade beads, worn in a deep collar.

fine. The Otavalo blouses are exquisitely embroidered. Both sexes wear hats made of felt, pressed into molds and hardened until very stiff. Worn over a headwrap, they offer protection against wind, and the upturned brims are used to carry small objects or food to market.

Ecuador has other tribes in its tropical, or *selva*, regions whose mode of dress is totally adapted to their environment. It remains unchanged because of these people's limited contact with outsiders.

In the southeast live the Jivaro, a tribe who wear wrap skirts, beads, and bamboo sections in their pierced ears. They decorate their hair with feathers and practice body painting, in the same way as the Colorado people of Pichincha province (*colorado* is the Spanish word for colored). Body painting has a protective purpose, as the materials used sometimes contain insect-repellent substances found locally, but it is also used for symbolic and aesthetic reasons.

PERU AND BOLIVIA

Like Ecuador, Peru has three climatic regions: humid coastal land, cool mountains, and jungle or *selva* inland. Peru's Quechua and Aymara people constitute about half the population of around 9 million, while the Amazonian region of Peru contains about 60 different peoples whose numbers total about 10,000. Traditional dress is hardly seen on the coast, but persists in the sierras.

The importance of dress legislation as a means of social control was not lost on the conquistadores. Peru was the seat of the Inca Empire, and in 1572 the Viceroy from Spain prohibited the wearing of native dress as a means of eradicating memories of the former Inca rulers.

Men were forced to give up the *uncu*, or sleeveless, handwoven, knee-length tunic, and to wear trousers and a short jacket. Women abandoned their wraparound robe,

or *anacu*, for a skirt and blouse. In common with other Andean people, they still wear some pre-Columbian accessories: the wrapping blanket (*lliclla*), the sash (*chumpi*), and the shoulder bag (*chuspa* or *alforja*, the Spanish word for saddle-bag).

In *Peruvian Peasant Dress*, Ruth Owen describes a dress variant among the women of Chivay, just north of Arequipa in the south of Peru, where full-length skirts with deep borders of embroidery and vivid mixtures of bright colors are very prevalent. Interestingly, in this area the men do the embroidery work and lace appliqué, on strips of stiffened nylon using treadle sewing machines.

Chivay women's vests are worked in chain-stitch to depict birds, fishes, and flowers within stylized floral box borders. The vests are worn over double-layered skirts. The top skirt is pulled up to form a useful pouch at the front and a decorative bustle behind. A jacket, or *chaman*, featuring embroidery at the cuffs and borders, completes the outfit.

To the north, near Huancabamba, on the border of Peru and Bolivia, the older wrap dress was still worn in the 1980s, again as described by Ruth Owen.

Many Indian women wear outfits that combine pre-Columbian and Spanish elements: a half-*anacu*, or wrap skirt, with a blouse and *rebozo*, or shawl. Men wear

Near the Bolivian border, the island of Taquile is also noteworthy for the survival of its crafts. Craft cooperatives generate income for the inhabitants. Men wear long-sleeved cream, homespun wool shirts, atypical for the region. They have gathered sleeve-heads stitched to the one-piece central section. A dark blue vest is worn with a sash over dark blue trousers. To make these, men work pedal looms; women use small backstrap ones.

Men also knit the long *chulla* hats, with a tapering end that forms a tail. The women wear all black: two or three wool skirts, shirts, and sashes. In order to help boost their economy, Taquileans are legally obliged to wear their costume, so that the pre-Columbian *lliclla*, *chumpi*, and *chuspa* will continue for some time to come.

Bolivia's highlands are occupied by the same indigenous people as are found in Peru: the Quechua and Aymara Indians. In the past 10 years the Simonianos, Toromonas, Borror, and Jova indigenous Indians have actually died out, while, sadly, others – namely the Chimanes, Mojos, and Morima – are under constant threat from the inevitable process of assimilation.

The costumes follow the same general principles as described for Aymara and Quechua of Peru. The prevalence of the derby hat on the Bolivian *altiplano* comes

European shirts, trousers, and woolens with as fine a poncho as they can afford as an outer cover. Ponchos vary in length and may be sashed at the waist or left hanging free. Ponchos and bags are made by local weavers on backstrap looms.

Women use the drop spindle, which they carry at all times, even spinning at bus stops, in the market squares, or when they are walking or running along pathways with their babies tucked inside shawls on their backs.

from the days of the British railroad workers who built the rail track there in the 19th century and whose headgear was much admired by all the local inhabitants. British hatmakers quickly set up an export trade. Another style of hat that is worn is the close-fitting knitted cap, which resembles a Spanish conquistador's helmet.

The biggest festival of the Bolivian *altiplano* is the *diablada*, or devil's dance, which takes place in the towns of Oruro and La

ABOVE LEFT AND RIGHT:
Children of the altiplano, *central Peru. Andean people consider all children a blessing, so young Indian children are often well dressed. These little girls wear double-layer skirts and trilby felt hats. The young Quechua boys from Ollantaytambo wear cheap, market-bought trousers, but over them, they have striking ponchos with subtly blended colors and lines of well-balanced geometric motifs.*

LEFT: *Two Quechua Indian women of Cuzco, Peru, with their llamas. They are wearing traditional short jackets (an adaptation of a Spanish jacket shape), full skirts and flat-felted hats, all trimmed with handmade braids, which are still sold cheaply in each town market. Llama wool is used for weaving and knitting (mixed with sheep wool), and the fur skins are used for large patchwork rug blankets, which are made to sell as tourist souvenirs.*

Paz. The people attending the celebrations wear masks that are made of plaster and primarily painted red. The festival uses some Christian symbolism featuring the Archangel Gabriel and Lucifer, but it also evokes older Incaic forms of worship of the sun, of its conquest of darkness, symbolizing in turn the yearly cycle of birth and death, seed and harvest.

CHILE

Chile, south of Peru, is a land of great physical variety, ranging from the hot Atacama Desert in the North to the fjords and icy islands of the South. The backbone of the country is the continuation of the Andes, but unlike the rugged *altiplano* of Peru, Bolivia, and Ecuador, it does not form a refuge for Indian culture. Only about 15,000 Aymara live in the north of Chile.

To the south of the capital, Santiago, 1 million Mapuche Indians are settled on reservations. These are the descendants of the Araucanians, the indigenous Indians of Chile, much reduced in number. Their name, *Mapuche*, means "people of the

*ABOVE AND BELOW: **Lake Titicaca, on the border of Peru and Bolivia, is the setting for a livestock market, and as everywhere in the Andes the women are vigorously involved. They are usually the buyers, sellers, and growers of market produce. They carry produce or their babies in their warm, homespun blanket (see below), leaving both hands free for work.***

earth." They spill over into Argentinian Patagonia, where they number only 36,000. Men wear a modified version of pre-Columbian clothing, related to the Mexican *tagora*. It is a generous rectangular length of cloth, or *chamanto*, used as a loincloth and gathered through the legs to form trousers, with an apron flap at the front and back. The Chilean name for this garment is a *chirpa*. Otherwise, very wide trousers tied at the ankles, called *charahuilla*, are worn.

Women wear the *chamanto* as a wrap dress, which is a pre-Columbian form of attire. It extends all the way from the shoulders to the feet, and is fastened at the shoulders with a tie or pin and is sashed at the waist. A second cloth forms the ancient rectangular cloak (similar to the Mexican *tilmatli*), and is secured with a silver fibula resembling an Incaic clasp.

Farther south, groups of nomadic peoples, like the Tehuelche of Patagonia, weave the wool of the *guanaco*, whose fleece produces a warm and silky-soft yarn for jackets and loin wraps (*chirpa*, as above).

elegant compared to the rough-felt sombrero of his Argentinian counterpart. On cold days a large, enveloping blanket poncho is worn over the outfit. *Huaso* originally meant an independent or freelance horseman. The symbols of his cowboy craft are the roweled spurs, the buckled, tasseled leggings, and high-heeled boots. Today the *huaso*, like the cowboy of the Wild West, has no role because his open places are fenced off, but the costume is still worn by the *estanceros* and their hands on festive occasions. Women's fiesta clothes are versions of Spanish-colonial frilled dresses, with lace-edged aprons.

ARGENTINA

The Argentinian *gaucho* is both a legend and a national symbol. Originally of mixed Spanish and Indian blood his name is thought to derive from the Araucanian word for "orphan." The great era for *gauchos* was the late 18th and early 19th centuries, when cattle roamed unenclosed *pampas*, or grasslands, of central Argentina.

The *gaucho* costume is worn for festive occasions and rodeos. It consists of *bombachas*, or baggy trousers, and boots. A *faja*, or woolen sash, is wrapped around the waist several times, and is covered with a stiff leather belt stamped with decorative discs and coins. The indigenous loincloth, or *chirpa*, is reduced to a vestigial square of colored cloth, tucked like an apron under the belt. A neckerchief, a soft black felt hat with a droopy wide brim, and a set of rolling

spurs as much as 8 inches (20 centimeters) in diameter all contribute to the *gaucho*'s rather romantic image. A *gaucho* seldom uses a saddle, preferring a thick sheepskin over a folded blanket instead. The working *gaucho* is now more likely to be a *mestizo peón*, or farm laborer, probably Guarani in origin, living in the northeast. In the south, across Patagonia, gangs called *comparas* still travel from one *estancia* to another looking for work as sheep shearers.

Argentina's few surviving indigenous people – remnants of 16 nations – now live on the borders of Bolivia and Paraguay.

Along with the indigenous Indian culture, there are legacies of Spanish rule, such as the Chilean *huaso* (cowboy) costume of the *estancia*, or cattle ranch. The *huaso* uses the term *manta* for his short poncho. *Manta* can mean many things in Spanish-speaking regions. In Spain it means cloak; in Mexico it means both a shop-bought cotton fabric and a man's shirt. The Chilean *manta* or poncho is worn over a fine shirt and is horizontally striped, usually red or yellow, and often woven of llama or guanaco wool.

The *huaso* wears a flat-topped, narrow-brimmed hat that is distinctly Spanish and

ABOVE LEFT AND RIGHT:
Typical southern Chilean and Argentinian male riding costume has common elements: baggy trousers or bombachas, **or more formal straight-legged ones worn with leather chaps, large spurs, and short ponchos. The little boy comes from Santiago, Chile, the older rider from Patagonia, farther south in Argentina. The "cowboy" is known as a** huaso **in Chile and a** gaucho **in Argentina.**

LEFT: A small group of Argentina's indigenous Mapuche Indians. Although there are no official figures available, there are over 400,000 Mapuches, Kollas, or Tobas, living mainly in the north and southeast of the country. The same elements of dress seen in other Andean countries are also found here – ponchos, blankets, knitted caps, derbies, or other adopted, molded felt shapes.

Countries of the North and East

razil is the largest tropical country in the world, and yet of all its population, which numbers well over 125 million, the Amerindian peoples represent less than one percent. Most of these people live in the vast empty recesses of the Goias and Mato Grosso states. The *mestizo* population, a mixture of Portuguese, native Indian, or African of slave descent, is centered around the coastal area. A larger Portuguese-Indian population live in Minais Gerais, the "general mines" region. Large-scale, speculative exploitation of resources has long formed a basis of the economy in Brazil, from the

BELOW: Brazil's Amazonian Indians live in protected areas such as the Xingu reserve. The Xingu wear little, but practice elaborate forms of body painting, which has functional, aesthetic, and symbolic motives.

sugarcane plantations that existed in the colonial era, to coffee and rubber booms and now, in the 20th century, mining in the jungle. Viewed in this context, the Indians of the interior have a slim chance of maintaining their traditional way of life.

The arts of the Brazilian interior are the most purely indigenous; the remainder of Brazil's style has developed largely from

the European (Portuguese) and African immigrants to the country.

Among the most colorful tribes of Brazil are the Karajá, who live around the 200-mile (320-kilometer) long Bananal Island in the states of Goias and Mato Grosso. Their language bears no relation to any other Amazonian tongue. Along with a few other tribes, the Bororo, Tapirapé, and Urubu-Kaapor, the men are outstanding feather-workers. They make masks and headdresses for personal adornment and for ritual activities. For example, one design is a boy's cap made of reeds, woven with a zigzag design, topped by a fluffy rim of chicken feathers and surmounted by three tall macaw feathers. As with many of the hunter-gatherer tribes, life revolves around age grades and rites of passage. The change from one kind of dress to another is part of the life process.

There are three main styles of featherwork. First, a simple head fan in a splayed shape, which is sewn to a headband and tied to the forehead. Second, a huge "nimbus" headdress that uses exotic feathers, such as macaw, egret, and Muscovy duck, which is worn by young men on special occasions. The feathers are sewn to a palm splint using homespun cotton and natural glues. Smaller feathers are used to form rosettes and flowers at the base of the curved headpiece, covering the quills of the longer feathers. The headdress is then tied to create a halo around the face. The third style is a crown shape, with vertical feathers that rise from a circular base.

Other ornaments produced by the Karajá are wrestlers' belts made of palm-leaf fiber, with feathers forming a pendant bustle, and arm and knee bands with little side tufts of feathers. Otherwise the males wear very little, usually just a breechcloth with a string of beads attached. They practice body painting, using juice from the *urucu* seed pod to make a red color, and the *genipa* plant to make black. For one particular rite of passage the Karajá make a complete costume of fibers: a long skirt, a collar that covers the entire chest and back, and a tall cone-shaped headcovering, topped with just a couple of tail feathers. These are very elaborate affairs, fetishistic creations, and especially dramatic when seen against the backdrop of the jungle.

ABOVE: **These young Kayapo Indians also live in the Xingu reserve. They are wearing ceremonial dance attire, which, as for many tribes, includes delicate featherwork for hats and other accessories.**

BELOW: **A Karajá Indian dancer wears a "nimbus" headdress, traditionally made with all kinds of exotic bird feathers: macaw, egret, or Muscovy duck. The Karajá live in the Mato Grosso and Goias states. It is easy to see the cultural provenance of some of the more elaborate costumes in Brazil's city carnivals.**

A similarly impressive object comes from the Tapirapé tribe. It is a wooden mask used in their Banana Festival by the Casa Grande dancers. Covered with feathers and inlaid shellwork, this great half-circle of wood with a fan rim is worn over the head, resting on the shoulders, during a purification ritual. It represents the spirits of the dead enemies. Other effigies are made of black wax and they are then decorated with feather crowns.

In the region of Bahia, one of the main landing places for the African slaves imported by the Portuguese, there are elements of West African culture to be found, mixed up with the Catholicism brought in by the Europeans. Animistic cults persist and African gods are incorporated into Christian festivities, in dance and in healing rites. African influence is revealed in the costumes of the numerous carnivals held in Brazil. Drumming rhythms and dance steps can be traced back to tribal groups of the Congo, Nigeria, Angola, and Cameroon. Each samba "school," or club, in the major carnivals, such as that of Rio de Janeiro, always contains a section of *Bahianas*, older women wearing the white, colonial crinoline-skirted dresses with puffed and flounced short-sleeved bodices, their heads wrapped in close-fitting white scarves topped with floral, fruit, or jeweled decorations. They dance in a stately fashion, carrying white lace parasols.

To the south of Brazil, cattle-breeding plains are managed by the *vaqueiro*, the Brazilian cowboy or ranch hand, who wears a form of the *gaucho* dress that is commonly seen in Argentina. In the northeast the cattlemen traditionally wore a full leather outfit, to give them protection when riding through rough thornbrake, but this is now seldom seen.

GUYANA AND FRENCH GUIANA

Brazil is home to several tribes of Wauwai people, but the majority of this group and other Carib-linguistic groups (the Akawaio, Pataimona, Arekuna, and Makusi) live in the neighboring country of Guyana. An Arawak-speaking group called the Wapisiana tribe also shares the dense interior region. The coastal American Indians in Guyana have largely been assimilated into the country's population.

is also followed by the women of both the Makusi and Arekuna tribes.

VENEZUELA

Venezuela, a more prosperous and westernized country than some of its neighbors, has several tribes. There are 150,000 indigenous groups, including the Bari, Wayuu, Yukpas, Paujanos, Piaroa, and Taurepan. In common with all the Amerindian jungle dwellers, men wear minimal clothing. Skirts or body wraps made of palm fiber or cotton are worn by all the women. Elaborate body painting helps define a person's age group and other social distinctions, or can be used purely for interesting decoration.

SURINAME, PARAGUAY, AND URUGUAY

In Suriname, a large indentured labor force from the Portuguese domains in Southeast Asia, brought over in previous centuries, adds to the mix of European, African, and Amerindian stock. Each group wears a style of clothing that relates to their place of origin. Carib-Amerindian women wear the aboriginal wrap dress. Indian women continue to wear their saris. There is also a very small number of Bush Negro communities, who are descendants of runaway slaves and represent one percent of the population. They wear wrapping cloths, beads, and feathers, and the bush women braid their hair in beautiful patterns close to the scalp.

In French Guiana there are only about four to five thousand indigenous people left. The Arawak, Galibu, and Palikuit live on the coast, while the Emerillon, Oyampi, and Wayana are inland peoples.

Various forms of body deformation, such as extended earlobes and restriction of body parts are often practiced. For example, the Wauwai people have a practice of binding a girl's legs below the knee to the ankle to produce enlarged calves, which they consider to be aesthetically pleasing. This custom

Paraguay has seven listed minority nations, totaling perhaps 80,000 people: the Toba, Maskoy, Ayoreo, Mataco, Mbaya, Ache, and Ara-Chiripa. The largest Indian group is the Guarani. The variations of primitive dress that have been described earlier in the chapter are found among the tribes who live on the borders with Bolivia and Brazil.

Uruguay's population is mostly European. The *gaucho* costume is often worn as cattle raising is popular on the Plate River plains near Argentina. The *chirpa* is worn as a shawl.

ABOVE LEFT: **Macumba** *is the name of an African-derived religion of the northeast region of Brazil; these two women devotees wear white Bahian clothing reminiscent of colonial Portuguese women's dress.* **Bahianas** *in more luxurious versions of this costume are seen in most Brazilian carnival parades.*

RIGHT: There are also indigenous Indian peoples living in the tropical regions of Venezuela. This is a Waika girl , wearing a fiber skirt and a nose ornament. Body beads are worn by both sexes.

ABOVE RIGHT: **French Guiana** *is a department of France; its western neighbor, Suriname, won independence from the Dutch in 1975. Both countries have a rich mixture of ethnic peoples, many of whom originally came from the Far Eastern possessions of their colonizers. This French Guianese couple from Southeast Asia are of Hmong origin and still maintain their culture and their dress customs, even when marrying in a Catholic church. The bride's dowry still has to be paid in gold bars.*

Latin America Map

There is a great variety of traditional dress in Latin America. Indigenous peoples' clothing relates to climate and location: rich decoration exists on clothing in tropical Central America; warm woven wraps are worn by Andean Indian groups; while feathers and bark or cotton wraps are favored by Amazonian minorities. The long rule of the Spanish and Portuguese empires has left its mark on the *gaucho*, or cowboy, dress of the *pampas*.

MEXICO

Otomi
Mazahua

Huichol
Mexico City •
• Veracruz *Maya*
YUCATAN
CHIAPAS
Oaxaca •

Zapotec
Tzotzil
Tzeltal
Lacandon
Tarahumara

GUATEMALA
Mayan
Kanjabal

PANAMA
SAN BLAS
ISLANDS
Cuna

Otavalo
Colorado
Paéz
Guambino
Amahuaca
Yagua
PICHINCHA
Jivaro
Rio Bamba •
ECUADOR
• Huancabamba
Aymara
Quechua
PERU
Andean
TAQUILE
ISLAND
Cuzco •
Chivay •
Arequipa •

COLOMBIA
Bari Wayuu Yukpas
Paujanos Piarea
Taurepan

VENEZUELA

GUYANA
SURINAME
FRENCH
GUIANA

Caribs

AMAZON BASIN
Amazon

Txcariana
Xingu

Kayapo
Xingu
Karajá

BRAZIL
BAHIA

Tapirape
BANANAL
ISLAND

MATO GROSSO
GOIAS

• La Paz
BOLIVIA
• Oruro
Tarabueo •
Callawaya

Mbaya
Ache
Ayoreo
ATACAMA PARAGUAY

MINAIS GERAIS

• Rio de Janeiro

Toba *Maskoy*
Kollas *Mataco*
Guaraní
Mapuche

Santiago •

URUGUAY

PACIFIC
OCEAN

Mapuche

C H I L E
A R G E N T I N A
PATAGONIA

SOUTH
ATLANTIC
OCEAN

Tehuelche

Ona
Yahgan

A Totopac Indian dancer of
Veracruz, Mexico.

A Cuna Indian of the San
Blas archipelago, Panama.

A Quechua Indian woman
from Peru.

A Callawaya Indian of the
Andean region in Bolivia.

A young boy from the
indigenous Txcariana tribe,
Amazonia, Brazil.

A woman of the state of
Bahia in Brazil.

Key

3,000 plus m (9,000
plus ft)

1,000–3,000m
(3,000–9,000ft)

400–1,000m
(1,200–3,000ft)

0–400m (0–1,200ft)

Sea, lakes and rivers

Note: peoples are shown in italics eg: **Maya**

WRAPPING BLANKETS

TOP ROW, LEFT TO RIGHT:

Peruvian goat herder wearing white wool blanket over his jacket and knitted hat under his felt derby.

Girl from Tarabuco, Bolivia, wearing a silver-beaded torque and locally woven wool shawl.

Ecuadorian mother of Andean region, carrying her child inside her wool blanket.

Mayan Indian woman of Chiapas region, Mexico, wearing a rebozo, or shawl, embroidered with traditional floral motifs.

Woman of Saraguran, Ecuador, wearing a blanket wrap held in place with an Incaic straight pin in studded metal alloy.

MIDDLE ROW, LEFT TO RIGHT:

Woman at a fiesta in San Francisco, Guatemala, wearing homespun fabric in two designs, for her skirt and wrapping blanket, in which she carries her child.

Indian man of Cuzco, Peru, wearing a characteristic wool tasseled cap and poncho woven on a narrow loom, two panels stitched at the center.

Indian man of San Andrés de Pisimbala, wearing a blanket poncho in a natural-dyed striped wool.

Indian girl of Andean region, Ecuador, wearing felt hat and simple wool blanket wrap.

Aymara Indians of La Paz, Bolivia, wearing distinctive natural wool-fringed shawls and the popular bowler hats.

BOTTOM ROW, LEFT TO RIGHT:

Woman of Chichicastenango, Guatemala, wearing a colorful handwoven huipil and rebozo, or shawl, for market day.

Indian of Cuzco, Peru, wearing entire outfit of homespun, handwoven cloth with long poncho robe and short cloak on top.

Indian woman of Guatemala with embroidered wrap. Her hair is braided with a gauze net strip.

Indian woman of Jaquisilli, Ecuador, wearing a blanket to hold purchases and carrying a pile of Panama hats for sale.

Cuna Indian woman of the San Blas islands, Panama, wearing a mola, or reverse-appliqué blouse, and a shawl covering her head.

45

EUROPE

In Europe, from the Atlantic to the Urals, the term "folk dress" is used to describe the costume of peasant cultures.

Jelka Radus Ribaric, in his book *The Folk Costumes of Croatia*, describes the social, geographical, and historical factors inherent in its production. "The costume worn by the population of a region behaves like a living organism adapted to its environment. It fits into the picture of the area, reveals the basic branches of economy, indicates the climatic conditions and the standard of living of the community at large, regardless of the standard of the individual. It also bears traces of the events which have shaped the history of the area. And finally, in the folk costume is the reflection of the workmanship, vivid imagination and creativeness of the people; thus clothing becomes a medium through which a community expresses its striving for beauty. It is a treasure from a time when life was harder but more poetic than today."

The clothes we recognize today as folk dress are more often than not modeled on festive dress rather than everyday working dress. These beautiful clothes, with their nuances of meaning, thrived on feudalism and neglect. It is no accident that they survived the longest in the eastern European countries, such as Hungary and Romania.

Here, the centuries-old way of life essential to the continuing production of folk dress was finally shattered by World War II. Traditions have a way of lingering on, long after the cataclysm that cuts their roots. In the mountains of Romania and Bulgaria, for example, it is still possible to see costumes on Sundays and at weddings. This was also true of former Yugoslavia, too, before the civil war started. Happily, the

*ABOVE: **At Saami gatherings in Lapland the best clothing of these reindeer-herding people is seen. Braids and ribbons are lavishly applied to all their dress.***

*OPPOSITE: **A Norwegian couple from Arendal wear fine examples of regional dress.***

folk-dance group Lado, based in Zagreb, still has its extraordinary collection of authentic dress gathered from the provinces and wears them for performing. Also notable are the costumes worn at church festivals in Catholic Portugal and Spain.

Folk dress was intimately bound up with the customs observed by patriarchal communities, and its characteristics were determined by strict rules. A collective life was essential to provide the range of skills needed to produce the exquisite refinements of fabric seen in these pages.

Styles were dictated as much by technology as by tradition and so changed very slowly. What is remarkable is the variety in the embroideries, colors, patterns, and weaves, that distinguish the dress of one

region from another. For instance, Ukraine has 30 or more regional variations.

The basic dress for women throughout Europe was the long-sleeved shirt or shift (sometimes called a chemise) in homespun linen or hemp, cut from lengths of cloth. This dress is still common in eastern Europe, but in the West the shift has been replaced by the blouse. Over the shift come the skirts, often layers at a time, the ubiquitous apron, and a sleeveless jacket, or the fitted bodice and shawl of western Europe. Generally, the starched and folded headdresses tend to be replaced by kerchiefs. In the West men's dress was based on the tailored jacket and breeches of the late 18th century. In the East the homespun fabrics dictated the looser shapes of the shirt or tunic, that were worn belted or girdled over draped or straight trousers.

The way of life that helped sustain this creativity was doomed as the Industrial Revolution and the urbanization that followed it spread across Europe. The decline started in the West in the late 18th century. Fortunately, by the early 19th century, a few enthusiastic intellectuals saw the value of their folk traditions as a vital part of their national consciousness. They set about collecting and recording stories, dances, and costumes. The Brothers Grimm were a part of this movement.

Today, folk traditions are increasingly held in high esteem. Old costume styles are now being revived in colorful hybrid forms, which may infuriate purists, but which nonetheless ensure their survival.

A useful test of authenticity is to ask whether the garment that is worn still has meaning for its community.

The Arctic Region

The Scandinavian countries and western Russia north of the Arctic Circle are home to the reindeer-herding Saamis, or Laplanders, whose Finno-Urgic language and culture are unique. Their ancient way of life, though challenged and endangered by western ideas, is undergoing something of a renaissance. Traditional costume, primarily reserved for festivals and family occasions, is still worn as working dress by inland Saamis.

The Russian Arctic peoples lead a similar life and still make clothing from the skin and fur of reindeer or walruses to protect them from the bitter Arctic winters.

THE LAPLAND AREA

The foundation of the Saamis' folk art has been their nomadic way of life. Their wanderings have dictated that their general dress, as with all their artefacts, be simple, economical, and practical. Within these limitations, the Saamis' feeling for color and design has produced beautiful and colorful articles. The clothes by necessity are seasonal: relatively hot summers of perpetual sunlight require smocks, and the extreme, cold winters demand furs. For men, women, and children the dominant colors for smocks, skirts, and tunics are deep blue and red, enlivened with an endless play of color provided by bands of bright ribbons and braids, and yellow inserts across the shoulders and around the collar, with fine lines of embroidery – also in red and yellow – along the seams. Under the smock are long trousers and, when the snow comes, braided bindings and the Saami boot.

Saami boots are a perfect example of man's ingenuity in making use of the raw materials around him to help him adapt to his surroundings. Ideally suited to function in the snow, the boots are made from skin taken from the legs of reindeer, where the fur is thick and protective. The pieces of hide are sewn together in a special order, so that the fur on the front of the sole goes in the opposite direction to the fur on the back, to prevent slipping.

Instead of socks, only the best hay, cut in August and preferably from under willows, is used. Small bunches are tied together, beaten against a stone or with a birch club to soften the strands, and, when dried, tied into rings and stored. Saamis learn as children the difficult art of stuffing their shoes. And these boots, with their lining of hay, allow the feet to breathe without the cold

region covers a vast area in which at least a dozen ethnic groups – about 300,000 people – live in a delicate balance between the modern and the traditional way of life.

The main groups are the Chukchi and the Yukaghir, the Yakut, Dolgan, Khanty, and Nenet peoples. There are only about 800 pure-blooded Yukaghir left, but they are determined conservers of their lore and crafts. Although many have given up their *yarangas* for Russian-style wooden housing, and some of their traditional prey, like the walrus, can no longer be hunted due to conservation laws, their prime activities remain fishing and reindeer herding. Their traditional clothing is ideal for these age-old tasks. They wear knee-length boots of walrus skin, with embroidered and appliquéd front panels, banded under the knee with woven ties. These are prized possessions. Long walrus or reindeer robes edged with braid, with hoods edged with fur, are worn by the women over long floral-print dresses. Westernized clothes are preferred by the men.

Women wear their hair in a single braid, and use folded lengths of floral material as headcovers indoors. Traditionally, the decorative motifs on Arctic clothing have been a mixture of Russian folk motifs, Eastern Orthodox church symbols, and local animistic images. Pendants of glass beads, Russian coins, pearl shirt buttons, and fur tassels are all found on coats and tunics. As in many hunting societies, red is particularly favored. Traditionally, red flannel is used for appliqué panels on skin clothing in which the fur is worn inward. One reason for the mixture of stylistic elements, according to Walter Fairservis in *Costumes of the East*, is that the Arctic people, though conquered by Russian invaders, were tolerated, and their lifestyles were left relatively undisturbed. Today, mixed marriage is not frowned upon, and higher education is widely accepted without loss of pride or interest in the native culture. The same adaptive tendency is also evident in all of their dress.

getting in. The boots have turned-up toes and are wrapped tight at the ankles with multicolored bindings, which are tasseled and braided.

It is interesting to compare Saami dress with the hunting clothing of the Inuits and Aleuts (see North America, pages 14–15).

THE RUSSIAN ARCTIC

The traditional way of life of the Russian Arctic peoples has always revolved around fishing and hunting. Their dwellings are round wigwam-like tents or *yarangas*, covered in walrus skins. The Soviet Arctic

RIGHT: **These Nenet women are wearing reindeer-skin coats to watch a sleigh race at a festival held in Yamal, Siberia, in the Russian Arctic. In common with many other Arctic hunting peoples, the Nenets used to make full use of a variety of hides for their clothing. Their boots are traditionally made of walrus skin, banded at the knee with woven ties. Robes were also made of walrus as an alternative to reindeer, but the former are now protected by conservation laws. Both garments are appliquéd with braid at the edges.**

ABOVE RIGHT: **The traditional way of life of Russian Arctic peoples has always revolved around fishing and hunting. There are at least a dozen ethnic groups in the region, trying to maintain their customs with some adaptation to modern life. Many now live in wooden housing instead of tents covered in walrus skins. This Arctic woman is watching a corral, her reindeer coat deeply bordered with darker brown hide in a customary design.**

Scandinavia

Norway, Sweden, Denmark, and Finland all have traditions of regional dress that are very much part of their contemporary culture. Most versions are either replicas or derivations of the festive or Sunday styles worn in the 18th and 19th centuries. Regional variations are scrupulously maintained, and every stitch is traditional. The garments do not vary much.

For women the costume consists of a smock or blouse with a bodice, skirt, and apron, over which is worn a jacket or shawl, accompanied by a headdress. Their accessories may be jewelry, belts, kerchiefs, and separate pockets. In a few regions, a more ancient form of dress has survived well: a pinafore, or *sarafan*, where the skirt hangs down from a high yoke or a bodice.

For the men, the costume is a shirt, long trousers or breeches, worn with a vest, jacket or coat, neck scarf, and topped with a hat or cap. Typically, traditional dress is worn more by women than by men, because men's trousers or knee breeches are quite fitted and become too tight as men get older. Although women do not always stay as slender as when they were young, their costumes are made for life and are therefore more easily let out (skirts have several inches of overlap hidden under the apron). The demands of pregnancy ensure that their clothing is adaptable, in a way that men's never has been.

NORWAY

This country has really cherished its folk traditions. It is a country of high mountains and deep fjords, with pockets of fertile soil where the land meets the sea. These factors provided ideal conditions for the growth of small independent communities, sufficiently in touch with one another to maintain a sense of national unity, but isolated enough for regional differences to be quite marked. Throughout the 19th century, Norway strove for independence from Sweden, finally achieving it in 1905. In World War II it was occupied by Germany. Such experiences make this nation very protective of its uniqueness and its indigenous culture. A

wool decorated with baroque flowers embroidered in a deep border at the bottom of the skirt, on the apron, and at the front of the vest. A final colorful flourish is added with a narrow double band of colored fabric to bind the bottom of the skirt, apron, and vest. The men's costume is breeches, an 18th-century waistcoat, short jacket, and elaborately patterned socks with small tassels at the knee, and buckle shoes.

Jewelry was always a great feature and is still very impressive and is mostly made from silver or silver-gilt. The finest exam-

ABOVE MIDDLE AND RIGHT:
These two versions of female Swedish costume show the typical elements generally seen now, which are based on rural dress of the early 19th century. This was the period when artists and writers first began to depict and record folk life in detail. As a rule, women maintain the custom of wearing folk dress longer than men, because they can alter their clothes more readily than the men's fitted breeches and jackets, so the man's outfit is a fine example of a rarer outfit.

LEFT: This couple from Ålborg in Denmark are wearing typical replicas of costume that is often made for the country's folk dancing groups. The man's dress shows the smart breeches, vest, and jacket worn by men up until the middle years of the 19th century. The woman's dress comprises a flowing checked skirt, an embroidered bodice and blouse, topped with a patterned shawl.

strong arts and crafts movement, formed at the end of the 19th century, ensured that many different costumes were collected and recorded, and out of this grew the *bunad*, literally meaning "clothes." Today, the term denotes a regional festive costume, which has been revived. Patterns of the authorized version for a region can be bought from many arts and crafts shops.

The best-known female style in Norway is from Hardanger, and many other variations resemble it. The white linen blouse is decorated at the collar and cuffs with beautiful Hardanger openwork embroidery. This crisp geometric style of needlework is still taught in schools. The skirt that is worn is black and finely gathered, except for a flat, overlapping panel at the front. The fitted

red flannel waistcoat is edged all around with a softly shaded, multicolored band, and in the front a separate panel of intricate geometric beadwork, or *plastron*, mounted on linen, is tucked and pinned in place with gilded silver pins with ornamental heads. The white apron is then decorated with a deep inset of the same geometric Hardanger work. Extra interest may well be added with long colored braids hanging from the belt, relieving the starkness of the white apron. The traditional stiffly starched headdress that accompanies this costume is rarely worn: apparently it is extremely difficult to starch correctly.

By way of contrast, though not in form, is the dress from Telemark, a redesign of an early 19th-century costume. It is of black

ples consist of filigree necklaces with dangling *paillettes* (coin-like disks), brooches – some like a large round boss from the center of a shield – and chain-laced vests.

SWEDEN AND DENMARK

As in Norway, for 150 years or so intellectuals in Sweden have been recording every detail of their national folk culture for fear it may be lost. It is to them that the Swedish owe their easy familiarity with revived folk dress in all of its regional variety. In Denmark the situation is different. It was first among its neighbors to prosper in the Industrial Revolution and the old dress was never consciously collected with the same fervor. However, folk dance societies hold records of authentic patterns from which revived outfits are made.

North Europe

In North Europe indigenous dress plays a colorful part in the everyday life of some peoples, while for others it is simply a historical remnant.

SCOTLAND

The Highland dress of Scotland with its centerpiece, the kilt, is often still worn in daily life. Around the beginning of the 17th century, Highland dress for men consisted of "the great kilt" made of 12 ells (1 ell equals about 90 centimeters of tartan fastened around the body. The kilted or lower half of the dress was first arranged in pleats tucked into a belt, and the upper half, or plaid, thrown over the shoulder and held in place with a brooch. Later, the kilt and plaid were separated. Today a man's kilt, always mid-knee length, is properly made with 7

yards (7 meters) of tartan, but the pleats are stitched in place with a small amount unpleated at either end to overlap across the stomach and form the apron. Strap and buckle fastenings either side of the apron ensure that the kilt should fit its owner from slender youthfulness to increasing girth in middle age – an essential feature, considering the cost of a good kilt. The finest are custom made and last a lifetime.

Tartan, the hard woolen cloth from which kilts and plaids are made, has a long history. Each clan, originally from the same region and bearing the same surname, had its own tartan. The Highlanders were a belligerent people and, until they united in the Jacobite wars in the first half of the 18th century to fight the English, were constantly fighting

among themselves. Some distinguishing mark was needed in battle, so each clan took as its distinctive pattern the one woven into the cloth used by its clansmen. The early 19th century saw such a revival of interest in tartan that every clan and regiment had at least one, if not two or three, to call its own.

Large numbers of Scots emigrated to America, Canada, and Australia and their descendants have returned to visit the land of their forebears and take home Highland dress to wear at Burns' Night parties, St. Andrew's Day dinners, and many other Scottish celebrations. Highland regiments, too, have taken the kilt all over the world.

In Scotland, the strict etiquette governing Highland dress is followed at all the special gatherings, but is easing elsewhere. The rules laid down by Lord Lyon, King of Arms in Edinburgh, may seem outmoded, but the result is magnificent: a man in full Highland dress is the equal of any tribal chief.

For a ball the kilt is worn with a black Prince Charles coatee, which is a waist-length fitted jacket with black silk facings, short tails at the back and square silver buttons. Underneath the coatee is a black silver-buttoned vest worn over a dress shirt. Legs are clad in white or tartan knee hose with solid colored garter flashes (the short

of little holes which are a reminder of a past practice when hunting or fighting men, who had to wade through rivers, would benefit from the holes which were punched through to let excess water out.

The place to see Highland dress in all its splendor is the summer games. The most famous are the Braemar Games, attended by the Royal Family, who are enthusiastic Highlanders. At the games, the dancers mix with pipers, local farmers, and dignitaries, and all sport the kilt. Women wear tartan skirts or kilts made with fewer pleats.

the fisherwomen is still worn by a few of the older people. Dressed in a simple blue short-sleeved blouse, a long dark skirt, and blue-and-white checked apron, with a cotton bonnet tied under the chin, the old fisherwives greet the herring fleet as it returns with the first fish of the season. At the same time, a ceremonial barrel of herrings is presented to the queen.

In the farthest arm of northeast France in Brittany, distinctive Breton costume, with its stiffened lace headdresses, is brought out for festivals and saints' days. Best known is

RIGHT: In the Zuyder Zee region of north Holland, different villages in turn celebrate their old customs and traditions on special days during the summer. These villagers are wearing a costume adapted from the superb examples of original dress housed in places such as the Zuyder Zee Museum in Enkhuizen.

LEFT: Three Latvian women display different modern versions of their brightly colored national dress. The cut of the basque bodices and pleated skirts harks back to styles recorded in the 19th century. Strands of amber beads are a reminder that Baltic peoples have traded in this semi-precious substance, a fossilized resin, for more than a thousand years.

BELOW MIDDLE: The starched lace caps worn by Breton women in Finistère in Brittany on special occasions have increased in height, even in this century.

tabs either side of the knee that are attached to garters). Shoes are buckled or laced. The elaborate evening sporran, hung in front, is often of seal or goatskin fur with fine silver tassels. Tucked into the top of the hose is the *sgian-dubh*, or black-knife, so called because it used to be hidden away in their clothing when the clans were at war!

Evening wear for women is often a long white ball gown and wide tartan sash worn diagonally over the shoulder. The sash might be pinned with the clan badge, a circular silver brooch with crest and motto.

Day dress is simpler, but the kilt is the centerpiece, worn with a tweed jacket and a vest with ornate horn buttons. Hand-knitted hose and brogue shoes are important. Brogues have a decorative patterning

THE NETHERLANDS AND FRANCE

Holland has a rich variety of beautiful regional costumes preserved in museums. Simplified models, copied from the originals, are worn nowadays only at summer festivals or to perform old events that are often associated with the sea. At the Scheveningen *Vlaggeties dag* in May, the working dress of

the delicate high cap with its long lace lappets attached at the back. France has played such a part in western European fashion that it is only in such remote places that truly regional costume has managed to survive at all.

LATVIA, LITHUANIA, AND ESTONIA

All these independent Baltic states have enthusiastic nationals in Britain and in the United States who make costumes for dancing and singing. Most decorative is the Nica dress from Latvia, with a white tailored vest, a red skirt, which is embroidered from top to bottom in shades of pink, yellow, blue, and green, and a white blouse with black embroidery. The crown-like beadwork hat, the *vainag*, is typical and similar to those worn in Sweden and Finland.

Northern Europe Map

All people love to wear decorative clothing, and will use whatever means are at hand to make their dress distinctive. Even in the frozen lands of northern Europe the reindeer herders work special embroidery and applied designs on fur hides. The Saamis of Lapland use wonderful woven patterned ribbons for their headdresses and clothes. The variety of woven tartans, used to identify Scottish clans, is still admired worldwide.

Eveny reindeer herder of Siberia, Russia, wearing a patterned hide coat.

ARCTIC OCEAN

NOVAYA ZEMLYA

East Siberian Sea

Chukchi

Yukaghir

Yakut

Nenet *Dolgan*

Khanty *Eveny*

Arctic Circle

RUSSIAN FEDERATION

Saami

LAPLAND

KOLA PENINSULA

Arctic Circle

White Sea

Kjölen Mountains

SCANDINAVIA

FINLAND

Norwegian

NORWAY

Norwegian Sea

HARDANGER

TELEMARK

• Arendal

HIGHLANDS

SCOTLAND

Scottish

NORTH SEA

SWEDEN

Swedish

BALTIC SEA

RUSSIA

ESTONIA

LATVIA

Ålborg •

DENMARK

Danish

LITHUANIA

Lithuanian

Dutch

THE NETHERLANDS

BELGIUM

ENGLISH CHANNEL

BRITTANY

Breton

FRANCE

A Scotsman in Highland dress with a pleated kilt.

A Saami man from Lapland, wearing a tall, colorful, beribboned hat.

Russian Arctic Key

Yukaghir people go across this area

Chukchi people go across this area

Khanty people go across this area

Nenet people go across this area

Yakut people go across this area

Dolgan people go across this area

Main Key

Saami people go across this area

Approximate area of provinces

1,000–4,000m (3,000–12,000ft)

400–1,000m (1,200–3,000ft)

0–400m (0–1,200ft)

Seas, lakes and rivers

Note: peoples are shown in italics eg: *Dutch*

Central Europe

RIGHT: The highly decorative clothes worn by men on special occasions throughout the Tyrol are a direct result of the interest taken in local peasant clothing by the aristocracy and bourgeoisie from the middle of the 19th century. These men and boys in Austria wear typical leather shorts and red vests rooted in this delightful movement.

BELOW MIDDLE: Usually a woman would be horrified to find another woman wearing the same hat as herself, but not at a folk gathering, where uniformity is a mark of regional identity, as shown in these older women's tasseled black felt hats, in Gotzens, in the Austrian Tyrol.

Folk dress is alive and well in Germany, Austria, and Switzerland. It lives on in a wealth of revived styles that bear a strong family resemblance. For instance, the *lederhosen* of Bavaria – the short leather trousers with embroidered suspenders – are Austrian also, and Switzerland has its own variation. The *dirndl* of Austria, that is adapted from the work clothes of the local peasants of the Salzkammergut, is popular in Bavaria too. *Dirndl* is an Austrian dialect word for "maid" or "dairy maid," whose bodice originated as a form of brassiere, and whose skirt was a petticoat. Adopted by the upper classes in the middle of the 19th century, it gradually became gentrified. Since then, the *dirndl* worn with its apron, has been universally admired and has never really gone out of fashion, which is hardly surprising since it has such a flattering design.

AUSTRIA

In Austria, as in Germany, *tracht* ("that which is worn," derived from the German *tragen*, "to wear") is a word used to describe all dress derived from the rich store of folk costume. It is an essential element in the wardrobe of all the more prosperous people.

Every province has its own variations that can be bought at a *Heimatwerk* shop, whose skilled dressmakers work according to the old patterns. *Tracht* is worn at weddings, at parties where the invitations would be marked "black tie," and at public functions. There are also occasions to wear traditional clothing at festivals of the Catholic church. The *festracht* (festival dress) is a sumptuous version made in silks and brocades for splendid occasions, such as the Salzburg Festival. *Tracht* has been reinvented as a fashion item, and designers study the extensive museum collections for inspiration.

Tracht has survived particularly in isolated mountain valleys, where changes are slow. Suede, chiefly of red deer and chamois, is widely used for leather trousers. The most popular material was, and still is, *loden*, a woolen cloth known to the first Germanic settlers who originated in the Alpine regions, where sheep are shorn two or three times a year. After the woven cloth was fulled (compacted) in order to felt and thicken it, it was pummeled with heavy pestles, washed, dried and stretched on frames. The pile was raised, originally with teazel heads, and finally cropped. The resulting cloth was water-repellent. Today, this hard-wearing cloth is widely used to make clothes for both men and women.

For men, the most common form of *lederhosen* are cut off above the knees. These leather shorts were originally a protection, worn over woolen or linen long pants, and are particularly suited for working in the mountains. In Styria, older men wear long linen breeches still, under their *lederhosen*. A characteristically Alpine protection of the calves is the docked (knee to ankle length) stockings. Leather suspenders can be richly embroidered with peacock quills. The wide-brimmed, felt Tyrolese hats are noted for their hunting decorations. The *gamsbart*, which looks like a shaving-brush, represents a plume of hair plucked from the withers of the chamois in its winter coat.

The widespread acceptance of country clothes is credited to two passionate and aristocratic hunters: Archduke Johann and

Emperor Franz Joseph. The former married the daughter of a postmaster, and thought it natural to dress like the Styrian people among whom he lived. His great-nephew Franz Joseph, emperor of Austria from 1848 to 1916, also thought it proper to wear the dress of the humblest gamekeeper in his beloved mountains, and his entourage fol-

lowed suit, wearing an outfit that was not only handsome but also thoroughly practical. The example of the ruling classes, the attraction for tourists, and a growing national self-awareness since the 1960s have led to the adoption of the suit of gray *loden*, with its green trimmings. These colors have been used by Alpine hunters for centuries. Emperor Maximilian wrote, at the beginning of the 16th century, in his *Secret Hunting Book*: "Thou shalt have gray and green clothes, partly gray, partly green. For hunting stag and chamois these are the best colors."

SWITZERLAND

In Switzerland, each canton (division) has its own costume, based on old festive styles. Costume varies from the exquisite and expensive style of the French- and Italian-influenced cantons, to the rural simplicity in the German-speaking ones. It is wholly revived, and dates from the end of the 18th century, the golden age of regional costume, when domestic agriculture and industries flourished under the developing sciences. The industrial age tolled the bell for traditional finery. However, in 1926 the National Federation of Swiss Costumes was founded to restore and to recreate, from old prints and paintings, this element of popular cul-

ABOVE MIDDLE: **Austrian** tracht *is smartest in Salzburg, where these women have gathered for a special festival. Austrian traditional dress, or* tracht, *is based on the costume of hunters for men, and of peasant women for modern women of all classes. What was once work dress is now worn as a cultural specialty by many women in town and country areas. The lady on the left is wearing a traditional golden bonnet.*

LEFT: **In Switzerland, as in many other countries in Central Europe, young Swiss children are also enthusiastically encouraged to wear revived styles of dress. These Alpine children are attending a cultural festival at Appenzell.**

ture. In German cantons to the east of the River Sarine some people wear folk costume on Sundays and at festivities. Otherwise, it tends to be reserved for costume festivals and folk dancing. The women's costumes have retained the separate skirt and rigid baroque corselet bodice, laced and hooked over the bosom, which is an opportunity for a marvelous display of silver and goldsmiths' work in the hooks, eyes, and clasps, from which hang pendants and silver chains. The sumptuous fabrics used in making the corselets are characteristic of each area. Switzerland is famous for its lace and ribbons, which are extravagantly displayed in highly original headdresses.

In Valais, the small straw hat is hidden under a wide embroidered ribbon encircling the crown. Around the brim a narrow black ribbon, which may be dozens of yards long, is twisted into an edging of tightly packed diagonal pleats. In Glarus, Thurgau, and Basle the *fichus de Milan*, with their fringes and tassels, were imported from Lombardy.

Men's dress bears traces of former working practices: the classic garment in the Bernese, Fribourg, and Vaud Alps is the *bredzon*, a smock of thick twill with short puffed sleeves that were designed to hold up the shirt sleeves during cheese-making.

The Burgundy smock, widespread during the 19th century, was originally the dress of the drivers who transported salt and wine from that part of France. In French Switzerland, the frock coat, knickerbockers, and three-cornered hat, which were common in late 18th-century France, were also worn in urban areas.

GERMANY

In Germany's Black Forest and in Bavaria, revived costumes are worn at festivals and represent local craftsmanship. The *trachtenvereine*, the societies founded in the 1880s for the preservation of costume, focused on gathering patterns of rural dress. The 16-day Munich Oktoberfest, which ends on the first Sunday in October, provides an opportunity for Bavarians to wear costume directly descended from earlier models. Despite being an international attraction for all, the Oktoberfest is still a true Bavarian celebration.

In a more rural setting, the Black Forest's mountains and valleys are home to interesting examples of women's dress. Here the laced bodice becomes a high-necked one, usually velvet, worn with a puff-sleeved blouse, brocade apron, and black skirt. The hats are fantastic: the Gutachtal has a straw Sunday hat piled with 11 woolen pompoms.

Hesse to the north, the birthplace of the Brothers Grimm, is the home of the most famous headdress of all: in the Hesse town of Ziegenhain, the unmarried girls wore the red caps that were the inspiration for the tale of *Little Red Riding Hood*. Local costumes can be seen at the Salatkirmes, one of the largest folk festivals in Hesse, during the second weekend after Whit Sunday.

ABOVE MIDDLE: **Elegant Catholic matrons from Appenzell, Switzerland, wear butterfly-like headdresses. The base is a small golden cap, to which finely pleated double wings of black and white tulle are attached. The outer black pleats enclose the inner pleats, which spill forward in a snowy white crest. Crimson satin ribbons tied in a bow add a flourish at the back. During the 19th century, the colorful clothing of this region gradually changed to darker tones until it became a funereal black, but this forms a perfect foil for a display of fine lacework.**

FAR LEFT AND LEFT: **Both these pictures illustrate costume worn at the Munich Oktoberfest, which is the best place to see Bavarian costume in all its glory and variety. The women wear chain-laced bodices, a major feature of the region's dress, as are the hairpins and white lace shawls and aprons. The men's attire is no less eyecatching, with scarlet vests, forest green coats, and decorated lederhosen.**

Eastern Europe

RIGHT: *Hungarian folk costume continues to thrive. Indigenous dress incorporates many elements, including the simpler Slavic styles seen in eastern regions. There is greater use of color and decoration in this area than is generally found farther west. The voluminous white shirts and wide* gatya *trousers worn by the men in the summer offset fine vests decorated with braiding or appliqué work.*

LEFT: *The village of Kazar in Nograd in the north of Hungary is the home of this gem-like dress with its headdress of beads and spangles, golden lace, and flower-strewn ribbons. Folk dress was still evolving in Hungary up to World War II, but then fell into a state of neglect. The richness of revived dress is largely the result of encouragement from the government after the war to keep old customs and culture alive.*

The finery of eastern Europe is less sophisticated, though more exuberant, than that of the West. It is closer to its roots, yet it is also influenced by European fashionable dress and exotic imports. Folk groups, which continue to encourage and maintain crafts and customs, are an important element of contemporary culture.

HUNGARY

In eastern Europe, Hungary is the nexus between East and West; its influence is found far beyond its boundaries, owing to the extent of the old Austro-Hungarian Empire, which ended at the conclusion of World War I. The distinctively indigenous dress incorporates many elements, including the simpler Slavic styles, an increased use of color and spread of materials such as *aba* (broadcloth), and cuts such as the *keftan* (kaftan), brought by the Turks, and later German influences. Folk dress was still evolving until World War II.

Today, a few notable regions keep the traditions alive. One of the rare developments this century is the almost gaudy peasant embroideries of Kalocsa, previously known for its crisp white cutwork blouses and skirts. The decorative floral elements of factory-produced fabrics and ribbons have blossomed into dazzling pink, red, yellow, green, and turquoise stylized flowers. These are embroidered onto a white ground to make blouses, bodices, and aprons with old-style, cutwork edgings. They are a uniquely Hungarian expression of folk art.

Also impressive are the needlewomen of Matyó, who tried to cover the whole surface of their material with multicolored embroidery. To dress splendidly was a spiritual escape from the poverty of their lives. Even men's clothes were decorated with thick bands of embroidery.

Skilled male artisans did the embroidery, appliqué, and braiding on leather clothes, and the stiff, handwoven, woolen frieze cloth of the *szür*, the long decorated coat of the shepherds. The *szür* was fashioned from rectangular pieces, proof of great antiquity. It was a prized article of clothing that every young man wanted to acquire by the time he was ready to marry. When going to propose, he would, as if by accident, leave it behind at the house of his intended. Next day, if it was hanging outside the house, it meant that his suit had been rejected. If not, he could confidently send along his best man to ask for the girl's hand in marriage.

trousers of the Plain), the simple shirts, and the women's chemises are all made from straight lengths of cloth, to avoid waste.

As prosperity increased in the 19th century, both factory-made cloth and the bright colors of synthetic dyes and yarns were seized on by embroiderers to supplement their subtle, organic-dye palette, always predominantly red. This was the time when peasants became major customers of the button- and braid-making artisans who had all previously worked for the nobility. Subsequently, a very large quantity of frog fastenings and ornate braiding appeared on trousers and coats, and is still a feature.

POLAND

In Poland vestiges of this passion for the braided and cord patterns can be seen in thick woolen clothing decorated with bold *parzenica* designs, which the Gorale men of the Podhale region in the Tatra Mountains continue to wear. It is the only place in Poland where elements of men's folk dress are still worn every day. The trousers, with their beautiful v-shaped, ornamented front panel and seam stripes, are worn with a wide-sleeved shirt, vest, and black *szür*-like short coat braided and embroidered in red and green. The black felt hat is decorated with a string of small shells circling the crown. The shoes of patterned leather, fastened with long crossover thongs bound around the ankle, are typical, and are as ancient a feature as the weighty stamped-

Although it would probably be made nowadays only for display, the noble *suba* must be mentioned. This long sheepskin cloak of the Hungarian Great Plain was made out of as many as 12 or more sheepskins, cut and stitched together like segments of a circle, hanging from a yoke. It protected its wearer against rain and cold, served as a bed and cover outdoors, was put on the back of a sweating horse and, when ragged, was made into a bed in the stable.

Hortobágy in the Great Plain is the region of the mounted herdsmen, who are a link with their horse-breeding ancestors, the Magyars, who came from the East in the 9th century and who gave the Hungarians their language. The summer festival here is devoted to the horse herders, and all the old costumes still appear. Their homespun origins are plain to see: the *gatya* (the wide

leather body belts inlaid with brass decorations, which are so wide as to require up to five decorated brass buckles for fastening.

Gorale women wear their flower-decorated folk dress only on special occasions. The highland bodice is made of velvet, black, dark green, or purple in color, similar in style to the basque bodices of Bronowice, near Cracow, with their gilded embroidery spangled with ordered rows and clusters of beads and sequins.

Among the costumes worn by the many dance groups, those of Lowicz to the north faithfully preserve the character of the wide brilliant orange and yellow stripes of the 19th-century costume, described by early ethnographers as "orange-peel colored." The vertically striped calf-length skirts, which might now be predominantly green or red, look wonderful with their black,

ABOVE LEFT: **One of the unique developments in Hungary this century is the gaudy embroidery of Kalocsca, previously famous for its white cutwork blouses and skirts. Both combine here in this girl's dress.**

ABOVE RIGHT: **A trio of musicians in Bronowice, near Cracow in Poland, show off their distinctive dress. The long blue sleeveless coats, decorated with scarlet tassels and fastened with white belts festooned with gold discs, have fascinated students of costume since the end of the 19th century.**

LEFT: **Dance companies, like this one in Poznan, eastern Poland, have been instrumental in keeping traditional dress alive. In past times, costumes as fine as this would have been reserved for great occasions. Lace caps of all shapes and sizes were formerly the correct attire for married women.**

flower-strewn bodices and white blouses. Men's trousers, too, are striped and worn with boots.

The bridal version of the Lowicz dress includes a huge headdress of fresh flowers. Folk beliefs assigned great magical powers to a married woman's hair, which is why she kept it covered. A reminder of the taboos surrounding married women's hair is the headscarf worn by older European women.

CZECH REPUBLIC AND SLOVAKIA

These countries are also a treasure trove of related yet different costumes, far too numerous for this book to describe in any detail. Here, as elsewhere, pockets of customs and crafts survive.

To nurture the Czech and Slovak culture, ÚL'UV, the Center of Folk Art Production, was founded in 1945. In Slovakia ÚL'UV works in cooperation with over a thousand workers, who continue folk-art productions linked to traditional technologies. Without ÚL'UV, many elements of culture would be lost. For example, the prevalence of blue-and-white prints, made with indigo dye, was a significant strand in Slovakian dress, as it was in the former Czech lands of Bohemia and Moravia, in Hungary, and in the Slavic enclave of Lausitz in eastern Germany. This fashion entered these regions at the end of the 18th century and was a great

BELOW: Hungarian influences are evident in the highly decorative clothes of Moravian Slovakia. The silhouette is bulky, but the wealth of embroidered detail is exquisite.

ABOVE: Young Czech girls wear indigo-printed material which became quite commonplace by the end of the 19th century as domestic dress throughout Central and Eastern Europe.

novelty among townspeople. The style probably originated with the batiks of East Asia, brought to Europe by the Dutch from their East India colonies. Slowly it filtered into the villages, and by the end of the 19th century a network of printers was producing the material that appeared in folk clothing. As the wearing of traditional costumes declined in the first half of this century, so did the print workshops. Then virtually extinct, this delightful fabric is being made again in Puchov, under the auspices of ÚL'UV, and can be bought in their shops, alongside other revived finery.

UKRAINE AND BELARUS

Despite centuries of foreign domination, Ukraine and Belarus, the two largest of the European republics to emerge from the breakup of the Soviet Union, have held on to their cultural identity. Both have rich funds of old dress with a marked Slavic base, and in some respects the forms overlap. However, there are also substantial differences between the two and, as always, it is in the details that one, region can be distinguished from another. Both countries excel at embroidery. Ukrainian costume is more varied and well known abroad, thanks to its celebrated dance troupes and expatriate communities. In North America alone, there are 1.5 million Ukrainians who promote folk traditions with great vigor.

According to a recently published study, *Ukrainian Folk Costume* (an immense task

undertaken by the World Federation of Ukrainian Women's Organizations in Toronto and Philadelphia), typical dress for a man was a shirt with embroidered front and open sleeves, wide baggy *sharovary* trousers made of blue matte woolen fabric tucked into red leather boots, a red sash tied at the side, a *svyta, a* coat of brown woolen cloth trimmed in black, and a gray Persian lamb hat. The trousers were comfortable for riding horseback and were also worn by Cossacks.

Typical costume for a woman included a calf-length chemise with a drawstring neck, a wide panel of embroidery on the sleeves, and a strip around the hem. Over this went the *plakhta*, a panel skirt woven in a square fancy pattern, which was put on around the back and was open at the front. The front opening was covered by a heavy narrow apron, a few inches shorter, and around the waist was a woven girdle. Over all this went the sleeveless *kersetka* (a waistcoat or vest), which fastened on the left and was trimmed in black velvet and decorated with tape or fabric zigzags. The *kersetka* could be hiplength or longer, and shaped with godets below the waist. A deep necklace made of strands of coral beads indicated how many fields the family had, and always bore a cross. On the head was the flower wreath with long ribbons hanging down behind,

BELOW: Farther east in the Ukraine, young unmarried women adorned their hair with a wreath of fresh or paper flowers, with a cascade of multicolored ribbons at the back. This popular custom is being revived.

ABOVE: **In the Ukraine married status was indicated by a close-fitting pillbox hat or ochipok, plain for everyday, finely embroidered for best wear, and covered with a white wimple or kerchief over the top.**

symbolizing womanhood. Fine red boots completed the ensemble.

Outer garments included the *svyta*, an ancient style of coat: the right side wider than the left in order to make a wedge-shaped overlap. Triangular godets sewn in under the sleeves to hem gave the characteristic trapezoid shape. The sleeves were set straight in the side seam, making a rounded, dropped-shoulder line. Variants were made by inserting extra godets in the back at the waistline.

The sheepskin clothing, the sleeveless *keptar* jacket, and enveloping *kozhukh* coat were the work of the *kushnir*, or leather-worker, a folk artist who would be hired by a family to come and live in for up to six weeks while he completed their outfits. Several sheep would be slaughtered in preparation, and the hides tanned and fitted. The *kushnir* would sew together and embroider the skins with a beautiful meandering pattern. It was strenuous work and required great skill. The style of the *kozhukh* was dictated by the shape of the skins. The slanted right-side overlap, with its sharp triangular corner, was made into a feature, with its handsome arc of embroidery contained within elaborate borders. Similar designs are seen in Mongol and Chinese skin-based clothing.

Although many authentic clothes still exist, dresses for dance groups are a stylized stage version of the old costumes, and

lighter to wear. The exquisite detail of the old embroideries, made as much for the pleasure of the making as in the wearing, would be lost on an audience. But the revived styles remain faithful to the patterns, colors, and shapes of the different regions.

The shirt is steeped in folklore. Just before a wedding the bride sent her groom a shirt she had embroidered. Mothers made their sons a special shirt when they joined the army. If the boy fell in battle, he would be buried in it; if he lived, it was a remembrance for him of his mother at home.

The shirt is also part of Ukraine's national consciousness. During the times of Soviet repression, a man could be sent to Siberia for wearing one. Now they can safely be worn again. The day Ukraine celebrated its independence, President Leonid Kravchuk and many others wore splendid shirts with a panel of red embroidery under their suits.

Belarus, formerly Belorussia, or White Russia, is landlocked, and its traditional dress has survived miraculously, and in a relatively pure form. The old costumes are treasured by the young, who wear them for country festivals, some of which have pre-Christian origins in celebrating the cycles of the sun. The country is renowned for its flax, now an important commercial crop. Flax is the subject of a museum at

BELOW: **Costumes from southeast Belarus are unmistakably authentic. The densely worked embroidery and deep, vibrant colors, mellowed with age, have a quality that cannot be reproduced.**

ABOVE: **Many Ukrainian girls possess at least one traditional blouse, and are still taught the art of embroidery, especially the geometric cross-stitch work that is seen on these front panels.**

Hudzievichy in the west, where women skilled in the production of linen teach the younger generation. Many of the old clothes were made at home until about 30 years ago, and in the country, it is still possible to see old women wearing beautiful dresses.

Garments for the women included the chemise; a heavy pleated, checked, or striped woven skirt; a linen homespun apron, and bodice, often worn with a basque. Complex pinned and draped headdresses, medieval in their style, have been replaced with kerchiefs.

For men, the white long shirt was girdled at the waist over straight trousers. The close embroidery was and still is a deep red, with black emphasis and outlines. Its symbolism is ancient. White, the color of homespun linen, was the color of heaven; red was the color of the sun, earth, and was protective of organic life; black was the color of the underworld and spiritual life.

The costume divided into three spheres: neck, shoulders, and sleeves represented the higher world; the waist, the middle region or earth; and the hem, the underworld. Different shapes of ornament were decreed for the parts to ward off evil. The reason that the woman's sleeves at the shoulders were heavily embroidered was that in an attack she would be seized there first. Men were thought to be vulnerable on the chest, which is why their chief ornament was at the opening of the shirt.

Central & Eastern Europe Map

Key

Approximate area of provinces

1,000–4,000m
(3,000–12,000ft)

400–1,000m
(1,200–3,000ft)

0–400m (0–1,200ft)

Seas, lakes and rivers

Note: peoples are shown
in italics eg: *Bavarian*

Within Central and eastern Europe, the greatest variety of headgear is seen. The most sophisticated hats are found in the rich regions, mostly to the west, that were industrialized early – such as Switzerland – whereas in the east there are pockets of rural communities where a love of less costly but expressive handiwork is typical. Up until World War I there were virtually feudal enclaves in many regions of Europe where styles of dress, now treasured or revived, were strong and simple. Certain basic hat shapes have survived here longer than anywhere else. The contrast is between burgher wealth and peasant ornamentation. Each type of society expresses its love of decoration in a characteristic manner.

An Austrian woman wearing a lace headdress.

A woman from Budapest, Hungary, wearing a traditional hat.

A Swiss musician wearing a felt hat.

A Moravian woman of the Czech Republic wearing a floral-printed headscarf.

BALTIC SEA

GERMANY

BELARUS
Belorussian

•Poznan

•Lowicz

•Hudzievichy

LAUSITZ POLAND

HESSE •Ziegenhain

CZECH REPUBLIC

UKRAINE
Ukrainian

Dnieper

BLACK FOREST

BAVARIA
Bavarian

BOHEMIA

Bronowice• •Cracow

Gorale PODHALE
•Zakopane

MORAVIA

Puchov•

Tatra

Danube

DANUBE VALLEY

•Munich

SLOVAKIA

•Basel *THURGAU*

APPENZELL

Austrian

JURA

Swiss GLARUS

•Vienna

•Matyó

HORTOBÁGY

SWITZERLAND

Tyrol

SALZBURG

STYRIA

•Budapest

GREAT PLAIN

VALAIS

CARINTHIA

HUNGARY
Hungarian

Alps

LOMBARDY

•Kalocsa

Tisza

ITALY

BLACK SEA

The Mediterranean Countries

The costumes of the west Mediterranean countries – that is, Italy, Portugal, and Spain – have all in their day been exceptionally rich and refined in style.

SPAIN

No one costume could capture the essence of Spain, a large country, which is really the sum of its regional parts. Here, old customs are being revived, and at festivals participants wear gorgeous clothes, many of them reproduced in the spirit of the old. In Galicia in the north, the form of dress is not unlike that worn in Portugal's Minho, but in detail it is quite restrained, which makes it look entirely different. The heavy red skirt is bordered by a double band of thick black

velvet ribbon. This skirt, the stiff crossover cape that replaces the shawl, and the round black velvet apron are all edged with a typical style of embroidery. This consists of a crusting of tiny black beads and faceted sequins stitched into swirls and edgings that give off a ghostly glitter. Overall, the costume has that unmistakably mannered elegance that is wholly Spanish – yet it is just one of many styles of related dress in the northern region.

In the mountain area of Salamanca, in La Alberca, the August fiesta in honor of the Virgin of La Asunción sees a spectacular display of dancing in the town square. The women wear skirts weighed down with dark

ABOVE MIDDLE: The Andalusian male in the south of Spain wears an immaculately fitted short jacket and trousers, a sober outfit which acts as a perfect foil for the flounced dress of his female partner. He also wears the famous wide-brimmed sombrero of the region.

LEFT: The flounced dresses of Andalusía, which are a feature of the Eastertide Feria of Seville, are not Spanish national costume, but particular to this region. In their present form, with their extravagant tiers of ruffles, they are relatively recent versions that reached their stylized height in the 1930s. Originally they were made in brilliantly colored fabric printed with white dots, but now many other patterns are used.

*ABOVE: **Musicians from Villanueva de la Vera in Spain wear fiesta dress that is quite modern, but cut according to tradition. Spanish costume is typically vivid in color, but simple and strong in style.***

spontaneous surge of interest in traditional dances, music, songs, and dress swept the country and local groups sprang up everywhere. Fortunately, the old ways of doing things survived in the people's memories and a younger generation have taken them up with enthusiasm.

The Minho on the Costa Verde (Green Coast), the fertile port-producing region of the northwest, has the most colorful costumes, and numerous festivals provide many opportunities to show them off. Every Sunday in the summer, bands of people congregate at local shrines and keep the festivities going until well into the night. The most splendid of these gatherings is the three-day festival held at the old town of Viana do Castelo, where the costumes – some old, most newly made, but in accordance with tradition – vie for brilliance with the fireworks of the grand finale.

Typical Minho dress is a vertically striped woven skirt, predominantly red, with a deep plain border heavily embroidered with flowers and beaded tendrils of electric hue. The white blouse is embroidered with blue flowers on the front, the shoulders, sleeves,

*BELOW: **The Minho or Costa Verde, the fertile port-producing region of Northwest Portugal, has the most exuberant costumes. Festivals like this one at Villa Franca provide an opportunity to display them.***

*ABOVE: **These Sicilian girls are celebrating the Easter festival in traditional decorated costume at the 15th-century Albanian town of Piana dei Albanesi in the uplands, south of Palermo.***

appliqué, and around their shoulders they wrap the soft, gold-embroidered silk shawls with their flying fringes, which were introduced into Spain from Manila in the Philippines. These islands were named after the Spanish king Philip II in the 16th century, when they formed part of the Spanish empire. Manila shawls became coveted items in the 19th century. Usually the hair is worn coiled up into a *picaporte* (door-knocker) style and left uncovered. The interest in the men's dress is in the silver buttons on the shirt and the velvet-trimmed jacket and vest.

The flounced dresses of Andalusia, which are a feature of the Feria de Sevilla held after Easter, are not national costume as many think, although they are among the most dramatic and photogenic. The Manila shawl has now been replaced with a smaller one, which is easier to dance with and not so precious. The men wear tightly fitted, waist-length jackets, frilly shirts, full-length trousers, a cummerbund, plus a wide-brimmed hat – called a *sombrero Cordobès*. The legendary *painettas* (high combs) and lace mantillas of the ladies of this region are sometimes still worn to bullfights, in particular by women from the most important families, who have ringside seats at *la barrera*.

PORTUGAL

A great delight is taken by Portugal in its folk traditions, which are actively encouraged by the Ministry of Culture. When decades of semi-dictatorship finally ended in 1974, a

and cuffs. The two-toned bodice, often red and black, is embroidered like the skirt and can be a masterwork of naive art. A printed kerchief covers the head, and a printed shawl tucks into the stiff woven apron of vivid geometric or floral style. The hanging pocket tied around the waist is a special feature, as are the black patent shoes embroidered with white flowers. Carmen Miranda was born in Minho; maybe her flamboyant taste in clothes was fashioned by the colorful costumes worn throughout the region.

Country weddings are the occasion to see further examples of Portuguese folk dress. The black velvet bridal skirt and jacket and small rounded apron, embroidered with fine gold or silver tracery, are reminders of Portugal's imperial past, as is the gold jewelry festooning the bride. The mass of fine chains, filigree hearts, strings of beads and coins covering her bodice are a form of dowry and a local craft tradition.

ITALY

Nineteenth-century Italy had a regional dress of unparalleled elaboration, as befits the country that was the birthplace of the Renaissance. Perhaps the style was just too ornate to revive on a large scale, and the costume is now virtually confined to museums, except partially in the Tyrol and the south, where it is still worn on special occasions by the established Albanian refugee communities in Calabria and Sicily. Albanians fleeing from Arab invaders first settled in Italy in 1448, and now there are over 70,000 living in southern Italy.

The Balkans

RIGHT: *A folk team in Sarajevo performs in costumes collected in Macedonia, a country famed for its weaving and embroidery. In women's dress the focus is the apron, thick as a carpet, densely woven with stylized symbols, and worn over a full-length chemise. The various garments are not cut and fitted but shaped by gathering or pleating straight-cut fabric lengths. This is also the basis of the men's wide breeches and full shirts.*

BELOW MIDDLE: *These dancers in Dubrovnik are dressed in a fashion entirely different from the Macedonian dress shown left. This demonstrates how varied costume from the numerous regions of the former Yugoslavia can be. It is a reflection of the ethnic mix of people in this region, which has such a complex political and cultural history.*

The Balkans take their name from the mountain range that sweeps in a shallow arc right across Bulgaria and then embraces Romania, Bulgaria, Greece, former Yugoslavia, and Albania.

Probably no other region has such variety of dress – no doubt a reflection of the complex history that has made it an area of extraordinary ethnic diversity. The Greeks, Romanians, Slavs, Turks, and Magyars, to name a few, have all left their mark and a host of influences. Some relate to western Europe; this can be seen in Slovenia (once owned by Austria), along the Dalmatian coast, and in maritime Croatia, whose dress bears a family resemblance to the extravagant costumes once worn in Venice. Turkish influence in dress can be seen in the baggy trousers, boots, fez and pillbox-shaped hats, tunics, and cummerbunds once used by men as pockets for their personal arsenal. The coin jewelry and the headdresses are

archaic. An ancient Slavic style of dress, which consisted of a long chemise worn with a wrap skirt or double aprons and a short or long leather or thick cloth jacket, often sleeveless, speaks of an early, simpler tradition, which gets more pronounced by degrees eastward in the region.

FORMER YUGOSLAVIA

One of the finest collections of authentic dress for men and women belongs to the Lado dance group based in Zagreb, capital of Croatia. Lado has dresses from all over former Yugoslavia, and by looking closely at the regional costumes one can appreciate easily the skills attained by the craftsmen and women and the degree of difference between one region and another.

Clothing was almost always made from homespun linen woven by the women, who were in charge of the production of flax: from sowing the seed through retting (soaking and beating the flax) and spinning, to dyeing and weaving. The various pieces of clothing were not tailored, but were made by sewing together straight lengths of fabric, which were then gathered or pleated into folds of varying width. This is the basis of men's costume, which consists of long, wide linen breeches and a long shirt, and of many forms of women's costume. Linen clothes would have been supplemented by wool, leather, and fur outer garments, such as vests, jackets, and mantles, bought from specialized furriers and tailors in towns and at fairs or from local master craftsmen.

A distinctive accessory was the primitive footwear called *opanky*. It is a type of leather sandal consisting of a broad sole that wraps around the bottom of the foot, tapering to an upturned or pointed tip over the toes, and lashed with thongs across the foot and around the ankle. Sometimes *opanky* are

which type of costume. For example, a young woman in her first year of marriage would be expected to wear garments with a red woven pattern because she should be protected against evil spirits and assured of a happy future – which meant, primarily producing numerous, healthy offspring. For older women who already had children, red garments were no longer considered the appropriate clothing. Therefore they wore less brilliant colors that were darker.

The women of Posavina were known to be expert embroiderers, and their best

great pains to decorate this, their most telling accessory.

Men's costume from Posavina was similar to that found throughout northern Croatia. The shirt and breeches were always made as a pair of the same kind of linen and with the same decoration. The breeches might be anything from one to three widths wide. In summer they were left loose and in winter were tied with *opanky* straps.

A most interesting costume historically comes from remote Baranja, situated between the Danube and Drava rivers, in

ABOVE: *A man from Sibenik on the Dalmatian coast, Croatia, wears his wool tasseled jacket cape-style.*
MIDDLE: *A church festival on the Aegean island of Karpathos. Coins and even banknotes were worn by young girls to indicate the extent of their dowry.*

ABOVE: *A dancer from the island of Lemnos, which lies at the entrance to the Dardanelles, wears a version of the skirted* fustinella. *The occasion was to greet the crew of the reconstructed ship Argo, as they re-enacted the mythic journey of Jason and the Argonauts.*

made with straps that criss-cross to the knee. Variations on *opanky*, often under different names, crop up everywhere in southern and eastern Europe, although in recent times people have shown a preference for boots and shoes.

Women's costume from Posavina in Croatia is one of the most striking elements in the Lado collection, with its bright red decoration and voluminous pleated blouse, full-length skirt, and apron.

In accordance with the old Slavonic color code, red is the prime color, and all others are subordinate. There were rules governing what color and pattern could be used on

decorative efforts were reserved for the cap (*poculica*) and the scarf (*peca*), which was worn over it. These pieces were the headgear of married women; young girls wore a red band decorated with coral beads and imitation pearls instead. The most festive caps and scarves were embroidered in silk spun from local silkworms and dyed with plant dyes in all shades of red, dark purple, yellow, blue, green, brown, and black. All this artistry was expressed in one motif, the floral baroque branch in its countless variations. Headgear, particularly the scarf, indicated the social position of married women, so that it is not surprising that they took

what was northeastern Croatia, but is now just in Hungary. It clearly belongs to the great family of Slavic dress that has its origins in the Slavic homelands to the north of the Carpathian Mountains and survived despite centuries of Turkish domination. It is an important feature in Macedonian, Romanian, Bulgarian, and other eastern European costume. There are two distinct variations, one from the area of the Danube and the other from the Drava. Basic to both regions is the sleeved linen chemise (*rubina*), embroidered with vertical stripes on the sleeves and bodice and with additional woolen garments worn over the top.

In the summer a thickly fringed apron was worn, made of a narrow length of cloth decorated with many colored stripes. In the winter, a skirt of similar material was adopted, arranged in pleated folds at the back and sometimes not even sewn together in the front, but covered with a wide woolen apron made of two lengths of cloth.

Along the Danube, instead of the skirt, two woolen aprons girded the body, tied front and back. Both styles developed from the same garment and represent what was originally one straight piece of material.

rain. It is surprisingly heavy and at the hem can be as much as 44 yards (40 meters) around. The dress uniform worn by the Evzones, the soldiers who guard the tomb of the unknown soldier in Athens, comprises a tasseled fez, a full-sleeved white shirt, embroidered vest, *fustanella*, white stockings, and red shoes that sport some enormous pompoms.

The most decorative of the women's costumes is the *Amalia*, which originated at the court of the first Greek King, Otto, and his Queen, Amalia, who came from Bavaria in

they were being sold for next to nothing in markets by peasants who had renounced their intrinsic culture.

These clothes had their roots in ancient history and were barely influenced by western styles. The underlying style was old Bulgarian, with Slavic, and what were originally Arabic influences that came via the Ottomans. Among the numerous clothing items worn by women over a long shift were the *saya*, a gown with a deeply curved bodice and sleeves, and the *sukman*, a closed tunic dress, which at its most shapely had

ABOVE AND FAR RIGHT: **Bulgaria is the world's major supplier of attar of roses, used in perfumery, and at the Festival of Roses in June, people come from all over the country to display their fine dress. The women's aprons relate to Macedonian styles.**

MIDDLE: **The embroidered blouse, gathered skirt, and lavishly decorated apron of this woman's festival costume from Crisului, Transylvania, Romania, shows the strong Hungarian elements in a region that was under Hapsburg rule for centuries.**

GREECE

In Greece, authentic dress is nowadays best seen in museums and in a simplified revived form at festivals. Folk costumes do not appear to be so important here as they are in the rest of the Balkans. Most startling is the men's skirted *fustanella*, with its 400 tiny pleats, which are said to represent the number of years of occupation by the Turks. It developed from mountain dress in Southern Albania, where the stiff skirt of fabric made of a dense mass of slender triangular pieces tapering into a waistband would be protective (that is dagger-proof) and practical for scrambling over rocky ter-

1833 and was keen to adopt Greek fashions. This graceful dress consists of a full, ankle-length silk skirt, a white blouse, and a fitted gold-embroidered velvet jacket. A trace of Turkish influence remains in the small red cap, with its long, heavy tassel.

BULGARIA

Folk traditions have survived well in Bulgaria. In the 1970s it was state policy to revive arts as an ideological weapon to fight "western capitalist influences." A particular form of nationalism began to bloom, and ethnographic sciences flourished. There was a new awareness that traditional Bulgarian costumes were beautiful, at a time when

godets inserted at the waist, giving a stiff A-line flare to the skirt. A gown from the Rhodope Mountains, made nearly 100 years ago in a woven lilac-blue and black stripe, is a most elegant item in the wardrobe of one of the attachés at the Bulgarian Embassy in London and looks like new. For the men, a shirt, baggy trousers, fitted from the knee and worn with a wide cummerbund, and short jacket were typical.

These clothes were rescued just in time to reappear at the regional festivals of performing arts, which are now a feature of Bulgarian life. These festivals are accompanied by a parade of colorful clothes. Not all are necessarily authentic – but a surprising number are. Good-quality reproductions are made by the Guild of Folk-skill Masters. Regional variations are striking in appearance, marked not only by whether a tunic is worn over the chemise, or the double apron, or a pleated skirt, but in particular by fine embroidery – a significant expression of Bulgarian folk art.

Peasant jewelry looks as if it has come from an archaeological excavation, with its chains of coins, big circular belt clasps, and headdresses interlaced with metal leaves and coins and with long dangling side pieces.

ROMANIA

The earliest picture we have of Romanian costume is of that worn by the Dacian soldiers carved into the spiral procession of figures on Trajan's Column in Rome. These soldiers, from a land subjugated by Trajan in the 2nd century, wear the high, slightly bulbous, conical hats that their descendants are still wearing today in the mountains of Romania.

There is a wealth of exquisite embroidery, leatherwork, weaving, and appliqué in the country, used with great flair in toning and also wildly contrasting color combinations on shirts, chemises, short sleeveless jackets, and coats, worn by both men and women. Among the finest weaving anywhere in Europe must be the long, gauzy headscarves worn by married women. Often knee length, they were draped around the head and under the chin and held in place with ornamental hairpins. They were worn with chemises with lavishly embroidered sleeves and the Slavic style of wrap skirt or double aprons, girdled with a woven belt.

In the men's costume, a very impressive feature is the wide leather belt, with punched and studded motifs, or braided with narrow strips of colored leather. Also remarkable are the short sleeveless jackets and vests made of sheepskin, with bright borders of embroidery and edges trimmed with fur or fleece. For rough mountain wear the shepherds have a thick rectangular cloak, much like a rug, with a hood at one end made by simply stitching one end together, corner to corner. It is held in place on the shoulders with a stout woolen cord, and at night it serves as a blanket. On Sundays and feast days, Romanians in remote country districts still wear their traditional clothes, which can also be seen in village museums.

The style is essentially Slavic, with a strong dash of Hungarian in Transylvania, which was carved out of the old Hungarian empire after World War I and annexed to Romania. The Hungarian influence is evident in the decorated men's breeches. The famous costume of this region comes from Maramures. Craftsmen take great pride in the jewel-like embroideries of sheepskin vests, which combine lush flower designs with soft leather appliqué and tassel decoration; at the Spring Festival, young girls wear them with the double-apron skirt with wide yellow and black stripes.

A glimpse of this charming country when the wearing of traditional costume was at its height is given in the book *Between the Woods and the Water*, by Patrick Leigh-Fermor, who walked through Romania in the early 1930s on his way to Istanbul.

"I fell in with a party carrying sickles and scythes and slung babies. Their ample white homespun tunics were caught in with belts as wide as girths and sometimes covered in iron studs, and except for those who were barefoot, they were shod in the familiar canoe-tipped moccasins and rawhide thongs. In Transylvania, the women's clothes had been varying all the time. Each village and valley enjoined a different assembly of colors and styles: braids, tunics, lace, ribands, goffering, ruffs, sashes, caps, kerchiefs, coifs and plaits free or coiled: a whole array of details announced whether they were betrothed, brides, married, spinsters or widows. There were bodices, flowing or paneled sleeves, embroidery, gold coins at brow or throat or both, aprons front and back, a varying number of petticoats and skirts jutting at the hips like farthingales, and occasionally these were accompanied by colored Russian boots. Their everyday dress was a sober version of their gala outfits; but these exploded on feast days and at weddings in ravishing displays. Clothes were still emblematic, and not only among peasants: an expert in Romanian and Hungarian symbols in a market place would have been able to reel off their provenances as swiftly as a herald glancing along the flags and surcoats of a 14th-century battle."

A girl wearing ornate hairpins for the Javea fiesta in Southern Spain.

A golden headdress worn by a young girl at Easter in Sicily.

Southern Europe Map

Throughout the Mediterranean regions, jewelry is considered a most important part of display in clothing. Festoons of coins, chains, and crosses are conspicuous as signs of wealth, status, and dowry expectations. In countries, such as Spain and Portugal, that had sources of precious minerals due to their empires, these materials predominate. Farther to the east, less precious metals and stones are used, and jewelry designs have an archaic feel to them, with straight pins, coin fringing over the face, and primitive pendant earrings.

Key

1,000–4,000m
(3,000–12,000ft)

400–1,000m
(1,200–3,000ft)

0–200m (0–600ft)

Seas, lakes and rivers

Note: peoples are shown in italics eg: *Greek*

A girl from Karpathos, Greece, in an ornate costume with gold coin jewelry.

Elaborate attire of a bride in the former Yugoslavia.

Bulgarian girl in embroidered costume at the Festival of the Rose at Kazanlúk.

A Greek girl wearing a sequinned headwrap and ornate silver headdress.

FESTIVE COSTUME

TOP ROW, LEFT TO RIGHT:

Lithuanian women's costume with elaborate cross-stitch embroidery, worn with highly prized amber beads.

Eighteenth-century-inspired Swiss finery seen at a costume festival in the Valais.

Back panel of an Arctic woman's hood, in Siberia, festooned with beadwork and braid.

Bodice of a Danish woman's folk costume, decorated with eyelets and lacing and a silver-clasped belt.

Lavishly patterned ribbons of a woman's headdress in Transylvania, Romania.

MIDDLE ROW, LEFT TO RIGHT:

Coin necklaces worn tucked into a Cretan girl's bodice.

Rich embroidered bands applied to a Saami man's costume in the Arctic.

Floral motifs worked in gold on a green brocade bow, as a final touch to a floral damask-weave skirt, worn by an Albanian woman living in Piana dei Albanesi, Sicily.

Ubiquitous flower motifs on a simple shawl worn by a Budapest woman, Hungary.

A young Austrian woman's white lace collar and elaborate bodice embellished with gold ribbon lacing and a red and silver sash.

BOTTOM ROW, LEFT TO RIGHT:

Short, back-pleated apron over a full-length chemise, is a strong Slavic element in this Bulgarian costume.

Chukchi fur and finery seen at a spring festival, in Russia.

A Sunday vest worn by a man from Zagreb, Croatia.

A silver-chain-swagged tracht bodice worn by a woman from Oberbayern, in the Bavarian Alps.

A basque bodice encrusted with spangles and beads for a Polish festival costume.

73

AFRICA

The people of Africa dress in many different styles of clothing. Communities living in Stone Age conditions coexist with those that are living in completely westernized areas across this vast landmass.

For the purpose of this chapter, the ethnographers' practice of grouping or identifying tribal people by their languages is followed. In Africa, perhaps more than on any other continent, the indigenous peoples pay scant attention to politically drawn boundaries. Nomadic people wander across frontiers and pastoralists go where their flocks can graze, as they have done for hundreds of years. In Africa climate will dictate movements far more than a government will.

Africa is here discussed by cultural areas and vegetational zones, rather than by countries; and the history, life, and customs of the people in each region are included.

Starting with the north coast, the subtropical coastal zone of Morocco, Algeria, and Tunisia is home to the Berber people. A stretch of steppe extends south until it meets the vast Sahara Desert. The origins of the Berbers are unclear; they are culturally and linguistically distinct from the Arabs, who came to this region between the 7th and 11th centuries.

Moving southward, the Sahel region is a belt of land running for some 8,046 miles (5,000 kilometers) through six of the mainly French-speaking West African countries: Mauritania, Senegal, Mali, Burkina Faso (formerly Upper Volta), Niger, and Chad. The Sahel is populated by nomadic and seminomadic peoples, perhaps the most well-known being the Tuareg and the Fulani. The Tuareg are stock breeders; the Fulani are pastoralists. Roughly 13 percent

ABOVE AND OPPOSITE: **Ornate beadwork is a prime feature of African dress, as seen above on these Pondo Red Blanket (Xhosa) girls of South Africa and the Samburu women of north Kenya (opposite) at a dance.**

of the population of the six Sahelian countries are nomadic.

The peoples of West Africa inhabit a region that is a mixture of both steppe and savannah landscape. These countries – from Senegal, through Sierra Leone, Liberia, Ivory Coast, Ghana, Nigeria to Cameroon – are known for the different types of cloth that they make. They are mostly factory made, but the finest are still woven by hand, carrying on an old tradition of craftsmanship that dates right back to the great

West African kingdoms before slavery was introduced to the continent.

Many separate and distinctive tribes live in the modern states of southern Sudan, Kenya, Tanzania, Somalia, and southern Ethiopia, a region described as the East African cattle area. On the Kenya-Tanzania border live the Masai tribe, while in the region's center lie the tropical highlands, home to some of the most endangered peoples of the continent, such as the Karo of the Omo River.

East of this region is the Horn, where ancient Jewish and Christian communities still eke out a basic living in the Ethiopian Highlands. Coastal Somalia has a completely different Islamic culture, one richly influenced by traders and settlers. An exotic mixture of Africans, Arabs, Portuguese and French have coexisted happily for centuries.

South Africa's peoples – Xhosa, Zulu, Swazi, and Ndebele – still wear their traditional beadwork and distinguishing headgear, but they are fast disappearing, although some traditional dress can be seen at tribal ceremonies or tourist attractions. As in other regions of the world, it is possible that the majority's achievement of self-determination – which black South Africans gained in 1994 – will be followed by a revival of interest in cultural history.

Sadly, the San, or Bushmen, of the Kalahari are rapidly declining in numbers, mainly because of disease and the scarcity of game and water. In 1990, there were roughly 50,000 Kung Bushmen still living in the northern area. In 1963, the Central Kalahari Game Reserve was established to provide a haven for the few still hunting, but they have no actual rights to the land.

North Africa

The Berbers are the indigenous people of North Africa and are scattered across Morocco, Algeria, Tunisia, Libya, and Egypt. They arrived in the region toward the end of the 2nd millennium BC and were conquered in the 7th century AD by the Arabs, who converted virtually all the Berbers to Christianity at that time. The Arab invasions of the 12th century destroyed their settled rural economy, imposed Islam, and forced many Berber peoples into a nomadic way of life. This continued with the Spanish, British, and French colonial conquests. Today, many Berbers are migrant workers all over southern Europe, while only a few remain as sedentary farmers in the Saharan lowlands in winter, moving their flocks to the High Atlas Mountains for summer grazing.

The nomadic Muslim of the past was polygamous, but his urban descendant is typically monogamous, mainly for economic reasons. A traditional wedding is the custom in Morocco, and it is expensive and impressive. The dowry, paid before a notary, is spent on the bride's trousseau and on new furniture. The jewelry a bride receives on her betrothal must be made of gold and comprises rings, bracelets, necklaces, and earrings. In addition, she is given two complete outfits, make up, and perfumes.

Marriage festivities are an outstanding event, especially for the bride, who leaves her family to join a new one, according to

BELOW: A desert scene at Imilchil, Morocco, where Berbers gather to negotiate dowries and discuss business or news. The scene displays the variety of male dress, from the hooded burnous to the loose djellabah or tunic, with turbans, scarves and caps.

the Koranic law. The complex ceremonies vary greatly from region to region: in the Atlas Mountains pre-Islamic practices have survived, but in towns the engagement is celebrated by prayers in the mosque. During the engagement period, which can last between six months to two years, the prospective groom sends his intended wife gifts of lengths of cloth, gowns, or perfume on feast days.

Five days before the wedding, a mattress, blankets, and other necessities are carried into the bridal chamber. The bride is given a bath in the *hammam*. This ritual bath is closely regulated by professional female wedding attendants called *negassa*. They apply some heavily stylized make up – including henna-stain designs, to the palms of the hands and feet. Finally, they dress the girl in her wedding finery of white robes which are often sumptuously embroidered. She is then placed behind a curtain, symbolizing her transition to a new life.

The following evening, the heavily made-up and veiled bride, sitting on a round table, is carried on the shoulders of the *negassa*, to a chorus of song and shouting, to the bridal chamber – but only to rest. The singing, feasting, and carrying will continue for another seven days. The *negassa*'s other ritual task is to verify the bride's virginity and witness her defloration. Today, the women are more discreet and stand behind a screen

during the act. Eventually, after a second ritual bath, the *negassa* leave the house and the couple are left alone.

The marriage ceremony would seem to emphasize the chattel status of the woman, in that she is carried, doll-like and heavily made-up, is not allowed to speak, and sometimes may not have met her husband before

the ceremony of engagement. However, a married Berber woman can go unveiled, has property rights, and can divorce easily and remarry. In cities or places where they will be seen or photographed by strangers, married women may choose to wear the *haik* or all-encompassing white robe and a *mandeel* or fall veil on the lower face, while being accompanied by younger, unmarried female relatives in jeans and blouses.

Berber costume is antique in origin. The *haik*, found widely in North and West Africa, is a derivative of the Roman toga. The undergarment, often a long length of fabric, is folded to form a panel across the breasts. It is held to the top of the shoulders with pins, and is of Byzantine Greek origin. It is called an *izar* in the south of Morocco, and is similar to the Tunisian *mellia*. The color varies with the locale. For a wedding, the *haik* will be white over a tunic of heavily encrusted brocade. For everyday wear in Morocco, a woman in Tiznir would wear black over a white under-tunic or kaftan. In Goulimine, the *izar* is blue over a black tunic. The Ait Hadidou of the High Atlas wear a white *izar* held at the waist with a woolen belt decorated with colored pom-poms. It is usually turned twice and is called a *batror* or *hamila*.

Apart from the kaftan, *izar*, and *haik*, other everyday costume items include the *chalwar*, which is a pair of loose, skirt-like, baggy trousers, or a skirt of brocade topped by an overhanging blouse. Sometimes a tight-fitting bolero, heavily embroidered in the Turkish style with couched gold thread at the neck, front opening, and up the cuffs, is worn with the *chalwar*. In winter a grand shawl of wool, called a *zlazil*, envelops the Berber woman. There is no tradition of hand-knitting among Berber women, as their hand-spun yarn is too weak.

The Berber women of the south side of the Atlas area wear highly decorative clothes and jewelry, and it is still possible to see tattooed faces among them. The jewelry of the Berbers is exceedingly varied and rich. The "trembling pins" that adorn the hair are perhaps influenced by the combs worn with Spanish mantillas that were once adopted by colonial women. Much older are the pins or fibulas, known as *bzima*, that the Berber women use to hold together all their traditional attire. Like the *haik*, these are very Roman in their design.

Necklaces often display circles or disks covered in granulation (little dots or beads of gold or silver). They are worn over the collarbone with a cord to hold the weight around the back of the neck. Coins of gold, silver, or copper are often featured. Head pieces may hang from the headwrap or turban, in front of the ears, with coral or pearls. Both of these semiprecious substances are symbols of fertility and ward off the evil eye.

The "hand of Fatima" is a frequently used design, symbolizing the female pudenda. Square anklets (*erdif*) and cylindrical ones (*khalkhals*) are 8–12 inches (20–30 centimeters) wide at times, and are decorated with cloisonné enamel or chased patterns.

The male costume is similar in origin and design to the female one. Normal street wear is the hooded *djellabah* (sometimes spelled *gelabiya*) made of cotton or wool, now worn over a European suit or trousers.

Traditionalists may wear an undershirt, with or without sleeves, instead of trousers. In the Magreb, a *jebba*, or square-shaped chemise, is worn with loose trousers: it is an unshaped garment with a slit neck that is threaded with a drawstring. In rural areas, the all-enveloping open robe, or *burnous*, is also worn over the *djellabah*. The favorite color for a city *djellabah* is blue with carmine trimming thread. A white *haik* may be thrown over it, or a scarf – *shesh* – in blue or white. For a wedding, men's *djellabahs* will be made of silk and ornately embroidered all around the neck opening. All Berbers wear turbans or caps with or without turban-wraps around the temples.

NOMADS AND TRADERS OF THE SAHEL

The Tuareg and the Fulani are the principal nomadic groups of the Sahel region. The Fulani have traded with the Tuareg for centuries, offering gold, grain, and slaves in return for meat, salt, and dates. Increasing desertification of the region is making traditional nomadic life harder, but there are many groups who persist in their traditional customs. Such a subgroup of the Fulani are the Wodaabe people who live in the central Niger region.

Sahelian nomads come together annually at a great market gathering, which the Wodaabe call a *worso*, when members of one of their sublineages gather to celebrate births, arrange marriages, and deal with

ABOVE MIDDLE: These Berber Bedouin men come from Mauritania. Their costume shows its ancient classic provenance: the pure white draped cloth or haik *is worn over a simple tunic or kaftan and contrasts crisply with their deep indigo blue-dyed turbans. Pure handwoven cotton is very practical: surprisingly warm for cold nights in desert areas, but cool in midday heat. The small box worn around the neck contains some Muslim prayers.*

LEFT: Berber people are the indigenous stock of North Africa, and ethnically different from the Arab people who came to the region in the 12th century AD Berbers maintain a strong and active separate cultural identity, which shows in their dress, song, and customs. These Moroccan Berber girls belong to a dance troupe; they wear typical coin jewelry and square neck collars, the shapes of which can be traced back to ancient Roman designs.

other community matters. This event takes place before the annual decampings, at the onset of the rains, to new pastures along centuries-old migration routes. At such meetings there will be trading of Nigerian cloth, Tuareg fringed camel bags, and silver or other metal goods transported down the trade routes from Libya, and Hausa leather-work. The finest clothing is worn by all those assembled.

The culminating event of the two- or three-day *worso* is when the young male groups or *surbaabe* dance to show off their beauty and skill to the marriageable girls. The youths adorn themselves elaborately. Their skin is lightened with a chalk paste and patterned with dots and lines. Kohl is applied to their eyes, lips are blackened, and their heads are wrapped in white turbans. Around their necks hang ubiquitous talismans. These little leather pouches contain numerous mixtures of herbs, written spells, and ritual objects believed to bring strength, charm, sexual power, and protection from harmful spirits or physical injury.

Long strips of brass-wrapped leather, bead strings, and straps decorated with cowrie-shell beads dangle from their temples and over the chest. Huge straw hats adorn their heads. They are loaded with feathers, wool tassels, beads, and anything useable, and the spectacular ingenuity and variety of the decoration adds to the festive atmosphere.

Specifically for the beauty dance, the males wear women's wraps pulled tight as skirt lengths from the waist, inhibiting leg movement but enhancing the effect of their high-jumping dance style.

The women's attire for the final beauty pageant is their best. They wear black striped cloth embroidered at the hem edge with many patterns, wrapped around the body and topped with a short, bolero-style jacket and an abundance of glittering textile

headwraps elaborately folded and often draping down the back. Bodices or boleros are richly embroidered, often in gold and red. The women put on an abundance of jewelry, wearing several huge hoop earrings in each ear, necklaces, bracelets, anklets, and upper-arm bangles. They also carry large multicolored umbrellas.

The traditional male garment of the Tuareg is a draped cloak or *k'sa*, also of indigo blue cotton or wool. This measures about 6 yards (5.5 meters) in length and is worn over a long shirt or *kumya* and pantaloons. Sometimes a long, West African all-purpose robe, or *gandoura*, may be worn instead. A headcloth, or *tagelmoust*, is essential as protection against desert storms and sand. Usually blue or white in color, the cloth is tied so that it covers virtually the whole face. A Tuareg man never lifts the veiling from his face even to eat, but slips his tea or finger-held food underneath it.

Tuareg women wear a similar cotton *haik*, or all-encompassing white robe, over a *chalwar*, or skirt, of brocade, topped by a loose, overhanging blouse and a veil over the lower half of the face. A second headwrap may also be worn. Sometimes a short, tight-fitting, bolero-shaped jacket is worn with the *chalwar*. Tuareg men will always ride camels, but the women ride donkeys to the gatherings. They often wear colored and draped saddle skirts of leather on top of

*ABOVE MIDDLE: **A stunningly handsome and richly dressed Tuareg woman from Niger wearing a tunic robe and wrapping cloth in the traditional indigo-dyed cloth. Berber jewelry is justifiably famous and prized by collectors. The women favor silver, pieces of which form part of their dowry (a nomadic people must keep its wealth portable). Ornaments are imported from far-flung places on trade routes from the Arabian Peninsula through North and West Africa.***

*LEFT: **The Tuareg are among the numerous ethnic peoples who inhabit the Sahel, a belt of land running through six countries north of the Sahara itself. Only 13 percent of the Sahelian population maintains a nomadic lifestyle today. These incude the Tuareg, who are often called "the blue men" because the traditional dye of their clothes can bleed and stain their skin, though nowadays synthetic dyes are often used. A Tuareg always keeps his face covered by his tagelmoust or headcloth, even while he is eating.***

their robes, with festive white lace blouses underneath and black cloths across their heads. Tuareg women favor elaborate silver jewelry, which forms part of their dowry when they marry. Many necklaces and earrings of North African and Arabic origin are also worn.

The Wodaabe carry everything on donkey, camel, or their own person. Possessions are kept to a minimum, and include collapsible beds and a large collection of exquisitely carved calabashes or dried gourds for storing food and valuables. The women wear a single piece of cloth, wrapped around the body and tied above the bosom, but carry a second piece of material to use as a cowl or covering at night, or to be folded decoratively on the crown of the head.

Men wear loose pantaloons, a sleeveless shift, and a small decorated Islamic-style cap or a taller, rounded-cone-shape felt hat. For ease of movement, the shift is often constructed with a number of gores to the skirt sections, and the sides are left open to give extra coolness.

There is some diversity in male attire from region to region among the Fulanis, Wodaabe, and other groups. For example, a man might also possess a long, loose, sleeveless robe called a *boubou*, or a long, full-sleeved white gown and perhaps two or

three other colored or patterned gowns. A special cap might be worn at ceremonial occasions, plus a large, shallow-crowned, wide-brimmed straw hat worn as protection from the sun. All these items will be bought at the Sahelian markets.

Fulani and Wodaabe society is hierarchical. Unmarried girls belong to the adolescent age group, or *sukaabe*, and on marriage enter another group, called the *yeriijo*. Boys and men belong to equivalent age groupings. A woman's status can be determined by the the number of braids and their position on her scalp, and by the richness of her jewelry. A prized possession is a fan-shaped silver hair ornament Women braid men's hair too, usually in four thick, short braids. Male hairstyles can also vary according to age groups.

The Hausa are a very different people from the Sahelian nomads. Originally from west Sudan, they have settled in northwest Nigeria and the adjoining region of Niger. They are a technically advanced people, and include specialized weavers, dyers, tailors, tanners and leather workers in their number. The women make the standard Hausa *guado*, or cotton blankets, mold pots, raise poultry, weave cloth, and practice indigo dyeing.

The men are also involved in weaving, but it is usually done secondarily to the main farming tasks. The majority of the Hausa are Muslim, although some of those living in the small, remote northern villages are pagan and worship nature spirits.

The costume of the Hausa male is distinctive, uniform, and widespread. He wears a handwoven round cap and a white full-length kaftan tunic, sometimes embroidered on the chest opening in gold or white, over loose trousers. Occasionally a sleeveless open robe is also worn on top of the tunic. Hausa men are seldom seen without their Muslim prayer beads.

Women wear a wide variety of cloths, some handwoven, some tradecloths, as body wraps, combined with headcloths and overblankets to guard against the bitterly cold nights. Unlike the Tuareg females, Hausa women do not wear the veil.

ABOVE MIDDLE: **Young Fulani girls in their finery watch the Sharo,** or virility test, one of a number of rituals performed by the eligible young men of their tribe. In common with a number of nomadic groups, Fulani society is structured in age groups with rites of passage for each change of status. Such rites always involve a change of appearance, such as cutting hair, adopting a different style of dress, or using a particular form of headgear. Unmarried girls generally go bare chested until they get married.

LEFT: **The Wodaabe, a subgroup of the Fulani pastoralists of the Sahel,** gather for their worso, or annual celebration, during which eligible young men perform the surbaabe, a courting dance calling for physical prowess and an ability to be both amusing and graceful in movements. To be judged champion, one must wear an elaborate costume. Face painting, tight-wrap skirts, feathers, and beads are included in an unusual, and intentional mix of feminine and masculine characteristics.

Northeast Africa

Peoples of the Horn of Africa in the northeast are grouped as Hamitic or Semitic, according to their language origins as the supposed descendants of Noah's sons Ham and Shem, who, according to tradition, founded their lines after the journey of the Ark. Highland Ethiopians speak Amhaic, which is related to both Arabic and Hebrew. Somalis speak a Hamite language closely related to the Oromo and Afar tongues of the people on the borders of Ethiopia today.

The Oromo people are the largest ethnic group in Ethiopia, which contains 74 ethnically diverse linguistic groups. About 95

ABOVE: The Christian Amhara people of Ethiopia practice one of the most archaic forms of the faith found in Africa. They still use old and treasured clerical robes of brilliant brocaded silks. Their gilded umbrellas symbolize celestial spheres, and the priests' cloaks are cut in the shape of a cross.

percent are settled agriculturalists and nomadic pastoralists, using ancient farming methods to eke out an existence. The minority tribal group is the Amhara, but they are the dominant group politically.

The Oromo practice a traditional worship of *Waq*, the sky, with a host of lesser deities. There are endless subgroups, such as the

Borana. Oromo women are distinguished by their colorful headcloths and unusual jewelry made from Austrian Maria Theresa dollars, which were trading currency in Ethiopia for many years. A subgroup, the Beni Amer, who also like hair with ringlets and Oromo-style jewelry, prefer large chest plaques decorated with raised round bumps and yellow beads. Beni Amer men favor white muslin tunics, worn under the ample folds of a toga-like robe.

The Christian Highland Amharas are a deeply religious people, who in spite of great poverty persist in practicing an archaic form of Christianity centered on the great religious sites of Axum and Lalibela. Although poor, they conduct their ceremonies in a blaze of splendor. Men wear white turbans and long side-slit tunics over western-style trousers and jackets. Women wear brocade tunics and white muslin head-covers, and carry brocaded and fringed parasols in vivid jewel-bright colors. The climax of their religious ceremony is the procession of the priests, who create visions of extraordinary medieval splendor with their rich, gold robes and gold or silver crosses.

in fat and ocher. Their women wear metal bangles on their upper arms, beaded belts, and soft hide skirts. Married Hamar women wear torques of iron wrapped in leather for life, while an upper torque or *bignère* with a penis-shaped extension may be adopted by the first wife, to signal her status.

Other tribes in the region are the Surma and Mursi groups, whose women still wear lip plates. Among the explanations for this are that it was intended to discourage slavers or to prevent evil spirits from entering through the mouth, that it indicates

mountains, Sudan's Nilotic swamps, and the Kenyan borderlands, the most endangered people, the Karo, struggle for survival. Related to the Hamar, the Karo also favor body painting using black (charcoal), red (iron ore), white (chalk), and yellow (mineral ore). They wear simple cloth togas, mold their hair with clay, and practice scarification. The women wear hide skirts and an abundance of trade-bead jewelry.

Afar nomads are another Hamitic tribe, living in dome-shaped huts made of skins stretched over curved branch supports. The

RIGHT: **Rashaida women who live in the Somali coastal zone show Muslim influences in their costume, with their fine silver jewelry and elaborately silver-embroidered face veils. Long, silver "chain mail" veils of silver links, called** arusi, *are also worn.*

BELOW: **Rashaida women also practice the Muslim custom of henna-dye decoration for the hands and feet. This decoration is widespread in Africa and India. Sometimes a plain dye is used in a simple pattern or in a stencil design.**

The Falashas of Ethiopia, located mainly around the ancient city of Gondar, are of ancient Cushitic descent. A mass migration to Israel to escape persecution in 1984, has severely depleted their numbers and only around 7,000 remain. The women wear simple homespun robes edged with intricate black embroidery, headwraps, and ancient silver jewelry. The men wear simple brown cloth wraps and brown shifts, with white headwraps. The Falashas are craftsmen, with the men doing weaving and tanning, and the women pottery and basketry.

In southwest Ethiopia, the Konso, a subgroup of the Oromo, herd cattle and practice weaving and pottery. They supply the neighboring Borana people with colorful cotton cloths, and both sexes wear the common body- and headwraps of the region.

Other neighbors, the Hamar, are semi-nomadic pastoralists who cover their bodies

dowry size, or – the favored explanation – that the plate is a bride price. A large lip plate is valued at around 50 head of cattle. Both the Mursi and Bumi subgroup practice facial and bodily scarification. The body painting of another group, the Surma, especially for warrior fights, is complex and beautiful.

Hidden in the lower Omo valley of southwest Ethiopia, between the Abyssinian

men grow their hair in ringlets and wear talismanic necklets and file their upper-front teeth for aesthetic reasons. They wear light toga wraps, belted at the waist with a knife slotted in, and tough animal hide sandals. Women go bare breasted before marriage, and wear a wrap of brown-dyed homespun cloth. After marriage, a black voile shawl, a *shash* or *mushal*, is worn. The Muslim Afar girls of the Djibouti Republic wear elaborate gold jewelry. They braid their hair with long fringes of jewelry to mask their faces.

On the Somali coastal zone, Muslim influences are also in evidence. The Rashaida man, for example, wears a long kaftan tunic over baggy cotton trousers and a rolled turban over a Muslim cotton cap. Rashaida women are colorful, and glamorous. After marriage, they wear vivid headcloths and black masks.

East Africa

The steppes of the East African cattle area are home to a host of tribespeople. In Kenya the predominant people are the Kikuyu. Nomadic minorities, notably the eastern Nilotic peoples such as the Masai, still adhere to a traditional lifestyle. They live on the southern borders with Tanzania, alongside related subgroups, the Samburu and Rendille. The Masai have two self-governing areas, the largest in Tanzania and the smallest in northern Masailand.

In recent years there has been strong government pressure on the Nilotics to replace their minimal dress and body paint with shorts or trousers and shirts. However, it has been found that skin diseases are prevented by their long-standing practice of rubbing grease and powdered ocher into the skin.

The costume of the nomadic groups of the East African cattle area shows similarities. Men wear clothing according to age groups. Young warriors or *moran* wear beaded necklaces, earplugs in their pierced earlobes, and seamless broadcloth, or *shuka*, lightly wrapped across the body and tied over one shoulder. A *moran* has his head shaved when he joins the *manyatta* or warrior group, and then grows his hair to create elaborate coiffures, built up with fat and ocher and decorated with cockades of feathers. When a young warrior becomes a young elder in another ranking ceremony, his mother will

BELOW: Tribespeople of Kenya demonstrate the variety of styles and materials used in their dress. Masai women may dress in fabric wraps or bead collars and aprons. Men wear fur, hides, or fiber skirts.

shave his hair, and the cockades disappear. For ranking ceremonies and other special occasions, large headdresses of lion's mane, feathers, or other accessories made from animal parts are worn. Eye-catching body painting in spots, stripes, and waves is also a special feature.

Unmarried girls go bare-chested and always wear a beaded wide leather belt. Longer beaded ornaments are specific to married women. Married and older women wear body wraps, ordinarily of a reddish-brown color, but sometimes of checked or floral printed tradecloth. Their necklaces are magnificent, resembling collars or ruffs in halo shapes, made of tiny trade beads and wire. Long, brightly colored beadwork and leather earrings are worn, denoting age

group and status. Older women often wear blankets over their wraps.

Similar dress is found with the Samburu tribe, except that they wear huge collars of beads, and the men like to wear a fringe of beads across their foreheads as protection from the sun. Sometimes the beaded roping extends to a swag under the chin. They apply red ocher grease when they participate in warrior dances.

decoration. Male elders wear bulbous, gourd-like lip decorations and beaded headbands with feathers and beaded tassels or disk pendants that fall over the ears.

Two other pastoral nomadic tribes who live in the Northern Eastern Province are the Boran (who were originally migrants from Ethiopia) and the Rendille. Boran women have a particular custom during pregnancy of letting their hair grow for braiding, whereas

Muslim influence. In the Lamu area, men wear a long, Arabic-style white shirt. Around Orma, male fashion is dominated by bright colors: green, orange, or violet cloths, or *kikois*, are tied at the waist and accompanied by long white veils knotted like turbans around the head and falling to the waist. Orma women are swathed in black and wear distinctive wide silver bracelets, also showing Arabic style. North of Lamu, the Bajun

ABOVE: *A woman of the Samburu tribe, related to the Masai of Kenya, wears a traditional bead necklace. Tribal beadwork is popular with tourists, and she is wearing one for sale over her head.*

ABOVE: *This grandmother of the Rendille people indicates her status with a horsehair collar.*

LEFT: *A Boran man wears cowrie shell work and carries bells. His dress signifies the birth of a son.*

The Turkana are pastoral nomads who live around the Lake Rudolph/Turkana area in northern Kenya. Like their Masai relations, young Turkana girls also go bare-chested and wear soft hides slung around the hips, with a longer flap at the back. The whole outfit is held in place with a wide beaded belt. The skirts are made from animal hide, which has been dried and treated by beating with sticks to produce a soft and fine texture. Like the Masai, married Turkana women favor high collars of strung beads, especially red and white, the size of which is a sign of their husband's wealth.

Males apply white chalk body painting for special occasions, and young warriors create clay hair extensions with ostrich feathers as

normally they shave their heads bald. They favor large collars of square shapes in aluminum, which form a kind of bib over the chest. They wear faded print dresses or *shuka* cloths tied around the waist. Like many of the northern nomadic groups, Boran males wear large, flowing, brightly colored toga-like outfits.

The Rendille originated in Somalia, but have since moved across the border into Kenya and now live on the Meru reserve, Northern Eastern Province. They resemble the Samburu in dress and customs, as do the Giriama people, who live nearer the coastal area, north of Mombasa, near Malindi.

Clothing styles of the East African coastal area are very different, reflecting the Arab-

Islanders wear the all-encompassing Arab *haik*. They are thought to be descendants of Arab traders or refugees who intermarried with the local Bantu people.

North of Kenya, but still within the East African steppe or cattle region, lies the vast land of Sudan, Africa's biggest state. The population of Sudan is divided ethnically between Arabs in the north (two-thirds of the total) and Africans in the south. North Sudanese dress is basically the wide robes (or vivid *tobes*) and headwraps of Islam, but without face veiling for the women.

The southern tribes of Sudan make up, in total, 6 million people, about 28 percent of the population. There are four main groups: Western Nilotics, such as the Dinka, Nuer, and Shilluk, in the south central region; Eastern Nilotics, including Bantu speakers such as the Turkana; Sudanic people such as the Moru and Madi; and lastly the Azande, who are in fact related to the West African people.

The Nubians of the savannah west of the White Nile have no fewer than 10 different ethnic groups. Some follow Islam, some are pagan. Others are of Bantu origin and wear

languages. Dinka women wear skirt wraps with a second cloth that is then draped gracefully over their shoulders. The Dinka men wear a beaded waist corset, the color of which varies according to the actual age of the wearer. Traditionally, nothing else is worn at all, although nowadays men are no longer allowed to enter into the town areas without clothing and are required to wear shirts and skirt wraps.

are the usual male rural attire, but western dress is seen increasingly in the cities. The ancient Bemba culture is now a matter of history, with few material signs of the cultures of the 70 tribes that once lived in the region. However, the Lozi people of West Province still conduct a spectacle, the *Kuomboka*, in remembrance of the annual migration of their people from the floodwaters of the Zambezi. The king, or *Litunga*,

ABOVE: A Samburu woman of Maral, west Kenya wears a profusion of beadwork collars. As is common among nomadic people, a woman's display of jewelry indicates her husband's status and wealth.

ABOVE: The headwrap and print fabric robe of this Zambian woman are widely adopted in Africa.

LEFT: This young girl's carefully arranged bridal attire demonstrates the value given to correct dress.

practically no clothing. Other Nubians resemble the Kenyan nomads in dress codes and wear minimal clothing, have chalk body painting, shaved heads, or haircuts that relate to age groups.

The Shilluk are sedentary agriculturalists who wear white sarong cloths tied togafashion over one shoulder. They practice a custom that is very common among certain East African groups: decorative scarification. Little cuts are made on a person's face, which are then irritated by rubbing in certain powdered plant substances. When these heal they produce a fine, raised, effect on the skin's surface.

The Dinka are a relatively small tribe and yet they can speak a total of 50 different

THE CENTRAL REGION

In the countries of Rwanda and Burundi, tribal clothing – hide girdles for women and togas with horsehair headdresses for men – is seen only for ceremonies. By government edict, western dress is adopted, and every child in Rwanda now wears school uniform.

In the Republic of the Congo, tradecloth is worn by men in a version of the toga wrap, in which two corners of a rectangle of fabric are crossed on the breastbone and tied around the back of the neck. Women wear simple shirt tops and skirt wraps, called *pagnes*. Poor quality European-style clothing dominates this region.

Farther south, in Zambia, tradecloth wraps for skirts with T-shirts and headwraps

wears a British Royal Navy admiral's uniform for this rite, and women paint their faces white with schoolroom chalk and sport tribal bead earrings. The boatmen wear traditional skirt wraps, made from West African batik cloths, and red turbans with feather cockades.

Ritual days are also observed by the Ngoni of the Eastern Province, who are descendants of the Zulu people. Women wear tradecloth wraps and turbans, while men bring out leopard-fur hats with ostrich-feathers and wear animal-skin dancing tunics, which are slit to produce fringing. A fillet of cloth wrapped around an old man's head is a reminder of the headband of clay once worn by Zulu chiefs.

West Africa

ABOVE *This man wears the classic African long, loose robe, called a* gandoura *or* leppi *(in West Nigeria it is known as an* agbada). *Loose-fitting pants are worn underneath the garment. Sometimes the robe is worn open at the sides, as can be seen on the man standing just behind.*

ABOVE: *The market of Bobo-Dioulasso in Burkina Faso is typical of West Africa, where three types of textiles will be seen: factory-made plain cloth for westernized clothing; Javanese or Dutch tradecloths, printed in patterns resembling batiks; and, thirdly, "country cloths" woven by local craftsmen.*

ABOVE: *A Cameroon man wears a print robe displaying President Paul Biya and the initials of the former U.N.C party. The use of tradecloths for political slogans or to commemorate events is widespread in West Africa, a colorful and popular alternative to the printed word or televized image.*

The states of West Africa, from Senegal down to Cameroon, have several dress features in common. The common style for women is full-length skirt wraps with loosely fitting, yoked, full blouses on top and high headwraps. Sometimes stoles and wide sashes are worn, or the skirt wrap is tied over the breasts. On the whole, West African women's dress is less elaborate than men's. Ghanaian men wear either western-style clothing or variations of the loose smock, called the *fugu*, which is worn over loose, short trousers. Men also wear full-length robes, called *agbada* in West Nigeria, *gandoura* or *leppi* in Cameroon (also the term for the handwoven strip fabric used), and *riga* by the Hausa. The shape is basically simple, the meaning and status of the person is shown in the choice and the beauty of the cloth used, and the quality of weaving, embroidery, or print decoration. Ibo men choose brighter colors than the Yoruba; Hausa men prefer white. Ibos will also sometimes wear western-style shirts over a sash or *lappa* cloth.

Throughout West African markets, the same three types of textiles are to be seen: firstly, factory-made plain cloth, which is made up into European-style clothing. Secondly, there are Javanese or Dutch tradecloths, which are printed in patterns resembling the batiks of Java or India. These may be manufactured locally, but the

Dutch imports are of the best quality and are widely distributed throughout all of West and Central Africa. Thirdly, there are the "country cloths," which are made by local craftsmen. *Leppi*, or *lappa* cloth, is made from strips produced on a narrow pedal loom. These strips are then stitched together to make the required width of a robe. Usually only men work these looms, while broadcloth weaving is done by women. The ways in which strips are stitched together provide a wide variety of decorative effects.

The *garri* cloths of Sierra Leone are hand-printed on cotton using a wax resist technique, while the *adire* cloths of Nigeria are produced using the wax-resist methods of batik and *plangi* and the woven-dye technique of *ikat*. The *adinkra* cloth of Ghana is stamped with abstract designs made by Asante women, but *kente* cloth is the most famous fabric of them all.

The very best *kente* grade was reserved traditionally for royalty, although it is still made today for special commissions. It is called *nsaduaso* and is produced in Asante. The cloth is characterized by its exquisite silk inlay work. In Asante weaving, colors have special significance: gold denotes warmth, longevity, and success; while silver, white, and blue signify purity and joy, and red, death and sadness. White is very important, evoking the gods and the ancestors.

Today, the yarns used are cotton, wool, silk, and synthetics such as rayon. In the

BELOW: **These tribal elders of the Akan people of Ghana carry their traditional symbols of office, called knobkerries (walking sticks), and wear the toga-like garment seen throughout West Africa, and made well-known worldwide by the former President Nkrumah. The most traditional high-grade cloth used for the wrap is called** kente – **generally identified with, but not specific to, Ghana. It is produced across West Africa by numerous peoples. In Asante weaving colors have symbolism; red signifies mourning.**

past, yarns were hand spun, but imported machine twist is more commonly used.

The Ewe weavers produce *adanudo* cloth for their chiefs and elders using high-grade cotton, silk, or rayon. In Sierra Leone, the Ivory Coast, and Nigeria the fashion is for batik and stamped cloth in ornate designs. Tie-dye textiles are made in both Nigeria and Guinea. Among the Bamoun and Bamileke women of Cameroon a blue-dyed strip cloth with white resist patterning called *ndop* is highly valued. Raffia is stitched over the fabric in a pattern before dyeing. The raffia is then removed, producing animal motifs such as lizards.

Tribal costumes used for dances and festivals can.have political connotations. Central to people in the Ivory Coast, Liberia, Sierra Leone, and Guinea are secret societies. The use of masks in their rituals is common. Both the Kpelle of Liberia and the Dogon of southwest Mali make use of masks.

Southern Africa

Namibia is a multiethnic country with over a million inhabitants that is made up of 90 percent Africans and 10 percent Afrikaners. Near the Angolan border, in extremely harsh conditions, live a semi-nomadic pastoralist tribe called the Himba, a subgroup of the Herero. Both sexes wear grease and red ocher all over as decoration and skin protection. Males wear their thick hair long and add grease and clay to it, before piling it up on their heads and adding a soft leather cloth at the nape of the neck. To sleep, they use headrests to protect their elaborate coiffure. They also wear a "hunger belt," which they tighten to ease the pangs of a meager diet, and skirts of a pleated material (formerly hide, now cotton cloth, or *etapi*) and sandals with soles made

from car-tire rubber. Back ornaments, or *eha*, made of leather, metal, and beaten wire threads, are favored, and a necklace, or *ombari*, made of heavy twisted-metal rope is often worn.

The women dress in pleated skin or fabric skirts, which have fur-skin, bustle-like flaps at the back. A customary piece of jewelry is a conch, worn on the breasts, with long strings of beads dangling from it. Before marriage, girls wear bead headdresses; after marriage they keep their hair covered with brown cotton cloth. The older women adopt a goatskin headdress over long braids.

The Herero men have adopted jackets, cut Tyrolean-style, to match the dresses of their women. These were introduced by German missionaries who disapproved of

nudity, but they are now still worn as a symbol of national unity. As many as five petticoats are worn beneath dresses that use up 13 yards (12 meters) of fabric. The Himba still apply grease and ocher to their skins; the Herero use dark shoe polish on their faces as a vestige of their former customs.

SOUTH AFRICA

At one time an infinitely varied and spectacular wealth of tribal dress existed in South Africa, but it is now seen only in remote areas, or at tribal ceremonials or tourist events. There are 29 main tribes in South Africa. In the Natal region, the Ngoni or Nguni group includes two subgroups: the Xhosa and Zulu, and Swazi and Ndebele peoples. The Ngoni, along with the Shonas of Zimbabwe, the Sothos of Lesotho and

ABOVE: **Women of the semi-pastoralist Himba people who live on the north border of Namibia. They wear hide or cloth skirts with a bustle effect. They live close to the Herero people of whom they are a subgroup.**

ABOVE: **The Herero women's clothing contrasts sharply with the Himba women's style. Adapted from German missionaries' dress in the last century, the puff-sleeved, flounced dresses and horn-shaped headwraps are now a symbol of their identity.**

ABOVE: *Most Zulu men are now sedentary farmers, but full war attire of feathered headdresses, lion's mane leg ties and armbands, oxhide oval shields, knobkerries (walking sticks) and assegais (spears) is used for weddings and other ceremonies. Leopard skin is usually worn only by Zulu chiefs, but occasionally a diviner will dress in a regal pelt, and chief councilors can wear a narrow leopard-skin headband.*

Zambia, and the Tswanas of Botswana (Central Plateau people), form the southeastern Bantu group of peoples. Another ethnic group, the west coast people – Herero, Ovahimba, and Ovambi – have been described earlier in the section on Namibia.

Today, the groupings of people in southern Africa are influenced largely by the unifying process, which begun in 1818 under Shaka, the Zulu leader, in response to European expansion in the region. He joined many tribes together under one banner, regardless of race and regional origin.

The collars, earrings, and other beaded regalia worn by the Ngonis not only are decorative but also help to define an individual's age group. Literally dozens of pieces may be worn for grand occasions.

The most important beadwork object of the Xhosa is the *danga*, a multi-strand turquoise necklace, worn by both sexes,

which reaches to the waist. It is worn so that they can be recognized by ancestors. Men's leggings are their next most valued object, followed by their beaded and tasseled goatskin bags, deftly made by pulling an animal's carcass out of the hide without splitting it. It is worn for ceremonial purposes.

A Xhosa-speaking girl of pre-marriageable age wears a short plain skirt above the knee and she goes bare-breasted. A token headcloth is worn as a sign of respect for older members of the tribe. A marriageable girl wears a longer skirt and turban, while a

married woman must cover her breasts and wear a more elaborate headwrap – the size of which relates to her status within the community. Such outfits are clearly described at a *ntlombe*, or gathering of eligible young people, in the Transkei region, by expert Aubrey Elliot in his book *The Zulu*.

The Xhosa are often referred to as "the red blanket people" because of their preference for that color, but the term may also indicate their ritualistic use of red ocher.

Other Xhosa subgroups, such as the Xessibe, prefer wire decoration to beadwork. The women twist spirals of wire around pads of animal hair, which are then squeezed over their arms and looped together with chains. A tight band is worn over the breasts by adolescent girls.

The Pondo people are noted for the long, plaited fringes worn by engaged girls. The red fringes (now dyed with chemical dyes instead of ocher) cover the eyes as a sign of respect. Married women make beautifully beaded, tube-shaped, padded headbands.

Women of another Xhosa subgroup, the Momvana, wear the more widespread Xhosa turban, but theirs are decorated with red pompoms. Another group of Natal, the Cele, are well-known for their beadwork, and their women wear blue fabric bands under their beaded headbands, several pendant bead collars at one time, and a multitude of fine belts and apron-shaped panels over their small wrap skirts.

Among the Xhosa, the age-grouping hierarchy calls for elaborate rites of passage: young males are initiated into manhood wearing heavy, palm-leaf skirts and cone-shaped headmasks for ritual dances.

Swazi and South Ndebele people are also from the Ngoni linguistic group. The Ndebele's origins are a bit obscure, but they regard themselves as Zulu. The home of the South Ndebele is in the eastern Transvaal highveld, northeast of Pretoria, while the North Ndebele form a separate tribe, more closely related to the North Sotho people. The artwork of the South Ndebele (often just called Ndebele) is, however, entirely distinctive from that of other Ngoni peoples, with spectacular, vivid geometric wall paintings and wonderful beadwork. As with all indigenous South African artifacts, these crafts are fast disappearing. Ndebele dress is

more uniform than that of other South African peoples. Girls wear thick waist cords and small, beaded front aprons; boys sport just a small goatskin loincloth. The aprons increase in size as the girls grow up. When they reach marriageable age, the aprons are replaced by stiff boarded ones, about 12 x 10 inches (30 x 25 centimeters) or larger, traditionally made of hardened skin, but nowadays of cardboard backed by canvas. These aprons are lavishly decorated with beadwork in brilliant geometric designs. On their upper bodies women hang a profusion of beads or copper bands, and huge neck col-

lars. On her marriage, the Ndebele woman adopts an even larger collar, or *rholwani*. It is normally one color, made of twisted grass heavily encrusted with beads, though two contrasting hoops (blue and white, or red and blue) may be worn simultaneously. Above the *rholwani*, tighter fitting copper neckbands are worn several at a time. Other *rholwani* are made for arms and legs, and are worn two or three at a time. Schoolgirls often cut through their neck-collars and add a lace-up closure so that they can take them off while doing their schoolwork.

As is common among many South African peoples, married women must cover their shoulders, though their torsos are not concealed. Trade blankets that feature red, green, blue, and yellow stripes are highly favored. As a sign of respect for her husband, a married woman keeps her head covered, with anything from a simple band of beads to a full-scale beaded tiara. In the past decade a new accessory has been added to full ceremonial dress: blue tennis shoes (*tackies*), which are worn for show, as Ndebele women usually go barefoot.

Ndebele men's clothing is much less elaborate. Up to the age of circumcision, few rules apply, but thereafter, the male must wear a front apron (*poriaan*), usually made from the skin of a genet or civet cat and beaded in geometric designs on the front. Knobkerries (walking sticks), spears,

ABOVE MIDDLE: **This Zulu woman's headdress defines her as a** sangoma, *or diviner. Both sexes of healer-seers wear similar beaded headgear, to which they add the gall bladders of sacrificed animals or the skin and feathers of red fowl, or a strip of fur.*

LEFT: **Beadwork dates from the arrival of Portuguese traders in the 16th century, and is the chief feature of South African tribal dress. The type of high hat worn by this Zulu woman was once made by knitting coarse wool into her hair, but it is now removable. Dried herbs and other small valuables are stored in the hat, which can be stained red with ocher or a chemical dye. Each clan has its own shape and decoration, though the flared upright shape is generic.**

and round cowhide shields with several thin sticks attached inside for a handle (and to make a rattling noise in battle), are part of the full regalia. Leather or fur headdresses and a small hide shoulder cloak are also part of traditional attire, but are rarely seen today.

The Swazi people also use beadwork and wear body wraps in distinctive, vivid reds (for the women) or browns (for the men). Their hairstyles also define the sexes: the women's hair is molded with clay, piled high and circled with a band, while the men's has a "marbled" appearance, made with blue mottled soap. Both sexes use a fine porcupine quill decoration.

The vanishing people of the Kalahari Desert, the San or Bushmen of the "thirst-land," who occupy an inhospitable region stretching across Botswana, Zimbabwe, Southwest Africa, and Southeast Angola should not be overlooked. The term "Khoisan" refers to all the Bushmen-Hottentot groups who speak a variety of "click" languages, the origins of which are unclear. Khoisan Bushmen wear very little. Women drape a large pouch, or *kaross*, of antelope skin over a shoulder, and wear a small skirt wrap, with necklaces made of ostrich eggshells. Their heads are shaved close to prevent parasites, but they make bangs by twining beaded pendants into the hairline. They also make beaded headbands and belts for the men, whose loincloths are often beaded, too, with little spiraling disks of color. Young girls wear pleated antelope-hide skirts and glass (or plastic) trade beads made into necklaces, bracelets, or anklets.

Madagascar and Comoros

Madagascar, a French colony until 1960, is the world's fourth-largest island. It is now divided into 18 regions (or "tribes"), based on its pre-colonial kingdoms. The population is made up of French, Comorians, Indians, and Chinese, reflecting its long trading history. However, the original settlers 2,000 years ago were Malay-Polynesian navigators, and in the 15th century Arabs and Europeans brought over Bantu slaves.

The *lamba*, a shawl-like garment worn over the head and shoulders, is the island's female national dress. The men wear a long shift, known as a *malabary*. On the coast, the Moroni women wear a wide black robe called a *bui-bui*, while on Anjouan, part of the Comoro Islands, the *bui-bui* is predominantly red and white. Elsewhere the sari-like *chirumani* is worn.

Moroni women paint their skin with a paste (made by pounding coral on a piece of wood and mixing the resulting powder with water) to protect it. On Great Comoro and Anjouan, which are lesser, more isolated islands, some of the traditional aspects of the earlier influence of Islam have died away – strict veiling has now been replaced by the *chirumani*, for example.

BELOW: **A market scene in Madagascar shows many fine examples of the female national dress, the** lamba, **a shawl-like garment worn over the head and shoulders. Men wear a shift, or** malabary, **and on the coast, Moroni women wear a wide black robe, or** bui-bui. **Elsewhere a sari-like** chirumani **is worn as here, left.**

Africa Map

Two main themes run through the immense variety of dress on the African continent, indicative of the wide range of cultures and ways of life. Of course climate has a fundamental impact on clothing; some groups of nomadic people who live near the equator in East Africa wear little more than body paint, breechcloths, and beads because their environment is hot, arid, and harsh. Yet clothing of a minimal variety can still be elaborate, such as the pleated hide skirts of the Himba of Namibia or the animal-fur headdresses of their unmarried women, or the complex beaded collars of many East and South African tribespeople, including the Masai and Zulu. Semi-permanent decoration, usually identifying age-group, is also found – such as the grease and ocher headdresses of many East African groups that incorporate feathers or wire – or the beaded work woven into the hair of the Bush people. As is found with many nomadic people, wealth and status are signified by portable goods, with brass, silver, wire, glass, or plastic beading or other valued materials used in ornately fashioned jewelry. Materials often have symbolic value; tribal warriors wear animal skins to denote their status. A Swazi man wears a leopard skin headband, a Swazi girl red feathers, to indicate her royal lineage. To this day, body painting or scarification is also included in this mode of tribal display.

The second style of costume is found, broadly speaking, in the north, west, and east central parts of Africa. This is based on the use of draped lengths usually or loosely fitted fabric for flowing robes, as seen worn by men and women in Muslim countries, and for body wraps, used by women in many parts of Africa. Climate zones govern styles of dressing but are not the only reason for styles. Both Muslim and Christian peoples, from the Muslim Hausa of West Africa to the Christians of Ethiopia, adopt similar robes. African textiles have a distinctive tonal range, using lots of red, white, yellow, blue, and black, a high level of color contrast, and a bold, strong style of graphic design. Motifs generally tend to be geometric and abstract in character, compared to the more vegetal designs of Indonesian batik.

A Tuareg man from Morocco wearing indigo-dyed robes.

A woman from Mali dressed in a printed robe.

A Fulani nomad of the Sahel region wearing a distinctive straw hat.

ABOVE: **These Swaziland herdsmen are wearing their national dress, a version of the loose, often open-sided robe found widely in West, Central, and southern Africa. Both narrow and broad cloth looms are used.**

ABOVE: **Girls of the semi-pastoralist Himba people of Namibia wear pleated hide skirts and ornate beading. They decorate their skin and hair with a mixture of grease and red ocher.**

Key

Subtropical areas

Rainy tropics

Steppe

Berber people go across this area

3,000 plus m (9,000 plus ft)

1,000–3,000m (3,000–9,000ft)

400–1,000m (1,200–3,000ft)

0–400m (0–1,200ft)

Sea, lakes and rivers

Note: Peoples are shown in italics eg: *Tuareg*

A Falasha boy of Ethiopia wearing a plain homespun cotton robe and turban.

A Samburu warrior from Kenya in beaded decoration.

A Zulu woman in popular red and white tradecloth.

Bejaia •

Aït Hadidou

MOROCCO

Marrakech
Haut Atlas

Tiznit • • Gimouline

TUNISIA

ALGERIA

LIBYA

EGYPT

Berber

Nubian

MAURITANIA

S A H A R A

MALI

NIGER

CHAD

Bororo

SENEGAL

Dogon

Tuareg

Fulani

Shilluk
Nuer

Moru
Madi
Azande

SUDAN

DJIBOUTI
REPUBLIC

GAMBIA

BURKINA
FASO

S A H E L

Oromo
Borana

• Gondar

Bambara

Orma

Hausa

Konso
Surma
Mursi
Borana
Hamar

Afar
Oromo

Somali Nomad

THE HORN

GUINEA
BISSAU

Fulani

NIGERIA

Amhara
Falasha

Karo
Oromo Konso
Hamar

SIERRA
LEONE

LIBERIA

GHANA

TOGO

Yoruba

Shuwa

ETHIOPIA

Afar

Boran

SOMALIA

Asante

Ewe

Ibo

CAMEROON

Omo River

Boran
Rendille

Rashaida

Kpelle

IVORY
COAST

Bamoun
Banileke

Lake Rudolph/ Turkana

Turkana

• Mogadishu

EQUATORIAL
GUINEA

KENYA

Bajun
islanders

GREAT
COMORO

CONGO

Samburu

Masai

• Lamu
Malindi

RWANDA

Giriama

• Mombasa

COMORO
ISLANDS

BURUNDI

ANJOUAN

TANZANIA

Lozi

ANGOLA

ZAMBIA

Zambezi

MADAGASCAR

Himba
Herero

Bushmen

ZIMBABWE

Ngoni

MALAWI

MOZAMBIQUE

NAMIBIA

BOTSWANA

Bushmen

• Pretoria
Ndebele

Swazi
Zulu

Ngoni

Gele

SOUTH
AFRICA

Xhosa

LESOTHO

95

HEAD AND FACE DECORATION

TOP ROW, LEFT TO RIGHT:

A Berber woman of Tunisia with stenciled henna patterning on face, hands, and forearms and wearing a "hand of Fatima" pendant.

A Shilluk girl of Sudan adorned with the raised marks of scarification.

A Himba woman of Namibia celebrating Independence Day, adorned with traditional ocher and grease on her body and hair and a hide headdress.

A Dinka man of Sudan with scarification marks on his forehead.

A Nigerian man with tribal markings across his cheeks.

MIDDLE ROW, LEFT TO RIGHT:

A Shuwa woman of Nigeria with scarification marks on her cheeks and nose.

A Dinka man of Sudan with partly-shaved scalp and a decorative painted face.

A Bumi woman of Central Africa with perforated, extended lower lip wearing a wooden lip plate.

A Bororo male, Niger, adorned in his best finery for the Gerewol festival.

A woman of the Yoruba people, West Africa, with a greased, braided, and coiled traditional coiffure.

BOTTOM ROW, LEFT TO RIGHT:

A Kikuyu tribesman of Kenya with body and face painting in chalk paste.

A Bush woman of South Africa with striking bead pendants braided into her hairline.

A Kikuyu woman, Kenya, wearing chalk paste skin decoration and beaded head rings.

A Kavango, or medicine man of Kambathi, Namibia, wearing ocher and grease in his coiled, beaded hair.

A Nigerian woman displaying delicately chiseled facial scarification.

THE MIDDLE EAST

This chapter discusses many of the eastern Mediterranean countries and includes Turkey, Syria, Lebanon, Israel, and Saudi Arabia, Yemen, Iran, Iraq, Kuwait, Bahrain, Jordan, Qatar, the United Arab Emirates, and Oman, although only a few are discussed in detail.

The Middle East was once known as the Near East, but now Asia is divided into the Middle East, Far East, and Southeast Asia – a subtle change in terminology that speaks volumes for the evolution of the area and how the spheres of influence and trade links have broadened into a larger world picture. Islam is the faith of all these countries, with the exception of Israel, in the northeast, where the Jewish people wear western clothing.

The Middle East was subjected to considerable European influence up to the late 19th century, when the Sublime Porte of the Ottoman Turks played power politics on an equal footing with the Russian and other western empires.

In the first half of this century there was a long period when several Middle Eastern heads of state, such as the Shah of Persia and King Farouk of Egypt, would be seen in western-style clothing.

Interestingly, the trend today has now been reversed: public figures, diplomats, and politicians will attend formal functions wearing the traditional dress of their own people, although their wives might still prefer to dress and be seen in expensive western-style clothing.

Another notable change is that many Middle Eastern women who have been professionally educated in the West have returned to their countries and adopted the

ABOVE AND OPPOSITE: **Typical everyday Middle Eastern male dress: the headwrap, known variously as a** ghoutra, shaal, *or* ihram, **which is worn with a** kaftan or thawb, **and often a jacket.**

veil. Dress is now used as a sign of political commitment to a way of life that rejects most of the western lifestyle. Islamic fundamentalism is as much a political response to domination from the West as it is a spiritual revival, and the dress worn in the region is one manifestation of this.

Some elements of Arab costume may, however, predate the Muslim era. Face veiling was known to the ancient Assyrians as records show that this existed as far back as 1500 BC. However, since the dawn of Islam covering the head has also been considered a sign of modesty and respect.

In the Yemen and Saudi Arabia veiling has long been the tradition, but restrictive forms of dress have been revived in Iraq,

Syria, and also to a lesser degree in Jordan.

In addition to religion, another unifying factor in these states is the climate. This is a barren, largely desert region made up of low-lying plains and mountain ranges. The style of dress of men and women has remained unchanged for thousands of years and consists of light, loose, but warm layers to suit the environment and the different climatic variations that occur.

The unchanging terrain accounts for the persistence of certain traditional cultures and lifestyles. The Bedouin Arabs are one of these groups who have resisted change implacably. The Marsh Arabs of the Tigris-Euphrates, with their unique style of architecture and traditional floating way of life, are only now being dispossessed by the destruction of their landscape. Rivers are being diverted, and devastation by Iraqi bombing campaigns seems likely to complete the destruction of this area.

One result of the Gulf War was the expulsion of Yemenis from Saudi Arabia and other countries of the region, in retaliation to Yemen's pro-Iraqi position. At the same time, many Yemeni workers have returned to their homeland from Africa, chiefly Somalia. In common with many other Arab countries, the only unifying factor within the region in the midst of political turmoil is religion: Islam.

The considerable influence of Islam, which stretches right across a vast distance from West Africa to northern India, means that ancient forms of costume have remained and are virtually unchanged throughout the Arab Peninsula.

However, Islamic law does not actually stipulate what clothing should be worn.

Turkey and Iran

RIGHT: *A holy man of Isfahan, Iran, wears a classic open robe that is known throughout the Middle East as an* aba, zibun, *or* baalto. *Underneath he wears a long white tunic. His immaculate white felt hat indicates his standing, as simple, clean attire is always well regarded. In general, in Turkey and Iran, traditional male attire is less seen in towns, where westernized dress predominates.*

LEFT: *In rural areas of Iran or Turkey it is still possible to see women wearing traditional clothing, which is surprisingly delicate and luxurious, given their strenuous working lives. Here, a Turkish farmer's wife wears a mid-length full skirt over baggy pants, with a flowered cotton blouse, perhaps market-bought, and a long knitted vest or waistcoat. Over her head she wears a white muslin cloth decorated with small trade-bead clusters. Sometimes, tiny coins will also be seen.*

Apart from the *chador*, or headcloth, and long coat worn as a religious requirement, remnants of traditional dress are still found in rural areas of Turkey and Iran. The classic straight-grain and gusset construction of Arabian costume is modified in Iran and Turkey by other influences from Europe: curved armholes, shoulder yokes, plus the addition of turn-collars to necklines.

Elements of 19th-century costume survive, for instance, in Kurdish women's preference for tight sleeves with shaped cuffs, underarm openings, and curved peplums to jackets. Much of this is dying out as people in towns are becoming westernized and displaced people, such as the Kurds, accept European clothing, which is often poor quality.

The Kurds are of Indo-European stock and for centuries they have occupied their region, which lies over the borders of Turkey, Iran, Iraq, Syria, and also the Commonwealth of Independent States (C.I.S.), in the Anti-Taurus mountain range. They consider themselves to be descendants of the Medes, who conquered Nineveh in the year 612 BC.

Although their authentic clothing is not very often seen now, married women's traditional headgear is an elaborate turban over which a back-fringed mantle is draped then tied over the breast. All unmarried women wear different types of dresses and headgear, depending on their region. Costume is frequently extremely light and gaudy, with a preference for Lurex-threaded nylons, silks, and laces. These are all juxtaposed in vivid, sometimes clashing ensembles, consisting of baggy trousers, gathered-skirt dresses, and vests or sleeved jackets topped with veils, shawls and stoles, and the all-encompassing black cloak. Fabrics for all these items are eagerly sought after in the town of Sanandaj, the capital of Iranian Kurdistan, where bales of imports are available from countries such as India and Japan.

Northwestern Iranian men wear the traditional voluminous trousers and a short jacket over a cotton shirt with long pointed cuffs. A broad sash is worn over the jacket, and a crocheted skullcap with another fringed length of fabric draped over it is standard wear. There is a tradition in this region for *buzu* cloth, a narrow handwoven woolen strip in dark colors, which is carefully seamed together to use for men's clothing. Today, a machine-made copy has taken up a large part of the market.

The Arab Peninsula

On this great peninsula, situated between the Red Sea and the Persian Gulf, costume requirements tend to follow the pattern of the annual festivals. So, for example, most Arab women would wish to have a new outfit for the Eid al Fitr festival, which follows Ramadan, the holy month of fasting, and for the Eid al Adha, which celebrates the holy pilgrimage to Mecca. The pilgrimage itself involves the wearing of simple clothing, which is invariably white.

The covering of the head and the face-veiling of women reached its maximum expression of authority under the influence of the Turkish Ottoman rulers. It is worth noting that farther afield many Muslim women in Africa, India, and Central Asia do not veil themselves.

One explanation offered for the adoption of veiling is that deserts and desert cities

demand the protection of the face and eyes from dust storms, or gusts of gritty winds, and from harmful exposure to the sun.

However, Berber women in North Africa, who traverse the bleakest areas of desert remain unveiled, except during sandstorms. All that is certain is that the standard attire worn throughout the Muslim world first originated in the Arabian Peninsula, probably with the nomadic peoples.

Most particularly, the turban originated from there. Certain features, such as the adaptation of the Arab kaftan so that the long wide sleeves would fall to cover the hands, are said to have been the Prophet Mohammad's own notion. Also, the prohibition in Islamic law of any representation of the human form in art has led to the evolution of abstract embroidery patterns. Notably, the use of geometric cross-stitch

ABOVE MIDDLE: Male clothing and hairstyles are similar throughout the Middle East. A kaftan or thawb is worn with or without a westernized jacket. Cotton or cotton-silk mixtures in white or cream prevail, with cloak wraps, as here, worn by a Dhofari tribesman. Arab men's outer clothing was designed to fall open at the front so that weapons could be drawn quickly, but nowadays these are worn only for ceremonial purposes as is this traditional dagger.

LEFT: In the old days it was said that a man's home area could be identified by valued details such as his weaponry and how he wore his headcloth. Such distinctions are less apparent nowadays, except for special occasions, like this wedding in Rahaba, Yemen, where all the men have dressed smartly and traditionally. They are in the process of escorting the groom to his new bride's home.

work on women's clothes, especially those of the Bedouin, and the surpassing variety and beauty of the arabesque.

The basic element of dress for men and women is the kaftan, which is probably Turkish in origin. As with many traditional homespun garments all over the world (such as the *huipil* of Guatemala or the robes of *kente* cloth in West Africa), its shape is determined by the width of the loom on which it was originally woven. It has a narrow central section, folded double, with a slit neck. Sleeve sections are added to the sides on a straight seam, and side panels are inserted. The absence of curved cutting or use of the bias grain is compensated for by the use of underarm gussets.

Handwoven and handmade clothing is hard to find in the Arabian Peninsula, although the practice is encouraged in Oman and Iran. There are still a few places where traditional crafts are practiced, such as among the Qashqa'i and Bakhtiari nomads of the southwest Zagros Mountains area and, until recently, the northwest Iranian Kurds.

In *The Art of Arabian Costume*, Heather Colyer Ross describes how, in the old days,

a man's home town could be identified by his weaponry, cartridge belt, buckling, the way he wore his headcloth, the way his rug was folded beneath his saddle, and even the way he walked.

Today, male clothing and hairstyles are virtually identical throughout the Arabian Peninsula and the same elements exist all over the Middle East. They consist of the kaftan, a full-length tunic otherwise called a *thawb*, over which is worn a man's jacket (a recent introduction, adopted only a century

ago). For special occasions a grander, traditional velvet embroidered jacket, originally made in Damascus, will be worn. The present-day *thawb* has simple straight sleeves and side panels widening toward the hem for ease of movement. They are made in cotton or a cotton-silk mixture in white or cream for the hot season, or in light worsted wool for the winter. Braid, piping, or *soutache* trimming is added, often with subtle restraint, which makes the outfit look very elegant.

Traditionally, the male outer garment is the *bisht* or *mishlah*, a large cloak worn draped from the shoulders. Neutral colors, from cream, beige, or honey to brown or black, are favored. Better-quality cloaks have a gold-embroidered neckline band, ending in little tasseled tie cords. An intermediate garment, worn over the kaftan and under the cloak, though less prevalent today, is a sleeveless wrapover garment, called *aba*, *zibun*, or *baalto*. It is worn more by the nomadic Bedouin than by the sedentary Arab male. In general, Arab men's outer clothing was originally designed to fall open at the front, for instant access to

ABOVE MIDDLE: **Women in the United Arab Emirates wearing fine gauze veiling over** milfas, **or face masks. These small face masks are more commonly seen in the northern part of Saudi Arabia. For the majority of Arab women in the south, a full face veil or** burga **is worn in addition to a cloak. Each Bedouin tribe has its own particular style of design.**

LEFT: **Turban headwraps have generally been replaced by fine white polyester cotton, or the ubiquitous checkered cloth with tassels, called** keffiyeh, **as is seen here worn by these Saudi Arabian Bedouin men.**

RIGHT: In common with most Muslim countries, a bride has her hands and feet patterned with henna stain at the baths, or hammam, *before her wedding.*

LEFT: Finger jewelery, linking rings to disks and bracelets, is prized in the Muslim world. This wedding jewelery is from Bahrain.

daggers and firearms, though today swords and daggers are now worn only for ceremonial purposes.

The headwrap is the most instantly identifying article of Arab clothing, and is known variously as a *ghoutra*, *shaal*, or *ihram*. It is a square of cotton cloth large enough to be wound around the head or to cover the face. Nowadays, the turban headwrap style is less common, and the cloth is usually folded diagonally, with a central peak in the fold placed over the middle of the forehead, and secured with an *igaal*, or head circlet. The two pointed ends are worn either in front, or with one thrown back over the shoulder, or both – producing a cavalier effect – ironic when one considers the respectful purpose of covering the hair.

Fine white polyester often replaces cotton these days, although the checkered cloth with tassels, called *keffiyeh*, is also widespread and is more for everyday use. A skullcap, is worn underneath; nowadays a small crocheted version is the most common, but older examples are often more elaborate with hand embroidery in metallic gold thread.

In rural areas where the temperature gets cooler, such as in the southeastern highlands, a thick sheep's wool overcoat, or *farwah*, is worn. Sometimes furs are used as very simple garments, the skin side stained red and decorated for wearing outward.

Women's kaftans are cut similarly to the men's, with flaring side panels and underarm gussets that are often elaborate in style. The fabrics used vary enormously, but are hidden, because once a woman leaves the house she will be wearing her black wool cloak, or *abaaya*, which hides her dress. Especially amongst the Bedouin women, rich embroidery is used to embellish the front opening, sleeve edges, side gores, and sometimes the hem of the kaftan. Colors are jewel-bright; reds of all shades, oranges, and greens are used. A wide variety of textiles, from velvets and silk brocades to satins and voiles will all be for sale at country or town markets. Only the wool weaves are actually made in the Arabian Peninsula; the silks and cottons have always been imported.

*ABOVE: These young girls attend a Koranic school in Oman and are wearing a variety of brightly colored wraps. In the coastal area of this country, vivid cloth wrappers that are imported from Indonesia and India are worn with a gauzy shawl (*lihaf*) that covers the head and shoulders and is then tucked neatly under the chin.*

Commonly throughout the Muslim world, a cherry red shade is chosen for bridal robes. In Arabia, the *omasa* worn by brides is covered on sleeves and bodice with Indian gold embroidery. A bride also wears a long red wrapper for her ritual visit to the *hammam* (the baths) for her hands and feet to be painted with henna before the wedding.

For the vast majority of Arab women in the Emirates, a full face veil or *burga* is worn in addition to a cloak, which is usually decorated with tassels, beads, shells, or white shirt-type buttons. Each Bedouin tribe has its own particular combination as identification. Only the Shammar and some Hijaz tribes in the south go without the face veil.

In the northern part of Saudi Arabia a small half-veil, or *milfa*, is more common and a few tribes allow their women to be unveiled. *Burgas* will be held in place by the *asayib*, or circlet, sometimes with decorative pendant attachments. In some parts of the Arabian Peninsula (see also Northeast Africa on page 84), hoods are worn by girls and married women. These, too, are decorated with buttons, beads, and cowrie shells, and are often long enough to cover the chest.

In rural areas of southwest Saudi Arabia the style of headwear is different, with men and women wearing conical straw hats in place of headcloths or veils. Women may also wear a scarf under the hat, so as to absorb sweat and protect the neck from sun during fieldwork. The hats are decorated with looped chains around the back. In southern Saudi Arabia, Bedouin women tend to wear their dresses slightly shorter than the Arab women of the North, with *sirwaal*, or trousers, revealed to mid-shin.

Farther south, in Oman, a variation on the elements of Arabian dress is worn by the men, with a tighter shaped body shirt, topped with a broad sash wound around the waist. The sleeves of this garment are extra-long, with wide triangular shapes ending in long points. Sometimes the sash, or *fanilla*, is worn over a western-style shirt instead, and on ceremonial occasions, a traditional dagger is always tucked into it or into a narrower leather belt. Close-fitting *sirwaal* complete the outfit.

Among Omani women, tighter bodices and shorter ankle-length skirts over trousers are worn for agricultural tasks. In central Oman, veils are seldom worn, although in the interior a half-veil is more common. On the Omani coast, bright turbans and wrappers of Indonesian and Indian cloth are worn with a gauzy shawl (a *lihaf*) that covers the head and shoulders and is tucked under the chin.

In what was called the Levant, an area now occupied by Lebanon, Syria, and Israel, a rich heritage of costume is vanishing fast. Women of Christian, Muslim, and Jewish faith all wore clothes that showed traces of the region's history – noticeable in the shaped cut for tight bodices and in the use of richly embroidered or woven textiles. They also had a variety of headdresses, versions of the *tarboosh* (or fez) and round caps, worn with a veil, white muslin *shash*, or *yashmak*.

Palestinian costume is particularly rich and varied in style. After the collapse of the Ottoman Empire, this region of the Middle East was ruled by mandate by the British until 1948. Palestinian traditional dress reflects the three main social groups: the sophisicated townspeople, who have had close contact with foreigners, particularly the Turkish, British and French; the villagers; and then the nomadic or semi-nomadic Bedouin.

Shelagh Weir's detailed study, *Palestinian Costume*, emphasizes her discovery that village women's dress is far more diverse than other people assumed: "Several distinctly different styles of dress could and did co-exist in each village or region at any one time. Some elements did indeed vary regionally but some were common to several regions, and some to the entire country".

Traditional Palestinian costume was handwoven, of wool or cotton, with indigo and other natural dyes being used in colors that indicated regions. Rarer silks were imported from Egypt and Syria – particularly the rich narrow striped silk weft and cotton-warp satins. A small amount of work on treadle looms still continues, even today in refugee camps.

More importantly, the traditions of richly embroidered tunic dresses are still very strong in the camps, where women's welfare organizations provide work and create income for the people living there. The modern Palestinian tunic dress is rather narrower in cut than older, flared, paneled styles and is called a *shawal*.

Older full-sleeved tunic dresses would have wonderfully worked cross-stitch or couched gold-thread panels on the front, over seams, and at the hem. The embroiderers of Bethlehem responded to outside influences, like the gorgeous frogging and other embroideries on official's uniforms, both Turkish and British, seen in nearby Jerusalem, and produced a distinctive style of gold couchwork.

Nowadays Bethlehem couched embroidery in lurex thread, done by machine, but simulating the classic handwork, is popular on more elaborate festive dresses of velvet. These dresses are called *malak*, which means "royal," but are they only a very pale version of the original regal robes of past times.

Dresses still reflect the immense variety of regional styles in Palestine. Costume collections such as that of the Dar al Tifl Museum based in Jerusalem, and the Folk Museum in Amman, keep alive the culture of a long displaced people, as do the numerous dance troupes well supported by Palestinians. The "village" dresses act as a visual sign of a people's attachment and claim to their land.

While most men now wear westernized clothing, the checkered black-and-white *keffiyeh* headcloth and cravat worn by Yasser Arafat has become a strong symbol of Palestinian identity.

In neighboring Jordan, the ethnic mix of peoples – Palestinian, Bedouin, Armenian, and Circassian (Cherkess) emigrés – try to keep all their old traditions alive.

A Bedouin man from Syria wearing a typical Arab patterned headwrap.

This woman of Bahrain wears an ornate headwrap and gold jewelry.

A traditional costume of a Yemeni woman living in Israel.

Key

Kurdish people go across this area

Palestinian people go across this area

Bedouin people go across this area

1,000–3,000m (3,000–9,000ft)

200–1,000m (600–3,000ft)

0–200m (0–600ft)

Seas, lakes and rivers

Note: Peoples are shown in italics eg: **Bedouin**

Middle East Map

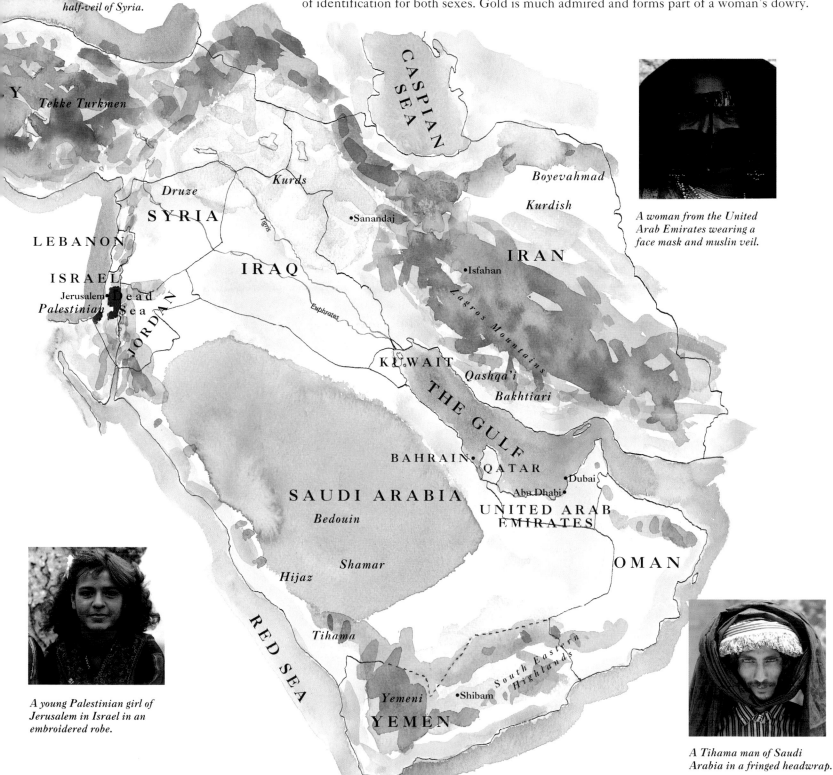

The predominance of Islam in the Middle East gives dress of this region a simplicity and uniformity prescribed by Muhammad himself. Yet within limitations, every country and region distinguishes itself by attention to the detail of its dress, and, for women, in a luxurious use of jewelry and sumptuous fabrics under veils and cloaks. Men still take pride in their weaponry, even if only for ceremonial attire. The use of headgear is the primary means of identification for both sexes. Gold is much admired and forms part of a woman's dowry.

A Druze woman wearing a half-veil of Syria.

A woman from the United Arab Emirates wearing a face mask and muslin veil.

A young Palestinian girl of Jerusalem in Israel in an embroidered robe.

A Tihama man of Saudi Arabia in a fringed headwrap.

107

FACE VEILS

TOP ROW, LEFT TO RIGHT:

A woman of the Boyevahmad tribe, Iran, with a head covering decorated with metallic floral shapes and coin fringing over gauze veiling.

A farmer's daughter of Shibam, Yemen, in a tight protective head veiling of black muslin.

A Saudi woman wearing a traditional mask with pillbox hat made from gold and decorated with pearls.

A Bedouin tribeswoman of Dubai, in silvered gauze headcover and stiffened satin milfa or face mask.

A woman of Bahrain wearing a blue floral embroidered head cover, tied under chin, and a gold face mask.

MIDDLE ROW, LEFT TO RIGHT:

A Harb Bedouin woman of Saudi Arabia wearing an ornate red face mask decorated with silver coins.

A Bedouin woman of the Sinai Desert in coin and chain-link veil, which reaches to the waist, held on by a lace headband under a black plush veil cloak.

A Rashaida nomad woman of the Sudan-Eritrea border region in silver-embroidered face veil stitched with rows of pearl buttons.

A woman of the United Arab Emirates (U.A.E.) wearing a head cover of black lace with gold coin fringing over face mask. Chandelier earrings and a silver strand necklace are also worn.

A Bedouin tribeswoman of Oman wearing full face mask with a hood, held in place by an asayib, or circlet.

BOTTOM ROW, LEFT TO RIGHT:

A woman of Oman wearing a bright yellow and pink kaftan hidden under a homespun black cloak and simple fall veil with forehead band attached.

A woman of Abu Dhabi, U.A.E., wearing a transparent silvered-gauze veil, a gilt pendant headpiece and finger jewelry attached to a bracelet.

A woman from the U.A.E. wearing a heavy, full face veiling of silvered gauze, under which a face mask, or milfa, and gold jewelry are barely visible.

A Bedouin woman wood-gatherer of Sinai, wearing a coin-trimmed headdress in red cotton, doubling as a face veil, under a heavy black hood.

A Bedouin woman of Qatar in a double-layered, light-silk fringed face veil, tied over long braids.

109

CENTRAL ASIA & THE CAUCASUS

The term "Central Asia" is broad, encompassing countries reaching from the Ukraine, in the west, to the borders of Manchuria, in Northeast China. In this chapter we cover Uzbekistan, Kazakhstan, Turkmenistan, Kyrgyzstan, Tadzhikistan, in Central Asia, and Georgia, Armenia, Dagestan, the Kabardino Balkar Republic, North Ossetian republic, and the Checeno-Ingush Republic, in the Caucasus.

Because of its vastness, the wide passes between mountains, the windswept steppes, and its position between China and Europe, Central Asia has always been home to the nomad, the migrant, and the displaced. Perhaps for that reason, its history is comparatively obscure to outsiders.

For a long time, until the Portuguese began the exploitation of sea routes, merchants crossed back and forth – bringing furs, gold, spices, slaves, silks, and gems from the east and north across the network of routes known collectively as the Silk Road. The wealth of the old oasis towns along this route – Bukhara, Samarkand, Kiva, Ferghana and Kashgar – is legendary. Empires rose and fell; each in its turn – from Sassanian to Roman, to Byzantine and Abbassid Caliphate, to Mongol, in the Middle Ages, sought to dominate or control the traffic and revenues of the Silk Road.

All these conquerors left traces of their cultures and added to the ethnic complexity of the region. One dynasty dominated Central Asia from the 16th to 19th century; these were the Uzbek Shaibanids. During the 19th century locally powerful ruling princes, Uzbek *begs*, emerged, such as the Mangits of Bukhara, the Min dynasty of Kokand or ancient Ferghana, and the

ABOVE: **A Kyrgyz mother and child: her vivid and richly patterned dress is typical of Central Asia.**

OPPOSITE: **Uzbek women of Samarkan on the Silk Road. Head coverings abound in this region.**

Khivan Khanate of Khorezmia. These khanates were political divisions containing a multiethnic population comprising Uzbek and Tadzhik or ethnic Persian farmers, Kazakh nomads, Kyrgyz sheep and horse-breeders, and Central-Asian Arabs who practiced pastoral nomadism in the mountainous regions to the east. Turkmen tribes in particular were commercially important, breeding and trading vast herds of camels and horses throughout Central Asia. More significant, however, was their trade in slaves, hostages of war or captured from raids on the Persian border towns.

As trade passed to the oceans via India, Central Asia became focused on itself. The 19th century was a time of social reorganization, political renewal, and religious revivalism, with an inward-looking development of

Islamic culture. Against this background, Russian conquest and absorption of the khanates early in the 20th century can be seen as one more step in a fluctuating historical continuum. The Russians wanted access to larger markets for industrial goods and control of the trade routes.

Trade still governs the success of these states: Uzbekistan, Kazakhstan, Turkmenistan, Kyrgyzstan, and Tadzhikistan. They are rich in mineral resources. Formerly part of the Soviet Union, they seek greater autonomy within the Commonwealth of Independent States (C.I.S), if not independence. These states have a growing sense of their separate identities and unique historic culture; from as early as the 1960s, many almost-forgotten crafts, such as *ikat* dyeing and weaving, have now been revived.

Dress plays an important part in establishing or maintaining cultural identity. Consequently the costumes of all the ethnic groups of the Central Asian states are varied, colorful, and still in existence – partly because they are the most practical working clothes in a lifestyle not much affected by industrial development, and partly because they foster national pride.

The Caucasus Mountains are not considered a part of Europe, even though "Caucasian" is used to define the European racial stock. That anomaly reflects the whole region's history. Russia has always maintained its security by dominating the peoples who live on or beyond its borders. The Caucasians are no exception.

In general, the costume of this area presents a romantic, medieval look, in keeping with the equestrian, chivalrous traditions of the people's warrior culture.

The Central States

In general terms the clothing of Central Asia can be categorized as specific either to a sedentary or a nomadic way of life. The sedentary population has worn clothing influenced by Persia and Islam: baggy trousers, long overshirt, sleeved robe, or *dolman*, which folds over at the front and is held in place with a sash, and a turban, or *kola*. But the costume of the nomadic groups reveals more of the various ethnic influences of conquests in the past, and the different techniques brought in their train. Quilting, felting, and weaving are part of their repertoire.

Turkmen horsemen, who still play the famous *buzkashi* game, a violent form of polo, wear thigh-length, quilted, and tight-fitting long-sleeved tunics, with a side slit

for ease of movement in the saddle, over wide, baggy trousers and knee-length boots. Nomadic populations make fabrics from wool and hair, whereas sedentary peoples grow and weave cotton as their staple. (Uzbekistan is the major producer of cotton for the C.I.S.)

Sedentary people tend to use many layers of cotton clothing for warmth and practicality. Women of these communities continue to wear brilliant and often delicate fabrics.

Central Asian nomadic people, by contrast, tend to wear fitted trousers with cut and shaped fur or wool jackets and coats that are more suited to riding and working with horses or camels; women's clothing is similar to the men's because their type of work is comparable. Central Asian nomads,

ABOVE MIDDLE: An eagle trainer and herdsman of Sarsembek, Kazakhstan. In a region where hunting in various forms is the basis of the culture, a mixture of furs and hides is often worn. Fur can be used as trimming for hats or sheared for garments such as robes and coats.

LEFT: A land of mountains, plateaus and fertile valleys, Kyrgyzstan has always been caught between its neighbors: Russia and China. It is now part of the C.I.S., but for cultural and religious reasons seeks closer ties with Turkey. The dress of its people reflects this link, as seen here in the little round kolas worn by the boys, the long dresses of the girls, and the veiling of the women. Many people are Muslim, while others are Orthodox Christian Russians. The Kyrgyz are still nomadic, and the women roll up their carpet-weaving when they move.

RIGHT: In common with many other Central Asian peoples, the Turkmen of Turkmenistan are fine carpet makers. This female weaver is in the middle of making a carpet. She wears a traditional and distinctive patterned high turban and scarf over a flowing blue-and-white striped robe.

LEFT: This Turkmen weaver is spinning wool on a hand-turned wheel before starting to make a carpet. She, too, wears the high turban, but her classic Central Asian long, loose robe is in a matching color. Both of these items of clothing have been dyed this rich color using a red synthetic dye.

whether male or female, wear leather or felt boots with their trousers tucked into the tops. A blouse or loose tunic is worn over the top, with a belted coat or ample cloak over all. In all the Central Asian states the crossover, full-length or "bagged-up" *dolman* robe or coat is seen. Shorter tunics are worn by horsemen, often with capes over the top for added warmth.

The Turkmen males, now living scattered across Turkmenistan and also in Iran and Afghanistan, generally wear cheap western-style clothing. Those nomadic tribes who have been pressured to settle wear the more traditional, conservative elements of their costume, such as the long crossover robe held in place with a cummerbund or narrow sash. These are frequently seen at special occasions, such as weddings, worn over western suits.

The traditional karakul fur or felt hat with side flaps is worn even if men wear western clothing. It is common to find traces of traditional styling when women copy old embroidery motifs by machine onto the fronts and collars of commercially manufactured shirts for the men of their family.

The men living in Tashkent, capital of Uzbekistan, wear white crossover-closing jackets, with long sleeves, a wide sash, and black trousers tucked into high black boots made of soft leather. Their hat is round and flat with a scalloped edge; it is called a *tibiteika* and is a national symbol of the Uzbeks. Women wear standard Muslim clothing, full-length floral-print dresses, headwraps, and veils. Occasionally the full-length white kaftan robe is seen worn by an older man.

Turkmen farming families who moved over the border into Afghanistan in the

1930s to avoid collectivization, revived silk-scarf weaving in some villages, and an itinerant Uzbek craftsman taught a simplified means of making *ikat*. This enterprise died out in the 1970s, although *ikat* weaving may yet be revived elsewhere in the border territories, if only to satisfy commercial interests.

Central Asian *ikat*-woven robes are highly prized. They are kept from generation to generation and are still worn in remote villages. A British expert is Pip Rau, who explains that *ikat* is the Malay word for what is termed *abra* in this region – from *abr*, or "cloud," in Persian (in Arabic it is *asab*; in Turkic, *ipekshahi*). A particularly subtle and colorful form of abstract pattern is made by dyeing the warp or weft, or both, in bundles before use on the loom. The penetration of

ABOVE: A village wedding scene in Uzbekistan captures the essential elements of Central Asia's heritage: a rich carpet hangs in the background, a symbol of a trade that stretches back to Greek and Roman times. A wonderful ikat-weave drape connects the textile culture of Persia with the Chinese silk trade in this region. The bridegroom wears a western suit with a traditional skull cap, while the bride is dressed in a beautiful gold lace veil and gown.

the dye is controlled by resist techniques – that is, tying up the fibers tightly so the dyes do not penetrate patches of the yarn. On the loom, the variously dyed and undyed sections of yarn meet and blend to give a slightly blurred, random but repetitive patterning – hence the use of the description "cloud."

In Central Asia this dyeing technique was applied to silk textiles. The origin of its use in the region is uncertain, but examples date from the 18th century onward, reaching their zenith in the 19th century. Central Asian silk *ikats* of this period are collectors' pieces, and they are copied by textile manufacturers. In the 1960s old designs were used on cotton garments, but updated with names such as "Sputnik."

In Chinese East Turkestan, incorporated into China in 1884, a Central Asian people, the Uigurs, still make handmade *ikat*-dyed fabrics. The women wear floral-patterned, knee-length cotton skirts or dresses with thick brown stockings on their legs, but they keep their traditional embroidered skullcaps, as do the men, but with western-style suits.

In the 19th century, different styles of hats distinguished groups of people. Today, the divisions are less obvious. Large sheepskin or lambswool hats were usually worn by the Turkmen; the gaily colored *tyubeterka*, like a *kola* or turban, by the Uzbeks; the *kalpac* or pointed beige cap, trisected by black felt lines, worn by the Kyrgyz; and the cup-shaped hat with a central peak favored by the Mongol men. The farther east one travels along the old Silk Road, however, the plainer the people's clothing becomes, and the less extrovert the wearers.

The Caucasus

RIGHT: *A Russian Cossack of Georgia wears the classic "mountaineer's" garb of belted tunic, baggy trousers, and tall fur hat, now national costume, but basically old military dress. In the 18th and 19th centuries, Cossacks gave military service to the tsar in return for land in the fertile south.*

BELOW MIDDLE: **These Chechen men of the Checheno-Ingush Republic are wearing another version of the tall fur hat, sometimes called** pa'a, *that is worn by all the mountain peoples who live in the Caucasus.*

LEFT: **Historic conflict between Russia, Turkey, and the southern nations resulted in waves of emigration out of the region. Descendants of Cherkess, Armenian, or Georgian refugees live in many countries of the Middle East, as well as the U.S. and Europe. This Armenian resides in Jerusalem but wears his traditional costume, which reveals strong Turkic influence in the fez hat and the gold embroidery of his jacket and waistcoat. Yet the majority of Armenians form an ancient branch of the Christian Orthodox church that long resisted Islam.**

In the 19th century, the ruler of Dagestan, Shamil, led the longest campaign of resistance that the invading tsarist forces had to contend with. The Ossetians, Chechens, Kabardinians, and other North-Caucasian mountain peoples were not far behind in their efforts to remain free. Georgia ceded its power to Russia partly because it had long been a Christian country, whereas the mountain people, or mountaineers, were and still are largely Muslim. After the Revolution oppression still continued, and whole communities of mountaineers were shipped out to labor camps, and the region was resettled by Russian communists. This was a continuation of the tsarist policy of settling Cossack farmers in the disputed area situated in the south.

The Caucasian people are still working for various degrees of self-determination. In parallel to the recent upsurge of political activity in the Caucasus, a keen interest in ethnic traditions has developed. Millions of

the indigenous people fled to other countries in the late 18th and early 19th centuries. The Cherkess (the people of the region north of the Caucasus Mountains on the Black Sea, formerly called "Circassians") have enclaves in the United States, Germany, Syria, Jordan, and Turkey. Many are entitled, and wish to return, to their native lands. In doing so, they will bring back their culture, which has been partially neglected by those remaining on the ancestral territory. In the diaspora, knowledge of dress, dance, poetry, and other cultural forms was carefully maintained, and now at every congress or reunion dancing troupes perform in their traditional attire. Weddings are also occasions for a people to display its authentic splendor.

The region comprises three climatic zones: snow-capped polar and alpine mountains, a humid region on the Black Sea, and a semi-desert area on the Caspian coast. The mix of nationalities is immense: in Dagestan there are scores of languages from one valley to the next. More than 50 nationalities inhabit the region, grouped linguistically as Ibero-Caucasian, Iranian, and Turkic.

All national costumes in this region – Georgian, Armenian, and Cherkess – generally have the same stylish elements and often draw on a common historical tradition. The Kabardinian female costume reflects the formal, hierarchical nature of their society. Historically, headgear varied according to status and group. Young girls went bare-headed, but marriageable girls wore beautiful caps, which they wore after marriage, until the birth of their first child. The dress was influenced by Ottoman costume: it is basically a long kaftan-shaped robe, either

open at the front and worn with an under-tunic, or closed and worn with long, soft trousers and a sleeveless vest or thick winter fur coat, usually fitted and flare-skirted. Materials were rich (damask, brocade, or silk), beautifully embroidered, and with varied and graceful sleeve shapes. Handmade trimmings, especially lace, are a feature of

both male and female costume. Wedding dresses of traditional design in luxurious lace are often seen today.

Caucasian women, although Muslim, do not go veiled, but wear long floating scarves over their round, pillbox-shaped hats.

Jewelry is ancient and elaborate, with silver predominating in the North Caucasus, while gold, carnelian, pearls, and corals are found more in Azerbaijan.

Traditionally, a chief feature of Circassian dress was the leather cinch belt. In former times a girl wore this through puberty to keep her waist tiny, and it was ritually cut off by her husband on the wedding night. Girls also ate sparingly, as a slim waist was considered the most important physical attribute. For men, too, abstinence and a modest diet were signs of good manners, and their self-discipline and hardiness of character were legendary. These traits were always much admired by the Cossacks.

ABOVE RIGHT: **Armenian national dress is worn only for special occasions and festivals; the women's costume is similar to that of many nations in this region, consisting of a long robe, a pillbox hat, and a veil. As with the male costume, there is a medieval, romantic look to this region's dress. This is partly a reflection of Armenia's militaristic and chivalrous cultural past, and partly because the costume has died out as a living, evolving form of dress. Turkic influences can also be seen here, in the veiling and use of coin decoration, and braid trimmings that were originally handmade.**

LEFT: **These Georgian men are wearing their national dress. In common with most other people who live north and south of the Caucasus, they wear a costume related to their militant history. (The Georgians like the Ossetians, are still in conflict with Russia, have only a provisional government, and their relationship with the C.I.S. is uncertain.) The tunics they are wearing have full skirts, for ease of riding, and "patron pockets" – now for decoration, but designed for gun cartridges. Armor was always a prized possession (many ancient examples are of Spanish provenance), and the short dagger is still a prized heirloom. Each nation wears different headgear: here not the tall fur hat favored by the Cossacks and Cherkess, but a rounder felt, stitched cap instead.**

117

If female costume emphasizes the delicacy and femininity of the female form, the male costume is its perfect foil, for it is a dashing ensemble – so much so that many Russian soldiers posted to the Caucasus (including Tolstoy) took to wearing it.

Men wear baggy trousers, tucked into soft leather boots (often made soleless, for better responses when riding), a tunic shirt (made of one piece folded at the shoulder), and a *cherkeska* – a full-skirted, tight-fitting, front-opening jacket with a stand-up collar. It extends to the mid-thigh and is perfectly designed for a cavalryman. The chest bears two "patron pockets" – originally for cartridges, but now purely decorative. Tucked in his tooled leather belt, the classic Cherkess fighter wore beautifully engraved daggers, or *camas*, which are still very much coveted. In winter he would wear a *burka* – a thick, trapezoid or bell-shaped cloak of sheepskin or astrakhan (a garment that hill farmers and shepherds still find most practical). When riding in bad weather, the rider turns the cloak so that the opening is at his back. The *burka* also doubles as a sleeping cover, making a virtual tent.

Fur hats of all kinds are found: the shaggy tall round hat of karakul fur was originally worn by the Cossack horsemen; it is still common to the herdsmen of the Caspian area. The Cherkess wear the *pa'a*, a tall fur hat, or a *bashlyk*, a hood made of broadcloth with a pointed top and long strips at the sides for tying at the neck, and often decorated with braid. More sedentary males used to wear kaftans, turbans, and robes in styles relating to those of other Muslim peoples farther along the Silk Route in Central Asia. These styles have not been revived as the classic costume by the new autonomous nations, perhaps because they are not reminiscent of their rebellious past.

Georgian countrymen still wear their version of the mountaineer's garb: knee-length tunics over dark trousers, wide at the crotch and tapering into boots. Daggers are tucked into their belts, and capes are flung over their shoulders. Georgian women's costume is a variation of the same regional pattern: long tunic-shaped dress, trousers, sash, embroidered or otherwise-decorated caps, and fur outer garments. Georgian jewelry of the lowland areas tends to be gold, while the people in the highland areas use silver, carnelian, turquoise, and glass.

Armenian traditional costume for women favors red, which is the color of womanhood, health, and fertility. Long red shirts and trousers, plus an outer garment called an *arkhalukh*, which is gathered at the waist with a silver belt or long scarf, are traditional female dress. The sleeves are then decorated with silver buttons or with silver chain links in the form of leaves and berries – perhaps old symbols for fertility. Armenian traditional costume, particularly to the west, includes lavish embroidery – wedding aprons with gold work are especially fine.

In Dagestan, to the east, traditional clothing is the order of the day, and not a matter of revivalism. Women wear tunic dresses richly embroidered in glowing colors (all the richer for the bleakness of their mountain habitat) over long trousers. They wear boots, often handmade, with felt uppers faced with leather, and decorated with some couched wool work. The upward curve of their toes prevents the boots from being splashed with mud. Glue is worked into the boots for waterproofing. Once again the Turkic influence is evident in the costume, with the round hats, long scarves, and elaborate jewelry.

A woman of Uzbekistan in turban and shawl.

A fur hat worn by a Chechen man from the Checheno-Ingush Republic.

Central Asia Map

Continuing in the Islamic dress traditions, Central Asian costume consists of long tunics and cloaks or loose open robes. Old traditions of silk manufacture, dyeing, weaving, and trade produce a stronger rate of survival for traditional costume than elsewhere. The region's inaccessibility and its old practices – hunting, herding, nomadic pastoralism – add to the endurance of ethnic dress. Hats are the group identifiers even where western dress is worn.

Boy of Uzbekistan in national male headgear, the tibiteika.

MONGOLIA
Mongol

KAZAKHSTAN
Kazakh

ARAL SEA

UZBEKISTAN
Uzbek

CHINA

TURKMENISTAN

•Tashkent

KYRGYZSTAN
Kyrgyz

CHINESE TURKESTAN

•Bukhara •Samarkand
•Dushanbe

TADZHIKISTAN
Tadzhik

Uigur

Turkmen

RAN

AFGHANISTAN

A Kazakh eagle trainer of China wearing a traditional hunter's fur hat.

A mullah in traditional cap and robe from Tadzhikistan.

A Kurdish woman from Armenia wearing a plain red headcloth and a shawl.

Key

Note: peoples are shown in italics eg: **Kazakh**

4,000 plus m (12,000 plus ft)

1,000–4,000m (3,000–12,000ft)

400–1,000m (1,200–3,000ft)

0–400m (0–1,200ft)

Seas, lakes and rivers

ROBES AND COATS

TOP ROW, LEFT TO RIGHT:

Tadzhik dancer in gold-embroidered robe.

Young boy in an embroidered chapan, or open robe, from Bukhara, Uzbekistan.

Georgian singers in ornamental version of their national robes of cavalry origin.

An Uzbek musician carrying his *rihab*, a stringed instrument, wearing a padded, quilted, striped chapan.

Young girl in national costume at the Navroz New Year parade at Samarkand in Uzbekistan. She is wearing a velvet silver-embroidered waistcoat and full-length, long-sleeved robe of 19th-century styling.

MIDDLE ROW, LEFT TO RIGHT:

Bride at Uzbek wedding in Samarkand, wearing a traditional silk brocade robe with appliqué cuffs of contrasting coloring.

Vivid ikat-weave chapan, worn by Tadzhik craftswoman of Dushanbe, Tadzhikistan.

Uzbek woman in quilted chapan.

Uzbek herb seller at a market in Samarkand, wearing a quilted vest and robe.

Georgian man in traditional national costume, including silver short sword.

BOTTOM ROW, LEFT TO RIGHT:

Turkmen wearing long side-buttoning closed robe and vest.

Fur-collared sheared lamb coat of an eagle trainer in Kazakhstan.

Simple cotton work chapan of an Uzbek farmer, worn over finer ikat inner chapan.

Muslim man in best striped chapan, worn for visiting the mosque in Tashkent, Uzbekistan.

Quilted modern coat of a melon farmer of Kazakhstan, worn over a traditional sleeveless fur vest.

121

SOUTHEAST ASIA

To the rest of the world, Southeast Asia has always been a source of great riches. Today its richnesslies in its ethnic diversity as much as in all its traditional exports of gemstones, silks, spices and other exotic goods. From the western boundary of the region (India's border with the Union of Myanmar [Burma]) to the eastern (China and the Pacific Ocean), the region is made up of deep valleys between high mountains running more or less north to south like the fingers of a hand. From the Malaysian Peninsula, like jewels shaken out from that hand, the islands of Indonesia lie scattered between the Indian and the Pacific oceans. The forested valleys of the mainland are at times impenetrable, and monsoons make traveling difficult. The high plateaus are equally inaccessible, accounting for the enormous concentration of population in the tropical deltas of the south, where the capital cities of the present-day states are situated.

The primary economy is rice growing; the primary religion is Hinayana Buddhism, although Confucianism and Islam also have adherents in certain areas. The standard dress of the Southeast Asian people is either western-style (adopted more widely by men and urban people in general), or a wrap-around fabric length worn by both sexes: as a skirt topped by a T-shirt or shirt by men, or in two ways by the women. A dress length is wrapped and tied over the chest, or a longer skirt is folded in pleats at the waist and worn with a fitted blouse or tunic top.

Farther eastward, the influence of Chinese dress is noticeable, with variations of shirt, trousers, and jacket widely accepted for both sexes. Everywhere the orange robes of Buddhist priests shine out, a vivid, spiritual

ABOVE: *Some Filipinos, such as this Ifuago tribeswoman, still wear traditional dress.*

OPPOSITE: *A procession at a temple in the Union of Myanmar. Sarongs are worn by both sexes.*

"traffic light" amid bustling crowds of people. But within the numerous ethnic groups hidden away in the high valleys and forests, animistic religions flourish, as do an astonishing variety of customs, dress, and rituals, still offering rich studies for anthropologists and others.

For contrast, there is the traditional clothing of much of the Union of Myanmar. It is a country where there is an extraordinary degree of equality between the sexes and where a particularly pure form of Buddhism prevails. There is no caste system or primogeniture in native Burmese society. There are around 35 million Burmese, one-third comprising minorities, such as all the hill peoples mentioned above, and two-thirds

the indigenous stock, originally Mongol, who settled in the area over 500 years ago. A second major influx was of Tai-Shans, Chinese in origin.

The Karen people originated near or in the Gobi Desert. The Union of Myanmar's population has, therefore, never been entirely homogeneous, but has always contained warring factions. Forty percent of the population, the ethnic minorities, contend for autonomy.

Indonesia is a collection of islands, each with its own unique history. The inhabitants vary from peoples of virtually Stone Age technology, with animistic beliefs, to long-established Hindu, Buddhist and Muslim communities, all of whom bear traces of the colonizing powers that have plied trade throughout this region. Hand-crafted clothing predominates in this exotic archipelago. Each costume requires a certain type of weaving, a specific type of thread and colors, to be accompanied by special hairstyles, jewelry, or headgear.

The range of textiles used throughout Indonesia is extremely broad. Cotton, silk, tree bark, and plant fibers are treated to different patterning techniques such as batik, *ikat*, and *plangi*.

Ikat has been described briefly in the section on Central Asia (see page 115). It is estimated to have arrived in Indonesia in the late-Neolithic period. In contrast to the weavers of West Africa, here only the women perform this craft. The accumulation of fine textiles is a sign of a family's status and prestige, as a degree of economic security is required to permit the time-consuming work of high-quality weaving to take place, and to release women from work more essential to a family's survival.

Hill Tribes of the Golden Triangle

The figures for some of the tribal peoples are substantial: the hill tribes of north Thailand, who have received most study, comprising the Karen, Hmong, Yao, Lahu, Akha, and Lisu, number around 415,000, yet are only a mere one percent of Thailand's population, and a very small percentage of the hill peoples who live in what is called the Golden Triangle of the Union of Myanmar, Thailand, and Laos. The hill tribes also live in Vietnam and China.

There are three main linguistic groupings. First is the Hmong (also known as the Meo and Miao), and the Yao (also known as the Mien), members of the Sino-Tibetan language group, the majority of whom moved across the Mekong from south-central China into Laos, and from there on into Thailand after 1975. This migration route was also followed by the Karen people, who belong to a second linguistic group. None of the Karen remain in China today, while four million are in the Union of Myanmar.

The third language group is Tibeto-Burman, to which the Akha people belong. The Akha are also known in Laos as the Kha Kaw, and as the Hani people in China and Vietnam, and speak a dialect that is found in Burma, northeast Laos, and the southwest of Yunnan province in China. At the last census, there were around 24,000 in Thailand. They have no written language, but a rich store of legends, proverbs, and rituals. Today, tribal radio stations broadcast taped songs and stories never before recorded or shared outside each group.

The Lahu people (of the Tibeto-Burman group) are also spread right across the region with around 250,000 in China, 150,000 in the Union of Myanmar, 40,000 in Thailand, and 10,000 in Laos. One-third of those in Thailand are nominally Christian.

Within every one of these groups, every subgroup may have its own costume, customs, and rituals. Nor are any of these static. For example, a Thai subdivision of the Lahu, the Lahu Shi, had converted to Christianity and abandoned their own traditional dress. Another group of refugee Lahu arrived from Laos and inspired them to readopt their former dress, at least for special occasions.

The most striking feature of hill tribe clothing is that it is still entirely handmade, of an elaboration and beauty that is extraordinary. The embroidery is not simply a manifestation of the skill of the hill tribes. Most are slash-and-burn cultivators of rice and maize, for whom life moves slowly.

Everything done is for a purpose and has a significance. It can be to appease a spirit, or to weave and stitch a burial cloth of the most exquisite fineness, which may never be worn. Both backstrap and foot treadle weaving frames are used. The basic shape

Hmong or White Hmong. The first make a blue batik material for their knee-length pleated skirts of cotton or hemp. The wax of the dyeing process is not completely washed out, so that the pleats are stiff and firm. Herringbone embroidery stitches anchor the pleats over the hip area. On top are worn jackets of black cotton or velvet with decorative appliquéd strips at the neck opening and front. White Hmong women do not use batik work but use embroidery, and specialize in the appliqué and reverse appliqué techniques. Aprons are a great

feature of women's attire: black for day and appliquéd ones for special occasions. Even leggings are made of handwoven cloth. Women generally wear their hair in a bun, but will add a bulky pointed headdress for formal dress.

Both groups make replicas of adult clothing for their children, with attractive pompon bonnets. They demonstrate their fine stitchcraft on baby carriers – consisting of two rectangles, a small one stitched to the short edge of a larger one, and the whole held on the back with broad red straps.

of Karen clothing is determined by the width of the loom. For a top, two strips of cloth are joined by a vertical center seam, with a head opening left at the center fold. Each strip is about 18 inches (45 centimeters) wide. The top is worn over a skirt made of two hand-woven lengths, placed one above the other and joined along the selvages, for a horizontal seam above knee height, and then joined in one vertical seam to make a tube shape.

This method enables the border patterns to be used to best decorative effect, and the top and bottom edges of the skirt, being selvages, to be left unhemmed.

The Hmong people are known by their clothing color schemes as either Blue

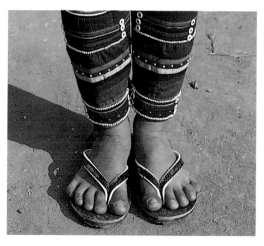

ABOVE: Handwoven leggings feature in many tribes' dress. Here they are worn by an Akha girl of Chiang Mai, north Thailand. Compare these with the dress of the Cuna Indians of the San Blas islands on page 34.

As with the Karen, Hmong men generally wear a somber outfit of black trousers and black jacket, but they will have a special version of silk or velvet with embroidery or other decorative sections on the crossover or button flap of the jacket, which again varies between communities as an identifier. Beautiful handwoven sashes, as much as 6 feet (5.5 meters) long, are wound around and tied like an apron in front. A black Chinese-style skullcap, with red pompom, is worn; otherwise the men go bareheaded.

The Lahu people wear clothing as rich and complex as the pieces described above, with the difference that the women's dress comprises richly decorated ankle-length tunics, with a stand-up collar and Chinese-style crossover front. The cloth is indigo-dyed homespun, although another group, the Akha, tend to buy their blue-black material from Thai merchants.

The beauty and diversity of Hmong and other hill-group clothing is the result of the marriage system. Eligible bachelors are very well dressed by their mothers. But young girls are the most extravagantly dressed because they carry their dowry on their person, in the form of massive, finely-crafted pieces of solid silver. Until fairly recently, any spare cash was nearly always converted into silver, though now flashlights or portable radios rate highly.

Brass and copper are also worn, and vast quantities of trade beads are used by all (most imported from China, though some older necklaces may be European). The color of the beads identifies a particular group: women of the Lahu Nyi and Lahu Shi wear red and white beads, while the Lahu Sheh Leh wear many rows of pure white, like a cowl neck. Twisted wire necklaces are favored by the Phani-Akha women; silver torques are preferred by the Lahu and Hmong.

ABOVE: A Karenni tribeswoman of the Union of Myanmar wears gold rings to stretch her neck into a "pleasing" shape (this practice is also found among the Palaung, although illegal). The gold is her dowry.

BELOW: Food vendors on the Irrawaddy River are wearing the simple and muted colors typical of the customary dress of rural Burmese people.

THE UNION OF MYANMAR (BURMA)

Burmese are modest and sober in dress: the women wear neat white blouses; the men wear shirts and jackets. Both sexes wear sarongs. The Shan Chinese are the only ethnic group whose men wear trousers, but even these are more like divided skirts, worn with the same crisp jackets and the ubiquitous shoulder bag. Their conical straw hats are called *khamouts*. Women draw their hair up in neat buns, decorated with combs and flowers. Older men may wear topknots with small scarves tied around them, but most men now cut their hair.

The Palaung people are of Mon-Khmer rather than Shan stock. The Palaung women used to stretch their necks to about 12 inches (30 centimeters) by adding gold rings, although this is now an illegal practice. As with the "deforming" customs in Africa, such as lip-plates, it is suggested that the practice may have been brought in to repel kidnappers, but this may be an imposed explanation for an unacceptable aesthetic. Palaung women prefer to wear striped sarongs with embroidered green velvet jackets and a cotton-tasseled "halo" headdress .

Malaysia and the Philippines

RIGHT: **There are 7,000 islands in the Philippine archipelago. Native people arrived in Paleolithic times, and today there are a total of 110 regional and ethnic groups on these volcanic islands, principally on Luzon, home of these Ifuago people, whose dress is similar to that of the hill tribes of the Golden Triangle. The Ifuago, along with three percent of Filipino people, still adhere to animist religions. They are protected by the Bureau of Northern Communities, which is staffed by the native people in each area.**

BELOW MIDDLE: **Three groups of people live in Malaysia: half the population is Malay, or Bumipetra, roughly one-third are Chinese, and the remainder are Indians. Islam is the religion of the majority of people, but the Chinese are Buddhist or Taoist, and most of the Indians are Hindu. This couple is dressed in traditional Muslim wedding clothing, including beautifully made gold-threaded silk for the bride's sarong and jacket. The bridegroom wears a similar pleated sarong and jacket and a jeweled cap.**

Malaysia is multiethnic, with the second largest proportion of ethnic Chinese of any Southeast Asian state. Malays make up half the population, Chinese 35 percent, and Indians 10 percent. Ethnic tensions exist between the indigenous Malays and the Chinese, who run many businesses.

The traditional dress of Malaysia is the *baju kebaya*, the sarong and long-sleeved blouse for women, and a sarong and shirt for men. But the ethnic mix means that in Malaysia you will see *cheongsam* of Chinese origin, Indian saris, Muslim *tarbooshes* worn with suits, and also western-style dress. Malaysian embroidery is very fine, especially *tekat menekat*, gold and silver threadwork on velvet and silk, with motifs derived from Malaysia's flora and fauna. *Kelantan kain songket* is a prized woven fabric: deep blue,

green, maroon, or purple silk shot through with silver and gold thread.

Some of the festivals held in Malaysia reveal its Portuguese history. At the Festa de São Pedro in June, for example, Portuguese Eurasians wear colonial-style clothing.

In the politically separate area of north Borneo live the Bajan people of Sabah (part of Malaysia). They wear riding costumes of green trousers and Raj-style jackets with white or gold embroidery. Kadazan women wear beautiful sarong skirts and black tops, with silver metal decoration.

The Ibans of Sarawak are a remote tribe, a subgroup of the Dayak (mainly living on the island of Kalimantan, Indonesia), whose clothing echoes that of other hill peoples.

The Philippines became a Spanish colony in 1571 and were then ceded to the United States in 1898. Independence was granted in 1946. The largely Roman Catholic people now wear westernized clothing, but there are hill tribe people, protected by state decree, who wear handmade clothing similar to that of the people of the Golden Triangle.

Indonesia

The wearing of the traditional *baju*, or shirt and sarong, is less common among men than among women in Indonesia, and varies from island to island. In certain places dress customs remain unchanged. Every aspect of life, including costume, is subject to *adat*, the traditional law of social behavior, part of an ancient belief system that governs the life of every island people. Most islanders have worked out a subtle blend of ancient lore and faith with whatever has become the general orthodoxy.

Variations on the blouse (*kebaya*) and sarong have different names and are subtly varied in cut, but what they all have in com-

ABOVE: Indonesia is a collection of islands, each with a unique history. The inhabitants vary from virtually Stone Age peoples of animist beliefs to ancient adherents of Hindism, Buddhism, and Islam, all bearing traces of the colonizing powers who have plied trade through this region. Hand-crafted clothing predominates, a prime example of which is shown here by the men of the Toba-Batak people, who are wearing fine sarongs and stoles in ikat *and other weaves.*

mon is that they are rectangles of fabric, cut with curved seams to side front panels, so that no darts are used and so that the bodice fits snugly, flaring out over the hips. Gussets are placed under arms so that a well-fitted blouse does not ride up when the arms are lifted to head height. The col-

lar is cut as part of the bodice front, folded in half for a self-facing, and then folded back on itself in soft curving lapels. Some blouses are collarless with a flat V-neck opening. The opening at center front is designed to reveal the complicated pleatings of the sarong, sometimes called a *kain*. The *kebaya* may vary in length, from the hip to almost the knee. Interestingly, the use of an individual's physical dimensions, such as the width of hand or fingers, is traditionally used as a measurement, so that the *kebaya* fits in perfect proportion to each body.

The sarong, or *kain*, is more accurately a tube of cloth, 2⅔th yards (2 meters) in circumference and 1⅔ yards (1.5 meters) in

RIGHT: **This market scene at Martapure in Kalimantan, Borneo, shows women wearing the** kebaya **and** kain – **blouse and sarong – in a variety of patterns. The accumulation of fine textiles is seen as a sign of family status in Indonesia. In contrast to the male weaving tradition of West Africa, in this region it is only women who perform the craft. The family also needs financial security to afford the time-consuming work of high-quality weaving. In both** ikat **and** batik **weaving, Chinese and Indian influences can be traced.**

length. When the pleats are formed, it is customary for there to be an uneven number. The sarong is then secured at the waist with a stiff cotton corded tie, or *stagen*. Sometimes a long stole or *selendung* will be draped over the shoulder.

Two older versions of costume are found in different localities: a voluminous upper garment, the *baju kurung,* found in west Sumatra, Sulawesi, and Maluku, for instance, which probably has affinities with the Muslim traders' robes from India, and the *kain,* used as a wrap dress in central Java.

There are also tribal groups in Indonesia whose clothing is of the utmost simplicity. This chapter moves from west to east, illustratively, studying both the smaller tribal groups and the broad traditions of each island. In Sumatra, for example, there are remote people like the Mentawai Islanders who normally wear only a breechcloth, but on special occasions make elaborate headdresses of raffia, leaves, and flowers, and wear finely beaded armbands decorated with flowers. The Toba-Batak people (Batak being a designation that is given to six ethnic groups numbering roughly 3 million) live mainly in the mountain region of Lake Toba, where they build *tambak* houses with distinctive peaked roofs for the remains of their ancestors. They make beautiful handwoven cloths in all grades, from those sold to tourists to special *ulos* stoles,

worn at all ceremonies. The blouse-sarong (*kebaya-kain*) costume is worn with fringed aprons and stoles. Men wear distinctive red-banded flat hats with their sarongs.

SUMATRA

The Minangkabau of west Sumatra are an example of the most exotic and rare cultural heritage of this region. A distinctive subgroup of the Sumatran linguistic group, they are of uncertain origin, but their myths and rituals are unchanging. Motifs woven into the sumptuous gold- and silver-threaded ceremonial clothes of these people symbolize the hierarchical and ancient order of their society. Women's headdresses are folded to resemble the horns of the water

buffalo, after whom the people have named themselves: *minang;* meaning victorious; *kabau,* signifying the animal itself. The folds of the clan leader's shirt and ceremonial hat will embody the rules of how a man should behave. Nature provides an alternative source of symbol, in exemplary tales of animal wisdom and skill; so even decorative textile motifs carry social meaning.

The basic *ikat* technique, with numerous and subtle variations, is found all over Indonesia, showing traces of Chinese and Indian influences but with its own distinctive character. The same is true of the region's batik, an Indonesian form of wax-resist printing. In *ikat,* pattern is created by resist-dyeing the yarn before weaving; in batik, a pattern is applied after weaving by drawing designs on both sides of the cloth in hot wax, using a special copper pen or *tjanting.* Alternatively, a *tjap,* or metal block with a motif on one side, is used to create the design.

KALIMANTAN

This island is the Indonesian two-thirds of Borneo; linguistically and ethnically different from the other third to the northwest, which is part of Malaysia. It contains three basic ethnic groups, coastal Malays, who are Muslim; ethnic Chinese, who settled here in order to trade; and the original inhabitants, the Dayaks, who comprise 200 inland tribal groups. Until recently the Dayaks were headhunters and built *lamin* or long-houses where the men gathered together, but these ways are being discouraged by the government.

The Dayaks are famous for their beadwork and make beautiful rattan carriers that are painted, beaded, and hung with coins, ivory decorations, and ribbons. These are carried, front or back, over their simple body-wrap cloths. Dayak women wear rattan bands around their forehead, on which are balanced huge sunshades for fieldwork.

SULAWESI

Still in Indonesia, the name "Toraja" defines several ethnic groups living in the mountainous interior of Sulawesi, the island east of Borneo. One such is the Sa'dan Toraja, of whom about 340,000 remain. They are farmers and craftsmen and weave beautiful, somber *ikat* textiles specifically to sell to tourists. *Ikat*, batik, and madras cotton sarongs are worn by both sexes. One of the main attractions of the Toraja is their architecture: they build *tongkonans*, with sweeping boat-shaped roofs traditionally thatched with split bamboo, although corrugated iron is now used. These structures are entirely portable, not requiring a single nail, and are for ancestor worship – kinship links

BELOW: This man belongs to the Sa'dan Toraja people of Sulawesi. They specialize in beautiful, somber ikat weaves. Ancestor worship is central to the culture; his shield is ritual regalia and identifies his kin group.

ABOVE: The Dayak make up 200 inland groups in Kalimantan and Borneo. These female dancers are wearing handwoven tops and sarongs in a mixture of red stripe weave with ikat panels.

being the source of status and identity among the Toraja. When a new house is first occupied, the young women dance a special *ma'gellu*, wearing monochrome, sarong-wrap skirts with scoop-necked bodices, on top of which they wear ritual ornaments: beaded and fringed overskirts, beaded headbands, and beautiful batik stoles. They will also carry sacred *kris*, or silver-hilt daggers, in their belts, and a *kandaure*, a beaded collar, over their shoulder blades.

BALI

A long, thin string of islands runs down in a curve south of Borneo, Kalimantan, and Sulawesi, and these include Bali, Sumbawa, Flores, and Timor, whose inhabitants are of the Nusa Tenggara linguistic/ethnic group.

In Bali, the Dutch exercised influence by treaty in the 19th century, but when they attempted to impose more direct control of the island at the turn of the century, the royal Badung household protested with ritual suicide, a shock tactic that helped to secure the continuity of the people's cultural independence. Here a special version of Hinduism mixed with ancient animistic rite is practiced, in which the sacred dance dramas form a central manifestation of the island's culture.

In *The Split Gate to Heaven* by Rudolph Mrázek *et al.*, the authors comment: "The dance movements are as elaborately prescribed as the movements of society itself." One such dance enacts the fight between Rangda, queen of the underworld, and the Barong, a huge and splendid animal god, lord of the jungle. Rangda is a witch figure, danced by a man, who wears an enormous maned headdress and long apron-fronted costume, trailing with ribbon streamers. True to the Balinese view of life, the fight is never ended, the conflict never resolved.

The Balinese woman's *kebaya* is hip-length, made of a fine sprigged muslin or organdy with a closed front, and is worn with a cotton *ikat kain* decorated with embroidered medallions in silver, gold, or colored threads, and a matching scarf wrapped around the waist, cummerbund fashion. The alternative style is a two-piece outfit: a sarong with matching tight bodice-wrap. A voile or chiffon stole is tied firmly over the bust and then draped down one side, until the loose end is tucked up at the center-back waist, under the edge of the bodice. Unmarried women wear their hair in a braid, to one side, and after marriage loop it up in an Indonesian chignon with flowers.

BELOW: A Muslim bridegroom of south Sulawesi wears a shimmering gold brocade sarong wrap with an orange and white brocade jacket and gold and red sash with matching headband.

A Nusa Tenggaran craftswoman believes that her sacred double-*ikat* textile *grinsing*, which plays a significant role in ceremonials, has great power. Both warp and weft threads are dyed with natural stuffs that can be gathered only during certain phases of the moon's cycle – this explains why it may take almost nine years to dye and weave one piece. *Grinsing* is considered a national treasure by the Indonesian government and may not be exported out of the country.

Numerous craftsmen make light, gauzy textiles with metallic threads, other than batik and *ikat* cloths. Judi Achjadi, in her book *Indonesian Women's Costume*, has noted four techniques for these: supplementary warp (*pahikungu* of Sumba, *so'e* of Timor); supplementary weft (*songhet/bertabur* of Sumatra, *paha* of Timor); floating bobbin (*pa'u* of Timor, *songhet* of Sumatra and Bali); and *pilih*, in which groups of threads are taken over or under the weft (*soutis* of Timor, and also found in Kalimantan). Traditionally, the finest cloths have been woven with 24-carat gold thread, now virtually priceless, and lately replaced by synthetics. Occasionally, an old *kain songhet* will deteriorate, and the valuable thread is unpicked and reused. The weaving of *kain*

BELOW : *A priest participates in the Pasola rite on the island of Sumba, the Sandalwood Island. His assistant's richly dyed* ikat *sarong and stole are typical of the islanders' fine textile work.*

ABOVE: Women take part in a funeral ceremony on the island of Bali, where a unique form of Hinduism prevails. The women are dressed in fine batik sarongs and fine sprigged muslin or organdy kebayas.

songhet is thriving, especially on Sumatra.

Balinese men take a casual view of clothing; in a temple procession, they will wear T-shirts and sneakers, with a sarong on top. Overcrowding and tourism erodes a lifestyle more decisively than colonial conquest.

FLORES, SAVU, SUMBA, AND TIMOR

The Flores warp *ikat* weaves are particularly subtle and rich, even though nowadays hand-spun cotton is rare and machine-spun imported yarn is taking over. Flores women wear two body wraps, as described for Bali, and wear their hair in a high bun, with western plastic combs stuck in alongside beaded and feathered straight pins. Ritual dances are now staged for tourists. For these, the men wear sarong wraps, together with beaded headbands, strands of bead necklaces, and stylish head-ties made of palm arranged in flat knots on the forehead.

Savu, an island kingdom, is also the center for fine *ikat* weaving and dance displays that mark the times of planting and harvest, or recall the islanders' warlike past. Cockfighting used to be a favorite sport; perhaps this is reflected in the pleated-paper fan cockades worn several at a time by male dancers and the feathers carried by female dancers. The men wear their sarongs in an

interesting fashion: skirt lengths are wrapped so that the warp – that is, the vertical direction of the design, is worn horizontally, and then they wear long (frame width) sashes crossed over the upper body, front and back, and tied over the right hip.

Sumba, also known as Sandalwood Island, is south of Flores and renowned for the finest ceremonial *ikat* textiles. To the west of the island they hold the Pasola rite, when many warriors charge one another on horseback, using javelins and wearing *ikat* hipcloths, shirts, and red-bordered turbans with a white peak inside. The Sumba men's two-paneled textiles are also remarkable, not least because the dyed fabric takes two years to complete. Some designs are called "power-shapes," and their symbolism is interpreted by clan elders.

On Timor, among the Atoni people, designs and mode of attire are a direct historic link to the 10 princedoms that once held sway. In certain areas, beautiful textiles are hung in "barriers" between the bride and groom; the male has to "buy" his way through these hangings to claim his bride. However, as is common in many groups in Southeast Asia, the best cloths of all are made to be buried with the dead.

BELOW : *A Maumerian family, all wearing the richly colored* ikat *sarong wraps that are in abundance on the island of Flores. Some of the finest warp* ikat *weave cloths are made here.*

JAVA

In Central Java, the heart of the batik industry, princes used at one time to create *batik* designs, for it was a noble calling. The hand-drawn form of batik, called *tulis*, is always done by women, but the blockwork of *tjap* is traditionally waxed by men. When the cloth is immersed in a cold dye bath only the unwaxed areas take the color. The wax is then removed by boiling. The non-waxed areas of the motifs come out in colors with white definition lines separating them from the background colors. There are numerous variations, such as reversing, in which motifs are covered in wax so that designs come out in white on a colored base.

The complexity and symbolism that pertains to textile manufacture throughout Indonesia are vividly illustrated by the Tuban people of Java (the island east of Sumatra). They have their own batik, which involves drawing motifs on a checkered-weave cloth called *lurik*, producing a delicate, shimmering effect.

Every type of cloth has a specific use, be it for everyday wear or for rituals or ceremonials. Although men tend to wear western dress, all social groups within the community can be distinguished by the textiles their women wear. These denote class, age group, village, and even region. Villages join together in a cooperative called a *mancapat*, in which every community has its own functions, from spinning to weaving and dyeing. This last always takes place in a central village because the ancient indigo vats are regarded as sacred – only the wife of the village Muslim priest or *modin* is appointed to this task, and the secrets of her craft are handed down from mother to daughter.

The eastern half of a village, where the headman's house is located is seen as male; the western half, where rituals such as textile dyeing are completed, is female. So the Tuban have mingled very ancient codes of practice with earlier Hindu hierarchical patterns and with their Islamic faith, adopted here in the 15th century.

Colors have great meaning for Javanese people: white is the non-color of the East, where the sun rises and life begins; red denotes the South, where the sun reaches its zenith; it is also the color of adolescence and youth. Yellow represents maturity and the West; and bluish-black stands for the day's end in the North, and death. Textiles made for the shoulder cloths reflect these stages: white for children, red and white patterns for young girls; *pipitan* (meaning yellowish) for "close together" (referring to the tight patterning) cloths for older women, with various color combinations of red and blue on a yellowish ground; and blues and brown for widows. This last cloth is called *irengan*, meaning both "black" and "lying fallow." Certain textiles are reserved for ceremonial use (normally light motifs on a dark background) and some for ritual wear, such as the shoulder cloths worn by mothers to protect their newborn babies, or a sick child.

THE SPICE ISLANDS

The people of the Moluccas, or the Spice Islands, form a separate, ethno-linguistic group. The Ambonese, divided equally between the Christian and Muslim faiths, belong to the *pasisir* area. This refers to a route winding around the coasts of the islands in the Banda Sea, where through trade a multitude of races have mixed over centuries and set up their bustling, cramped towns. The Portuguese were the first Europeans to trace spices back to their origins, landing here in 1512; they were followed by the Dutch in 1605. The small island of Ambon became the center for clove cultivation.

On Banda island you can see ceremonial dances where men wear Dutch helmets, carry blunderbusses, and wear red breeches and black, braided jackets. Similar traces of colonialism are found on Bouton, southeast of Sulawesi, where ruffled shirts and tailored jackets are worn for ceremonies, along with Chinese-style headdresses.

In south Halmahera, a small Spice Island, the Giman people practice the ancient custom of teeth-filing, a pre-Islamic practice, though subtle adaptation of a Koranic legend lends it orthodoxy. On another Spice Island, Babar, men wear unusual, very long, old cloths for a traditional dance called the *seka*. These *basta* cloths are of Indian origin and have ceremonial and economic value. With yellow background and red motifs, they are worn crossed over the chest and folded in a complex way to make a long apron at the front. A straw headband is also worn.

A woman of Chiang Mai in Thailand wearing a locally printed sarong.

A Karen tribeswoman from Thailand in a homespun embroidered tunic top.

A floral-patterned sarong worn by a Burmese woman.

Southeast Asia Map

No other region in the world offers such a complex and rare display of textile manufacture as Southeast Asia. Thousands of islands maintain separate cultures and identities and reveal their varied histories in their cloth. There are Indian, Chinese, Spanish, Portuguese, and indigenous influences on the *ikat*, batik, silk, cotton, and metal-threaded textiles, which are still made by hand in this region. Qualities range from the purely commercial to the wholly ceremonial. The most sacred craftwork is saved for the burial cloth, the finest grade of which is never worn or even displayed between the loom and the funeral.

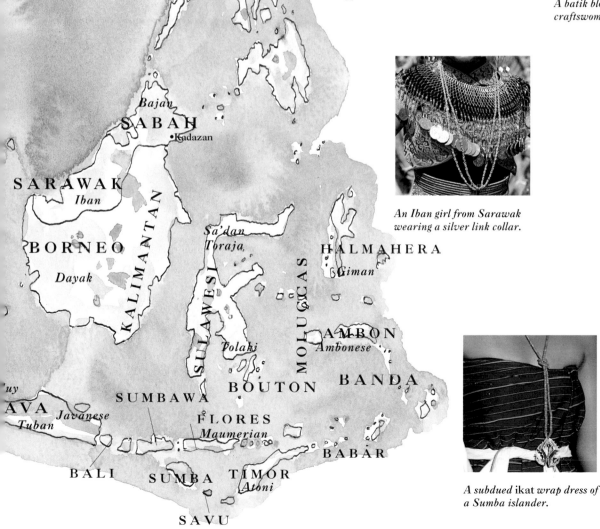

SOUTH CHINA SEA

Ifuago
Filipino
LUZON

PHILIPPINES

Bajau
SABAH
•*Kadazan*

SARAWAK
Iban

BORNEO

Dayak

KALIMANTAN

Sa'dan Toraja

SULAWESI

HALMAHERA
Giman

Tolaki

MOLUCCAS

AMBON
Ambonese

BANDA

SUMBAWA

BOUTON

AVA *Javanese*
Tuban

FLORES
Maumerian

BABAR

BALI
SUMBA TIMOR
Atoni

SAVU

ha

uy

A ribbon-trimmed bodice and cloak of a tribeswoman from the Philippines.

A batik blouse worn by a craftswoman in Java.

An Iban girl from Sarawak wearing a silver link collar.

An elaborate ikat-weave sarong worn by a Savu woman islander.

Key

Note: peoples are shown in italics eg: ***Iban***

Approximate area of peoples detailed

1,000–3,000m (3,000–9,000ft)

200–1,000m (600–3,000ft)

0–200m (0–600ft)

Sea, lakes and rivers

A subdued ikat wrap dress of a Sumba islander.

SARONG CLOTHS

TOP ROW, LEFT TO RIGHT:

Embroidered panel over a pleated wrap skirt, worn by a Hmong hill tribe woman, North Thailand.

Balinese women in batik kain and kebayas, blouse and sarong ensembles.

Thai woman in a striped weave sarong.

Burmese woman in a plain cotton sarong.

Iban dancer of Borneo in ikat-dyed wrap skirt and solid silver belt.

MIDDLE ROW, LEFT TO RIGHT:

Iban dancer, Sarawak, wearing batik skirt wrap and silver belt.

Girl at a dance school in Cambodia, wearing a divided skirt wrap.

Kris dancers in the Barong dance, Bali, wearing plain white sarong cloth wrapped to form pleated trousers.

Dancing girl's gold-weave sarong, for the Barong dance, Bali.

Batik sarongs worn by women of Bali.

BOTTOM ROW, LEFT TO RIGHT:

Village boys in ikat and batik and plain sarongs at a temple ceremony, Ubud, Bali.

Toba-Batak dancers in fine stripe-weave wrapping cloths, Sumatra.

Complex ikat-weave woman's textile skirt wrap typical of western Sumatra.

Dayak girls in ceremonial silver-linked garments over sarongs, in Sarawak.

Female dancer in vivid block-print skirt wrap, at the Badoyo festival, Pranlanon, Indonesia.

137

INDIA

Historical and cultural links bind India with the countries that surround it: Pakistan and Bangladesh (both formerly part of India), Afghanistan, Nepal, Bhutan, and Ladakh (part of Kashmir), also called Indian Tibet. This is why they are included here.

The population in India itself in the early 1990s reached a total of 844 million, 83 percent of which are Hindu. The remainder of the population is made up of 75 million Muslims, 18 million Christians, 14 million Sikhs, and 5 million Buddhists. Altogether, India is a homeland of people speaking 15 major languages. To describe the dress and custom of so diverse a nation is a vast enterprise, and must of necessity be illustrative, rather than definitive.

Since environment is a major factor in connection with all clothing, the physical features of India need to be examined. Throughout the world, it is the places that are most inaccessible to visitors where religion, custom, and dress are to be found unchanged for centuries and in their greatest variety. The northern borders of India are defined by the Himalaya Mountains, and here in the northeast and northwest corners of India and Pakistan the area is filled with rich examples of traditional styles. Old ways also survive in the mountain areas of Kashmir, Nepal, and Bhutan. In fact, in the Kingdom of Bhutan, which is still very religious, national dress is obligatory.

The Hindus of India are a mixture of two races, the indigenous Dravidians and the Aryans, who migrated eastward and settled in the Indus Valley around 2000 BC During the centuries, Hindu society developed a complex caste system, with four main groups: the Brahmins (priests and

ABOVE: **Young tribal girls from Baroda, Gujarat, wearing brightly colored headwraps.**

OPPOSITE: **Women in a northern desert town wearing the national dress, the draped sari. With many regional variations, it is worn everywhere.**

theologians), the Kshatriyas (rulers and warriors), the Vaisyas (traders and farmers), and the Sudras (craftsmen and workers). With the rise to power of the Brahmins in southern India, beginning in the late 15th century, the dress for Hindu women, the sari, evolved its system of folds and drapes, one for each of the caste subclasses. Men wear the *dhoti*, a loincloth ample enough to look like draped trousers. Although the caste system is officially abolished, it is still adhered to, particularly by country people.

The people of the southern provinces are more Dravidian by descent than those in the north, and they practice a purer Hinduism. Southern Brahmin women are very strict about wearing the correct dress.

There are many other regional variations in sari style. For example, in the prosperous and industrial province of Maharashtra in

central India, saris are double the length of those in the north. Farther south, in Andhra Pradesh, Karnataka, and Tamil Nadu, there are numerous variations of draping the sari.

The most vividly colored dress occurs in the northern provinces of mountainous Jammu and Kashmir, Himalchal Pradesh, the fertile Punjab, and arid Rajasthan. It is also found in poorer Uttar Pradesh, the Hindi-speaking heartland on the Ganges plain, cotton-growing Gujarat, and the northeastern provinces. The northwest area has always been open to western influences, and this is seen in their richness of dress.

The use of tailoring to shape garments with cut and sewn seams was introduced to India by the Muslims. Until then, bulky woven strip cloth was worn draped, as can be seen in the carvings on the walls of ancient temples: sari for women, *dhoti* for men. It is in the north that tailored clothing predominates. Rajput women prefer the pleated or gathered skirt, the *ghagra*, and the *choli*, a tight bodice; while in the Punjab the *salwar-kameez* (baggy trousers and tunic top) is preferred.

In Bangladesh, dress is simple. *Lungis*, skirt wraps, are worn by the men, saris by the women. However, the dwindling hill tribes provide a colorful contrast to their lowland neighbors. Similarly in Pakistan, the hill peoples' dress is elaborate. There, the Kalash women of Kohistan braid their hair and wear long silver chains and trade beads and, for ceremonies, magnificent headdresses.

Where orthodox religion plays a greater role, dress codes are strict. In Muslim Afghanistan, women wear a dark *burqa* (also called a *chadri*). Underneath, they wear luxurious clothing and decorative jewelry.

Northern States of India

To the northeast of India are situated the provinces of Assam, Manipur, Nagaland, and Meghalaya. Here the style of dress resembles the clothing of the countries that border on this region, namely Bangladesh, to the west, and the Union of Myanmar (formerly Burma), to the east. The traditional female outfit is the *mekhala*, a straight-cut sarong skirt worn to ankle length, lavishly embroidered on the bottom half. It is worn with the *chadar*, a similarly embroidered stole wrapped around the upper torso. Married women add a *riha*, or scarf, with a fringe of tassels, wrapped around the midriff. In Nagaland, an alternative style is a sarong-type, one-piece garment

wrapped over a short-sleeved fitted blouse. Naga dress is renowned for the quality of its embroidery. At its most festive and formal, Naga female costume can consist of as many as a dozen pieces.

In the remote Brahmaputra valley of Arunchal Pradesh, to the north of Nagaland, live the Tsanglas. Here the dress is plain and simple, reflecting the lifestyle of the people. Both sexes wear skirt sarongs, western T-shirts, and plain headwraps. The Adi also occupy this region. They practice an animist faith and go hunting for wild boar with poison-tipped arrows, and eat squirrel, monkey, beans, and fruit. For everyday wear, men wear simple western-style khaki shorts

ABOVE CENTER: **Well-dressed mourners at a Rajasthani Muslim funeral. Unlike western people, they do not wear somber clothing, and all have used colorful braiding around their headcloths and in their other dress. This consists of colored or white shirts and skirt-like sarongs that are usually worn for working in the fields. Funerals are very much a part of everyday life in India and are treated as a public event, with many people from the deceased's village attending the ceremony.**

LEFT: **In Rajasthan, women's dress is particularly brilliant, and gold-embroidered saris, ghagras (pleated skirts), and cholis (bodices) are commonplace. On special occasions, Rajasthani women parade with lavish displays of jewelry, indicating their status, prosperity, and class. The ghagra can be made of more than 20 yds. (18m) of fabric, with as many as 64 godets to give it a wonderful swinging fullness.**

with homespun jerkins, while for special ritual occasions, elders wear red robes and a huge bowl-shaped headdress that is completely covered in bear fur.

Generally speaking, the bleaker the landscape the more colorful the dress. For example, Bihar, to the west of Bangladesh, is particularly bare and arid, and the women dye the traditional *kurti* (sleeveless bodice) or *choli* in bold primary colors The local style of draping the sari displays half the border pattern across the breast and half over the hip. The Santal women, who occupy the borders of Bengal and Bihar, are distinguished by wearing white saris with red borders, worn to just below the knee, and long silver necklaces. Wandering musicians belonging to the Baul sect also live in the Bengal region. They wear unusual robes of multicolored patches, or white cloaks, and pull their uncovered hair up to be tied into a sleek topknot.

Uttar Pradesh is where the Benares sari – the dream wedding dress of all Indian women – is woven. The capital, Lucknow, is also famous for its *chicon*, a fine white embroidered sari cloth, and for its *ghararas*, or wedding outfits, which were formerly 30 or 40 yards (27–36 meters) long, worn with a *dupatta* or scarf so heavy that it might take four persons to fold it. Uttar Pradesh women tend to drape the sari, leaving the left arm free. The spare fabric is then brought up the back and over the head, leaving the border or *palloo* gracefully draped across the front of the body.

In the northeast of India, the *ghagra* skirt is widely worn. This reaches to mid-shin or near ankle and is usually worn below the navel and pulled in by a drawstring. The

ghagra may contain as many as 20–30 yards (18–27 meters) of cloth, which is either tightly pleated, gathered, or cut in flaring panels. In terms of design, regional varieties abound. Gujarat and Rajasthan versions are notable for their tie-dye effects, while Kathiawar and Sind areas incorporate mirror work with some embroidery or appliqué. Saurashtra or chain-stitched embroidery is particularly popular. In its original form the *choli*, or bodice, served as a bust support. It was often left open at the back, with two simple ties at the neck and across the shoulder blades to hold it in place.

Today, commercial blouses frequently replace the traditional *choli*, although some-

ABOVE: Traditional Hindu weddings are extremely elaborate social occasions. A bride's sari is traditionally red with gold decoration, the most coveted being made of Benares silk. Brides will normally wear a massive display of gold jewelry, a mixture of family heirlooms and dowry gifts. Men wear long fitted jackets and trousers, as seen here, but nowadays Western cut suits or jackets are also appropriate attire.

times a more closed variety, with front or back opening, is worn over a bra. However, this type still reveals the midriff.

The alternative dress in the northeast is the *salwar*, or trousers, with the *kameez*, or tunic. *Salwar* are cut very long with a band at the ankle, so that the fullness falls in folds and conceals the shape of the leg. Traditionally, the *kameez* is slightly flared at the hip, with a side slit, but modern tastes often call for a more figure-fitting look. A long scarf, or *orhna*, that is just over 2 yards (1.8 meters) long and 1½ yards (1.3 meters) wide in voile, fine silk, or other light material is worn over the tunic. As a mark of respect – for example, when a married woman meets her husband's relatives – the *orhna* can be worn as a head or face veil.

In Rajasthan, the warrior-prince caste of the Rajputs has left an indelible mark on Indian society. Their glorious traditions have imbued the people with a love of color and luxury that is fully expressed in their crafts and costumes.

Rajasthani women like their saris colorful in pattern and intricately woven or embroidered. The *ohrna* or scarf is so richly embellished that it has long been a subject for Rajput love songs.

It is interesting to note that in Rajasthan, unlike other regions of India, a person's career possibilities are not so wholly determined by the caste system. The Muslim minority in Rajasthan is valued for its industry and commercial talents. Muslims practice many crafts related to clothing, dyeing, textile printing, and jewelry making. Although largely agriculturalists and pastoralists, the Rajasthanis also produce 40 percent of India's wool.

foreign invaders through the Khyber and other western-range passes. This explains the influences in dress from neighboring Iran (Persia): pointed shoes, colorful turbans, richly woven brocade, and *ikat*-dyed coats and tight trousers. Muslim and Hindu dress alike here, and no veiling is seen. The *salwar-kameez* are worn by both sexes.

A distinctive feature of Kashmiri dress is the man's hat: a circular-shaped piece of cloth or lambs' wool. Kashmiri men also wear a loose, sleeved robe, or *pheran*, which they belt at the waist to form a pouch. A version known as a *chola* is worn by the Gaddi people of Himchal Pradesh and is loose enough to allow mountain shepherds to carry lambs in the pouch. The Kashmiri woman's robe can be covered by a sleeveless vest of embroidered velvet, and in cold weather a warm over-scarf is worn, sometimes with the ends tucked into the woman's skullcap, or *kasaba*. Some jewelry is worn on top of the cap and is combined with two plaits or braids of hair to form the distinctive style of the area.

Kashmiri fleecy shawls, or *pashmina*, are world famous. They are made of a fine-grade wool from a species of hill goat, which is sometimes mixed with silk fibers. The fineness of the *kashida* work is outstanding. *Kashida* is derived from the Persian word "to draw" and denotes all the basic stitches of Indian embroidery in silk thread: running, satin, stem, chain, and herringbone. The best-known motif is that of the *chenar* tree, a trailing ivy design, which can be

found across the region. Although saris are not worn so much in this region, Kashmir silk saris are exported to all of India.

South of Rajasthan, in Gujarat, both the *ghagra* and the sari are worn by women of the lower castes. The sari is usually worn over a petticoat, which, like the *ghagra*, is embellished with embroidery. Gujarati saris are usually about 5 yards (4.5 meters) long, and more than half of the fabric is gathered together into the pleats of the skirt. The right arm and hand are covered by the draped section, leaving the left hand exposed. A deep, red-brown shade is favored for daily wear, but, as elsewhere in India, a fiery red with lavish silver or gold embroidery is the choice of the bride.

North of Rajasthan lies the region of the Punjab, home of the Sikhs, and the exquisite high valleys of Jammu and Kashmir. Punjabi women wear the *salwar-kameez* and the *dupatta* or *ohrna* draped across the upper front. The *kameez*, or tunic, is often quite close-fitting. Both men and women wear the *salwar* trousers, although the women's versions are made of finer material. Men wear the loose muslin tunic, or *kurta*, over the *dhoti*, with a wrapper, or *chadar*, and/or a western-style jacket.

Farther north in Kashmir, a great variety of costume styles reveals past influences: Hindu, Buddhist, and Muslim. One well-known scholar called this region the "zone of attraction," because it has always enticed

ABOVE LEFT: **A Rajput woman displays the love of bright color and ornate decoration that is typical of this "land of princes." The sari used to be worn only by certain castes, but the rules are less strict today. Her gold bracelets denote her married status.**

ABOVE RIGHT: **Kashmir shawls have always been prized possessions, and are still used even when western clothes are worn. Here, one is worn by a nomad from Sekiwar, Kashmir.**

LEFT: **In the northern states, women and girls of both Hindu and Muslim faith may now wear the salwar-kameez, whereas in the southern states only Muslim women wear the style. However, schoolgirls everywhere find it a useful, comfortable uniform, with Hindu females reverting to the traditional sari as they get older.**

Pakistan and Afghanistan

RIGHT: An Afghani woman seen in Quetta wears the long-sleeved floral print dress found among Muslim women of north India. In another group, the Hunza, women prefer red and orange colors, with pillbox hats and a long, soft white shawl over the top. For Pathan women, floral prints are also popular, and their shawls, or chadors, are embroidered in motifs that identify their tribe. The boy here wears typical northern male dress, with a long shirt, baggy pants, and embroidered round cap. In traditional villages, children's clothing is often just a scaled-down version of adult wear.

LEFT: This elegant Gilgitis man wears an ornate gold-embroidered waistcoat over a typical loose white shirt and baggy trousers. Sometimes, a turban or skullcap will be added to this ensemble. As is common to many northeastern regions, Persian influence is seen in the motifs and coloring of the silks used in embroidery. This is because of the centuries of trading activity between East and West through the mountain passes. Care is always given to a meticulous, clean appearance as a tenet of the Muslim faith.

Pakistan contains a part of the Punjab, which has been described earlier in this section. In general, costume is similar to that of northwest India, while encompassing a rich variety of both regional and tribal differences. Standard male dress comprises a vest over a white tunic and trousers, with a turban or skullcap.

Near Pakistan's northeastern borders, a Tibetan influence is seen in the dress. Hunza men, living in the shadow of the Karakoram Mountains, wear belted shirts, khaki wool trousers, and flat rolled caps, as do the Gilgitis, with the addition of a long, open robe over the top.

The Northwest Frontier Province is home of the Pathans, a subgroup of the Afghani people, who are historically linked to Iran in their culture and customs. For example, turbans were banned when Iran became more westernized, but persisted in Afghanistan in a more informal way: a Pathan man will wear his with one end loose, which he uses as a washcloth. On more formal occasions, a *kola*, or little round embroidered hat, may be worn, over which a turban can be more carefully wound. The folding in the front is always of importance, as it sets off the male features. More importantly, the forehead is always exposed for prayer practices.

Women wear bright floral-print dresses with embroidered pillbox hats and white headshawls. Baggy floral trousers are worn underneath. Sleeve cuffs are always richly embroidered, and a thick wool robe is worn over all. A Pathan woman's *chador*, or shawl, embroidery identifies her tribe.

Perhaps the most colorful of the hill peoples are the Kalash of Kohistan, near Nuristan in eastern Hindu Kush, who still follow an ancient pre-Muslim faith. Men wear the usual mountain clothing, while women wear floor-length black robes, sashes, and ornate jewelry. For special occasions, the men will wear precious brocade robes and trim their hats with feathers, sprigs of juniper, or other mountain herbs believed to bring good fortune.

In Sind, Central Pakistan, the women wear strong colors: red, yellow, and black, and also favor a hand-blocked *ajrak*, or wrapping shawl, over a tunic dress and narrow trousers. The Sind region is famous for its mirror work and embroidery, and the clothes reveal a strong Persian influence in shape and decoration. Sindhi language is heavily influenced by Arabic.

To the west in Pakistan, the influences appear to be more Iranian and Afghani. Women of Baluchistan wear black tunic dresses over enormously wide trousers, so long in the leg that they wrinkle to a double thickness when worn. The tunics are decorated with floral motifs and embellished at the center front yoke with geometric designs in cross-stitch.

Baluchi women's dress shows how practical layers of heavy (often homespun) cotton can be in a cold climate. Tunics are tightly gathered to the yoke for thickness and left open at the sides so that a woman feels comfortable when pregnant. When breastfeeding she can also put her child under her tunic easily. Thick wool shawls over the top of the ensemble add warmth, and a second, lighter headwrap is added. Baluchi women like a rich, reddish-purple tunic, and the embroidery patterns they use vary from tribe to tribe. Elaborate silver coin jewelry completes the outfit.

AFGHANISTAN

The Afghani overdress, the *burqa*, which is more all-encompassing than the Iranian *chador*, is worn among the more affluent women. The *burqa* is the attire of the urban Muslim women of the merchant class, while

ABOVE: In Pakistan and Afghanistan strict female adherents of Islam will wear the total veil. The burqa *is an all-encompassing fine wool cover. Women find it possesses a subtle allure and fashionable quality: posture, walk, cut of fabric are telling. Beneath, bright, luxury fabrics are worn, unseen by male strangers.*

the *chador* is preferred by village and nomadic people. Herati men still claim that they can tell a lot about a woman from her style of shoes, the cut and quality of her trousers glimpsed below the *burqa* hem, her posture, and also her walk. A *burqa* is carefully designed and can hang beautifully if it is made of a fine fabric. It is considered a fashion object by Afghani women, rather than being an imposition to wear.

Underneath the *burqa*, wealthy Afghani women wear shimmering brocades or glittering metallic fabrics made up into loosely waisted dresses over silky white trousers with deep borders or lace trim at the ankle. Even indoors, women wear a long chiffon scarf, called a *qadifeh*, edged with lace. Gold earrings, bangles, necklaces, lockets, and rings are highly prized. *Hammam* wrappers (for use in the communal hot baths) of red, gold, or purple *ikat* woven silk are a precious item in such a woman's wardrobe.

Afghani men wear the *chapan*, a fold-over coat or robe, also of Asian origin. If it is made from good-quality *ikat* silk, this will be a treasured possession. Silk turbans and fur-skin hats are also stylish accessories. Underclothes, shirt, and trousers are usually just white.

Even less affluent rural tribesmen still wear the most subtle *ikat* robes. Lined with cotton or wool fabric, they are beautifully made and are also practical and warm. The traditional *ikat* textiles influence the designs of commercially produced striped cloth for the *chapans*.

Many Afghan women's tunics (such as those worn by the Baluchis) show how the traditional styles are strong enough to overcome, but also incorporate, outside influences into their dress. For instance, zippers are torn apart and rolled into "Catherine wheel" shapes to be appliquéd onto the bodice panels. Snaps are then added in rows to make a purely decorative pattern.

RIGHT: A proud villager of Rawalpindi in Pakistan wears a magnificent robe showing many of the features of northwest regional work: lavish mirrorwork, embroidery, and bead appliqué. In medieval times, silks, spices, and crafts flowed through the Sind region, to be exported as far away as Africa. Vestiges of this mercantile splendor remain in the culture, in spite of later economic decline. Sindhi people love color, song, and dance, and seductive costumes.

LEFT: The Kalash women of Kohistan wear a long black cotton robe, or cheo, *pulled up to form a pouch at the waist and belted with a red homespun sash. Long silver chains swing from their hips. Their headdress, or* kupasi, *is a heavy rectangle of stiff cloth in a panel covering the neck that is stitched with cowrie shells, beads, pompoms, and bells. Hair is braided in five* chui. *Collars of red and white trade beads and silver disk pendants complete their festive dress.*

Bangladesh

This is a very poor, predominantly rural country, and the clothing materials and styles worn reflect this simplicity. Men wear the long, draped *lungi*, or skirt, topped by a shirt or vest, while women wear the sari. Boys wear nothing but *lungis*, and the majority go barefoot.

Plain-dyed saris with no more than a basic border pattern or a simple block-pattern design predominate. It is quite common for women to wear little or nothing underneath their saris, yet their modesty is maintained by the graceful way they drape their cotton saris over their heads.

However, up in the hills a completely different style of dress is adopted by the Mru, Marma, Tippera, and Chakma tribes. Chakma women wear homespun indigo-dyed wrap skirts and black blouses and put on short cloaks tied over one shoulder for going to market. The women do the weaving, incorporating exquisite rhomboid patterns on their skirts, or *wan klai*. For normal wear, the skirts are worn wrong-side out and the rich pattern is revealed only for festivals. To secure the skirt wrap, Chakma women wear elaborate chains and belts, primarily in red, but green, white, yellow, and black patterns are also seen. Masses of silver jewelry, including upper-arm bangles, complete the style. Men wear loincloths and turbans and handwoven short, sleeveless tunics.

A lesser tribe, the Marma, also wear homespun indigo-dyed cloths, but they are incorporated in full-length sarong skirts. Men wear headwraps, which are decorated with flowers, or topknots decorated with headcombs resembling bird crests. Young men blacken their teeth for purely aesthetic effect. It is worth noting that not every custom of an ethnic group has any significance beyond that of fancy or fun.

BELOW: In poorer, rural areas, saris may be worn without the choli *bodice underneath or with a market-bought cheap, bra. However, the drapes of the garment provide a practical modesty.*

RIGHT: A woman of Poratal village near Jessore carries water from a well. Her sari is worn local style, with the drape thrown from front to back.

BELOW: A fisherman from Beel Dakatia in Bangladesh unloads his catch. His hat, which is more reminiscent of a Thai worker's, serves as a reminder that function defines style as much as ethnicity does. As with a woman's sari, the man's lungi *can be tucked up out of the way for practicality.*

Nepal, Kashmir, and Bhutan

The Karakoram-Himalaya mountain chain includes some of the highest peaks in the world, and its valleys support small peasant communities, sheep and goat herders, and barley growers. Buddhism flourishes in the area, and the temples and monasteries now provide a new source of commerce – tourism. Thirty-five different ethnic groups, which are characterized by dialect, area, dress, and religion, live together in the kingdom.

The population of Nepal is predominantly Hindu, although many of Katmandu's Newers, or indigenous people, will profess to follow both faiths. For example, it is possible to be Hindu by birth but Buddhist by calling, or merely to keep up Hindu prac-

tices where they concern village deities. Nepal is the center of the Tantric cults. "Tantra" is a Sanskrit word for the basic warp thread of a loom, and Tantrism emphasizes the Buddhist concepts. Nepal is the home of the living goddess, or Kumari, who, during the Indra Jata festival, is paraded through the streets in gold cloth, wearing flower garlands and a jeweled headdress.

Red and gold saris are worn for women's festivals, as red is Nepal's national color. For the men, the distinctive features of dress are the knitted mittens, wool shawls, and *topis*, flat woven wool hats with round roll brims. The hat is often called a *dacca* because the fabric originally came from the capital of Bangladesh.

In the southern Nepalese valleys, the sari is common among the more sedentary people, as is the *dhoti*. Block-printed fabrics are made in Katmandu at the village of Pashupatinath near the ghats (steps to river), where women come to purify themselves after menstruation and then change their saris. Thicker shawls are made of Nepalese red, black, and orange checkered cotton cloth, faced on both sides with a layer of muslin, which gives a soft pastel effect to the print and adds warmth. The Kashmir goat-wool shawls, called *pashmina*, are also worn here. Sheep and yak wool are woven locally for winter wear and then made up into long tunic tops, loose trousers, jerkins, and wide-waist sashes worn by the Murmi and Tamangs of the eastern and central hills. "Tamang" means "horse traders," although today they more commonly work as small farmers. A *khukri* knife is thrust inside the wide sashes. Some Tamang women wear short saris of homemade cotton cloth with a blouse underneath and few ornaments. Others prefer typical Nepalese flowery dresses with long sleeves and a wide sash over the waist and hips.

High-caste Brahmans and Chatris are also farmers, but hold government administrative and educational posts as well. Women

elements in dress. For example, Rai women wear mixtures of colorful cloths, often red, with wide sashes, body wraps, and head covers. They also wear bangles and gold nose rings. Nomadic Tibetan families also live in the mountains of Nepal. The women wear fur-lined sheepskin coats of Mongol origin in a crossover wrap shape over long dusky-pink, tunic dresses. They wear long earrings of blue and white beads with coral stones for luck. Nomadic women still produce homespun cloth, dyed in blue and red stripes. They also make their own fur-lined

dahlias. One figure, Indiani, wears an orange mask covered with eyes (no one can hide from the goddess); Maheswari wears a white mask (representing the female aspect of Shiva) and Brahma yani wears a yellow mask, representing the human aspect of Brahma the creator.

KASHMIR – LADAKH (INDIAN TIBET)

The eastern region of Kashmir, Ladakh, comprises a cold, mountainous, desert region, with a unique and complex culture. Typical Tibetan clothing is seen here: even little boys wear the long, black wool tunics, wide-

wear typical Nepalese long cotton wraparound skirts or full crossover robes with sleeved blouses underneath and sleeveless jackets on top. Headwraps and characteristic nose rings complete the attire. Men wear standard Nepalese baggy trousers, wraparound tunic tops with undershirts, and sometimes a jacket and/or wool shawl.

The Sherpas also live in the central and eastern parts of Nepal. Women wear long black tunics under striped woolen skirts, held in place by narrow, woven belts. Silver and coral are favored materials for necklaces, as both are supposed to have auspicious qualities. Middle hill people all tend to be called Ghurkas, but include other ethnic groups. All tribes wear distinctive

boots and baby carriers shaped like giant slippers. The women keep their coats on in the tents, but often slip an arm out of one sleeve to tend to a child or a duty such as churning yak-butter tea.

Festivals and dances form a central part of Nepalese culture and draw pilgrims from all over India. One of the most colorful events of Katmandu is the Asta Matrika dance of the autumn festival, when the goddess Durga's triumph over the buffalo demon Mahisasura is celebrated. Men and boys dress to represent the mother earth goddess, wearing silk skirts and short-sleeved tops in white or orange, braided in gold. The masks are generally fierce and extraordinary, heavily adorned with colorful flowers, especially

ly sashed over loose trousers, accompanied by fur boots and knitted hats with a pompom trim. Men wear a greatcoat made of yak fur and hoods sometimes encrusted with triangular panels of turquoise stones. Women wear the distinctive high, black quilted hat with its out-turned rim, a silhouette similar to the shape of the temples. Women's robes are full length and red-brown in color, with black homespun cloaks draped over them. Sometimes, to keep warm, women wear yak skin, fur side inward, draped over the body toga-fashion, and tied on one shoulder. Red Kashmir shawls with embroidered motif designs help to add a note of finery to this necessarily bulky, but also functional, form of dress.

BHUTAN

This small country is devoted to a religious way of life. The landscape varies from lowland jungle to high peaks that are covered in snow all year round. Access to the region is fairly limited; bartering is still an accepted form of commerce, and the government seeks to protect its culture and people by only a gradual adoption of selected elements of foreign influence.

National dress is obligatory for all the Bhutanese, with the exception of footwear: the traditional boots with upturned toes

necessities – loose paper money, lunch, needles, and coins. A small, straight sword is worn at the girdle by all men.

Women's dresses are handwoven masterpieces. Each valley has its own version. Floral eastern elements are locally woven of silk in double-sided or damask-weave patterns. The skirt wraps are neither cut nor sewn, but are made of three woven strips, each an elbow-length wide and traditionally four "ells," or 21½ inches (54 centimeters), in length. They are carefully pleated and draped around the body and worn with a

beautiful version of this ensemble, winding their silk lengths to form figure-hugging, tube-shaped skirts with a fringed edge falling down over one thigh. A wool tunic top and short, black-dyed long-sleeved cotton jacket complete the outfit, together with hand-embroidered fur-lined boots and the customary coils of coral beads.

In rainy weather, Lunana women adopt a red woven blanket cover. This is made of sheep's wool, and the natural lanolin it contains helps make it impervious to any snow, rain, or wind. Cloaks that are trimmed with

ABOVE: Sumptuous clothing worn by a Ladakh family: the man's robe is the classic Tibetan shape with side-buttoning. His brocade-cloaked wife wears a stunning headdress, decorated down the back with cowrie shells.

ABOVE: Traditional dress is obligatory for all in Bhutan. Their robes are best seen at festivals such as this one at Paro. A Lunana man wears a variation on this style: a handwoven cloth wrap, belted to form a pouch.

ABOVE: Bhutanese women at Paro wearing their handwoven wrap dresses. The motifs and colors of their clothes are centuries old, and as tradition dictates, they also identify their home village.

have been superseded by western styles. On special occasions, boots of soft leather with appliqué work on the legs are worn by both sexes. The toe shape of the boots is very practical, as it sheds the snow with each step. Men wear pantaloons, which they tuck into the boots, and a silk or cotton long-sleeved undershirt with a broad white collar and cuffs. Over the top they wear a sumptuous wrapover robe of Tibetan style. The robe is lifted at the waist to form a pouch and is sashed with a slim handwoven tie, often wrapped double around the body, with two fringed ends falling to one side. In the pouch the Bhutanese man carries all his

long-sleeved, crossover, handwoven top, together with a wrapping stole of twill-weave wool. Buckles may hold the stole in place at the center front, from which dangle some lucky golden charms. Once fibulas (metal brooches) were commonly used, but these are rarely seen today. Necklaces of coral or turquoise are strung with silver amulets. Most valued are the oval "tears of the gods," otherwise called eye stones. These are rare agates with a dark brown tiger stripe, or eye rings, and nine is an auspicious number to hold. The name speaks about the pattern in the stone. A subgroup, the Lunana people, wear a particularly

yak tail are also made for the Lunana men.

Young Bhutanese herders wear yak-felt hats with characteristic "horns," which divert any rainwater from the face, and fur jerkins over loose pants. In warmer weather they favor the Tibet-style shirts. Women wear a crown hat, too, of similar shape, which has a fur-trimmed, upturned brim. Small children wear scaled-down versions of all the adult clothing. Girls dress in long black or flowery robes with little kimono-shape jackets folded tightly across them that are padded for extra warmth. Very young children are carried in the back of the fabric wraps that their mothers wear tied in front.

Southern India and Sri Lanka

In the state of Maharashtra and farther south, women's saris are almost twice the usual length of the northern style and are decorated with a narrower border pattern. Some can be as long as 11 yards (10 meters). The extra length permits the right-hand half of the wrap to be brought through the legs from front to back, then tucked into the waistband. The effect is similar to the men's *dhoti*, in that the middle section raises the folds over the back of the leg, slightly revealing the calf. Maharashtra women love brightly colored saris and patterned borders, of which there are numerous varieties. Bodices in this region are particularly colorful and gaily embroidered.

Still farther south, in the provinces of Andhra Pradesh, Karnataka and Tamil Nadu, the long sari also predominates. It measures from 9 to 12 yards (8–11 meters) and has endless regional variations in draping: left to right, right to left, pleats at the side or center front, end drawn through the legs or not. In general, the sari does not cover the head, as in the north.

In *Family Web*, Sarah Hobson describes rural workers in the state of Karnataka as wearing a practical and decent sari that can be adapted for the squatting position for planting, or cooking over a fire. She describes how the woman always keeps her legs covered, as if wearing trousers, and wraps the spare fabric into a ball in her lap. Village blouses are looser than town blouses. The women mentioned are the poorest class, possessing no underwear except for a market-bought bra. They color their eyes with *kadige*, or kohl, and continue the practice of wearing a cotton thread tied around the waist for protection from harm during pregnancy and labor. The jewelry worn is minimal: a gold disk as a memento of marriage, a gold charm, a string of glass beads, and a silver belt to hold up the pleats of the sari at the waist. For wedding ceremonies, the bridegroom wears an impressive new white *lungi*, accompanied by a western-style jacket, a gold turban, and a traditional marriage shawl. Women guests wear simple saris, while the bride appears resplendent in a red-and-gold one.

Color and pattern are varied in the southern provinces. They are noted for more striking colors and combinations of pattern and tone than the north. Traditionally, Indian women have favored contrasting colors – for example, green with pink – but western influence has led to a taste for subtler color matching, such as two complementary shades of orange.

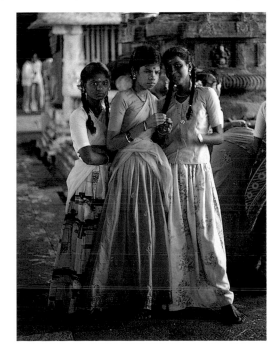

Male costume consists of the *dhoti* and maybe a shirt. The nationalist movement resulted in the rejection of western attire and the adoption of "khaddar" or homespun cloth by many orthodox Hindus. The high-collared coat, or *achkan*, and tight pants, or *churidar*, have become accepted wear. White is standard. The Nehru cap, at first the badge of a freedom fighter, became part of the national dress after 1947, and turbans, which once defined every man by caste, class, and region, began to lose favor. Only in Rajasthan or among the Sikhs or orthodox Hindus in the south is the *pugree*, or turban, head covering, still worn. Otherwise, in spite of the blazing sun in many areas, most men go bareheaded.

In Andhra Pradesh live the Konda or Hill Reddis, one of the "scheduled" tribes of India. Scheduled means identified as needing special assistance for their economic and educational development. Their clothing is very basic: men wear a *langoti*, or breech-cloth, tucked into a belt of twisted copper, while women wear distinctive gilded nose ornaments and sari lengths bought from neighboring plains people. In the same province dwell the Chenchus of the Deccan, who are related to the Veddas who live in Sri Lanka. These aboriginal people still have a Stone Age lifestyle and are also a scheduled tribe.

In Madhya Pradesh the Gonds, also known as Marias or Murias, still practice face tattooing. Girls load their torsos with trade beads and wear sarong skirt wraps. These are often tied at both ends and crossed over the bust behind the neck, or over one shoulder, to make a sheath shape.

Dancers wear elaborate masks trimmed with cowrie shells and bison-horned head-dresses for marriage ceremonies.

Another group not related to the indigenous people are the nomadic Banjara of Maharashtra. Women wear long tunic dresses of multicolored material, heavily embroidered and sometimes appliquéd or mirrored. Nose rings and silver jewelry are

worn in abundance. They are migrants from north India and their style resembles that of Rajasthan. Their black coin-trimmed skirts, decorated with patches of vivid reds and oranges, also show affinity with European gypsy costumes.

SRI LANKA

The indigenous majority population of Sri Lanka are the Sinhalese, whose religion is Buddhism. The minority people on the island are the Tamils, who are Hindu. They came to the island in two waves: first as migrants and secondly as plantation laborers. These two cultures, historically in conflict, produce different dress styles.

Overall, the ethnic dress of Sri Lanka is fast dying out, although saris are still worn by traditional women, including the tea-plantation workers. White is a favorite color and many textiles are imported from India. Red and gold cloth is still favored by Hindu brides, but bridegrooms have now adopted western-style dress. Buddhist weddings in

ABOVE: **Tamil girls in Sri Lanka wear saris and headwraps similar to those worn in the Indian subcontinent. Sri Lankans – particularly those who live in the main towns – are generally adopting westernized dress.**

BELOW: **A Sri Lankan fisherman wears a batik wrap patterned sarong and a striped stole that is more in keeping with the dress style worn throughout Southeast Asia. The indigenous majority population of Sri Lanka is Buddhist by religion, and its cultural links are more allied with Indonesia than India.**

the town of Kandy are still elaborate, with the man wearing a style of dress that is more akin to Southeast Asian costume. The groom wears white under-trousers, a pleated gold gauze overskirt with gold embroidery, and a short red jacket. The bride wears a long, straight, tailored blouse and a full-length wrapped skirt in gold-worked red silk. The main difference is that Southeast Asian costume is cut and fitted for the top half of the body, combined with stiff pleating for the skirt wraps. Hindu Indian dress is essentially all drape.

The best gold jewelry in Sri Lanka is from Kandy. The finest island costume can be seen there at the midsummer festival of Perahera, where a venerated relic, a tooth of the revered Buddha, is paraded. As with the Kandyan bridal outfits, the male dancers wear stiff head-crowns, bold embroidered jackets, and appliquéd pleated skirts, similar to those more commonly seen in festivals held in Southeast Asia.

India Map

The clothing of the Indian subcontinent can be broadly categorized as either drape or cut. The indigenous dress of Hindu people in India is draped, as in the classic sari for women, which has many styles and regional variations – full-pleated or simply draped, with the loose end pulled across the head or upper body. For men, the oldest, briefest drape garment is the *lungi*, or loincloth. An alternative is the *dhoti*, which is full enough to resemble trousers and can be folded and draped in many ways, depending on the region.

While the earliest known textile is Chinese silk, textile weaving in India is indisputably an ancient art. The first wool came from the mountains of Kashmir. The word "shawl" comes from the Sanskrit *sala*, meaning a floor or room, because the earliest square shapes were used as carpets, hangings, and coverlets. Fine weaving techniques passed from India to Assyria and Egypt, and through Phoenicia into Europe. The very names of basic commodities indicate their centuries-old provenance: calico from Calicut or Calcutta, strong cotton cloth or muslin from Mosul, chintz from *chint* or *chete* – Hindu words for variegated and dotted textiles – became known as "chita." ("Satin" derives from Zaytoun in China and "damask" from Damascus, Syria.)

Scissors, threads, and the art of cutting patterns, unknown to ancient India, came with Muslim invaders via the northwest. It was during the Moghul dynasty (1526–1857) that tailoring thus gained prominence. This explains why the northern states of India have many varied forms of dress, from wide *ghagras*, or pleated skirts, to *choli*, or tight-fitting tops, worn as a blouse. The *salwar-kameez*, a long tunic worn over baggy trousers in the Punjab, is widespread in Pakistan. The male's knee-length and slightly flared muslin shirt, or *kurta*, is found widely in north India. A Chinese influence is noticeable in the cut of the man's long button jacket, or *achkan*, with its stand-up collar and slight flare at knee-level.

This dualism between West and East, Hindu and Muslim influences can also be detected in embroidery techniques. Some stitchery, like satin stitch, originated in China; while the interlacing stitchery of Kutch, Kathiawar, and Sind was first introduced by Arab traders in the ninth century AD. In Indian Tibet and Nepal to the northeast, bordering China, clothing of the cross-over front shape originated in the use of animal hides by hunters. In Sri Lanka to the far south, the sarong-skirt style of dress, worn by the indigenous Buddhist Sinhalese, has closer links with dress worn in Southeast Asia.

A Kashmiri man dressed in fine wool clothing.

A Sikh bride from north India wearing an elaborate red-and-gold sari.

A Sindhi man from Pakistan wearing an intricate patterned shawl.

ABOVE: **At the Hindu ceremony of Udappuwa in Sri Lanka, one can see fine ceremonial draped clothing, such as this richly dyed sari.**

ABOVE: **A girl of Rajasthan wears a close-fitting blouse and under-bodice, or choli, which is typical of the north Indian shaped clothing styles.**

Key

 3,000 plus m (9,000 plus ft)

 1,500–3,000m (4,500–9,000ft)

400–1,500m (1,200–4,500ft)

 0–200m (0–600ft)

 Sea, lakes and rivers

Note: Peoples are shown in italics eg: *Sikh*

A woman of Ladakh in a finely tailored robe with turquoise and silver jewelry.

An Indian Tibetan village woman wearing a crossover robe of Manchu origin.

Hindu Kush

Herati

NURISTAN
Kalash

Gilgitis
JAMMU

Karakoram

•Kabul

Khyber Pass

Hunza

LADAKH

AFGHANISTAN

Afghani

•Peshawar

•Rawalpindi

KASHMIR
Kashmiri

NW FRONTIER PROVINCE

Sikh

Gaddi
HIMACHAL PRADESH

Lahore•

•Amritsar

Himalayas Sherpas
Gurkhas

Pathan

Quetta•

PUNJAB
Punjabi

NEPAL

•Katmandu

Newers Tamang
Murmi

Lunana

Tsanglas Adi

BALUCHISTAN
Baluchi

HARYANA

UTTAR
PRADESH

BHUTAN

ARUNACHAL PRADESH

PAKISTAN

Delhi•

•Agra

•Lucknow

ASSAM

NAGALAND

SIND
Sindhi

RAJASTHAN
Rajasthani

Jaipur•

MEGHALAYA

Bauls

MANIPUR

•Hyderabad

•Allahabad

Ganges

BANGLADESH

MIZORAM

INDIA

BIHAR

Santall

WEST
BENGAL

•Jesore

RANN OF KACHCHH

•Bhopal

•Jabalpur

Gonds

Calcutta•

•Chittagong

GUJARAT

KATHIAWAR

•Bhopal

MADHYA PRADESH

Mru
Marma
Tippera
Chakma

Rabari

Narmada

Gulf
of
Cambay

Banjara
MAHARASHTRA

ORISSA

A Banjara gypsy woman adorned with jewelry from Hyderabad in India.

•Bombay

Chenchus
ANDHRA
PRADESH

•Hyderabad

KARNATAKA

Krishna

A woman of Bangladesh dressed in a patterned sari.

Konda

Bangalore•

Toda

Melagiri Hills

TAMIL
NADU

KERALA

A Hindu woman of south India in a brightly colored sari with a full drape.

SRI
LANKA

Veddas
Tamil •Kandy
Sinhalese

A ceremonial musician of Sri Lanka dressed in an ancient cut and shaped costume.

155

HEADDRESSES

TOP ROW, LEFT TO RIGHT:

A man wearing a mirrorwork and embroidery hat, typical of the ornate craftwork of Sind.

A handwoven, ribbon-trimmed wool cap worn by a man from Himachal Pradesh.

A Bhutanese woman's plain woven straw sun hat.

A Sikh priest's ornate turban, worn at the Golden Temple, Amritsar.

A Punjabi man of Gangotri, wearing a turban of bright yellow, a typically vivid color of north India.

MIDDLE ROW, LEFT TO RIGHT:

A white turban worn by a Pakistani man of Lahore, whose features indicate his strong Aryan ancestry.

A black tie-dyed shawl and silver jewelry worn by a Rajasthani tribal girl on a pilgrimage to Armakantak, Madhya Pradesh.

Silver and metal headdress of a Kandyan male dancer at the Perahera festival in Sri Lanka.

A Muslim man of Fatephur Sikri, Uttar Pradesh, wearing a gold-and-red woven cap.

A woman from Gangotri, northern Punjab, wrapped in a typical shawl. She also wears a nose ornament and a silver necklace attached to her braids.

BOTTOM ROW, LEFT TO RIGHT:

Rajasthani migrant worker of Poona, wearing a simple head covering and elaborate silver pendant earrings, plastic beads, and gold nose ornament.

A village woman from Ladakh in a peyrak crown hat, decorated with chunks of turquoise.

A Pakistani man of Wazir with an indigo dyed turban.

A man wearing a chemically dyed yellow turban with a fringed drape, typical of Fatephur Sikri in Uttar Pradesh.

A girl of the Kalash tribe, Nuristan, Pakistan, wearing a cowrie shell-beaded headdress, which is decorated with some bead fringing, coins, and woolen pompoms.

157

THE FAR EAST

This chapter covers Mongolia (once part of China, but now independent) and China, Tibet, the islands of Taiwan, Hainan, and Hong Kong, Japan, and North and South Korea. China and Japan make a most interesting comparison in the current state of their costume. Chinese dress provides some visual evidence that when politics shapes every aspect of public and private life, it has a profound effect on people's sense of identity. Up to the beginning of this century, traditional dress in China was an effective indicator of rank, and consequently was seen as a symbol of oppression.

In 1911, when the last emperor was overthrown, the Republic ordered all men to cut off their pigtails, which were a symbol of foreign domination, and dress codes soon followed. Under Communism, the Chinese leader Mao Zedong, made the wearing of any form of ethnic costume illegal. A radical, simple, and very effective form of social engineering was brought about by the introduction of the "Han" suit across the entire country. This plain uniform of blue or gray linen jacket and trousers reduced both individualism and elitism.

Today there is a revival of interest in pre-revolutionary cultural history. The Cultural Palace of the National Minorities exhibits the crafts and costume of the non-Han Chinese; although these minorities amount to only 6 percent of the population, they inhabit roughly 60 percent of the country's territory. Ancient crafts are being revived, but only those that are useful for commerce and export. Hand-crafted clothing tends to survive well in societies where custom and tradition, rather than a western notion of progress, is a principle of the way of life.

ABOVE: **A woman and child from one of China's most distinctive minority peoples: the Black Miao, who live in many of the southern provinces.**

OPPOSITE: **Japanese girls in traditional dress, Kyoto.**

Throughout Taiwan, Hainan, and Hong Kong, western-style dress has been very widely adopted by the populace, but some indigenous dress is still to be found. An example is the *cheongsam*, tight dress, *mwa kwa*, mandarin-collared jacket, and a round satin hat.

In Japan, too, there is a revival of interest in traditional costume, the wearing of which had virtually died out. Now, however, educated women wear western clothing by day and go to academies in their spare time to rediscover the art of wearing the kimono. The kimono is almost a part of an attitudinal or philosophical approach to life, which is seen as uniquely, exquisitely Japanese.

Textile makers, dyers, and weavers are designated as "living treasures" by the government. The Republic of South Korea has undergone a similar development: after absorbing western ideas and dress, it has

now developed a greater interest in traditional costume, which is worn on festival and feast days.

Japan is ethnically fairly homogeneous, whereas the number of tribes in the large country of China is extremely diverse.

Apart from race and language, China differs in customs, historical development, and religions from Japan. The whole basis of the Chinese Empire was created by the indigenous Han, in the Yellow River basin area. The Great Wall, built in the third century BC, effectively kept all other peoples out. Over the centuries, as this nation developed, large numbers of outsiders were absorbed into it. But during this time both positive and negative attitudes toward minority peoples persisted.

Therefore, during some periods, cultural differences, including dress, were freely permitted; during others, differences from the cultural norm resulted in persecution. For example, during the Great Leap Forward (1958–60) and in the Cultural Revolution (1966–76) the rights of all minorities were restricted. However, in recent years their rights have been reaffirmed, with the freedom to develop their own language and culture, and economic assistance and limited regional autonomy is being granted.

However, China's policy toward Tibet has been one of acculturation, and ancient Tibetan dress really exists only in the remoter areas of the country. Nowadays the traditional costumes that survive best are those that relate to work or climate.

In Mongolia some old traditions remain. Fur coats, snow-proof boots, and ear-hugging hats are still worn by the people as protection against the area's bitter climate.

Mongolia

RIGHT: *These two gentlemen of Ulan Bator, Mongolia, wear the crossover front robes typical of a region where hides were originally used for clothing (the whole uncut skin was used to the maximum width). The use of toggle closures is also a mark of a hunter's clothing, as these work better than sewn-on buttons on furs and hides. Shorter-length robes and the use of trousers mark a culture that has hunting and horse riding at its heart.*

LEFT: *This wolf hunter from eastern Mongolia wears a bearskin coat over his homespun rough robe and knee-length riding boots. During the colder months, all the people of Asian nomadic groups wear an extra outer garment, cut like the* dolman *(a sleeved open robe), or the* del *(a crossover robe) – both made from fur. The variation in cut, length, and hides depends on the tradition of the ethnic group.*

Mongolia gained independence from China in 1921, with Soviet support. It is a bleak, enormous region of high plateaus and mountains, where only one percent of the land is cultivated. Over half the population lives in towns, but a significant minority, concentrated right up in the north, are nomadic pastoralists.

A nomadic existence defines the dress: as seen in many other areas of Central Asia, the prevailing cut of the clothes has origins in the old hunter-gatherer tradition – in this instance, that of the Manchu people – who ruled China throughout the Qing dynasty (1644–1911).

The nomadic dress style contrasts with the southern, indigenous Han traditions of weaving, in which the design of garments is defined by the strip products of the loom.

The northern nomads used the skins of hunted animals for their clothing, a tradition that accounts for crossover openings on tunic fronts (using a whole uncut skin to the maximum), side slits in thigh-length tunics, for riding, and the prevalence of trousers for one or both sexes. The use of toggle closures is also a mark of a hunter's clothing, as these work better on furs and hides than using stitched buttonhole closures. The calf-length Mongolian crossover-fronted and belted robe is called a *del* and is usually worn with plain black boots below loose pants. In winter, a heavier outer robe of fur or hide is added, cut like a *del* or *dolman* (sleeved cloak). *Ikat* dyeing and embroidery differentiate each community.

The Hulanbeier, who are nomadic herdsmen of Inner Mongolia, wear the traditional Han Chinese jacket and trousers, but the women wear brightly colored headscarves and full-length tunic dresses with a curved overlap front. These dresses are indigo-dyed, sometimes with a gold thread in the textile, sleeve caps are slightly gathered into a fitted armhole. Trims and froggings are often of a color contrasting with that of the main body of the dress, which may be held in with a wide sash of another bright color for contrast. Finely stitched, soft leather boots for both sexes are also a feature of these nomadic peoples' dress.

China

As one might expect, the pattern in China is for centralism, so the most traditional costumes are seen among the people who live on the fringes of the state. Even here, many people will wear the Han suit for daily labor and bring out their finery for special occasions. The costume that survives is the one that is distinctive due to function, such as the sarongs worn by the Dai people of tropical Xishuangbanna.

NORTHWEST CHINA

To the far west of China lies the Xinjiang Uigur Autonomous Region. ("Autonomous Regiones" refers to areas that are allowed some degree of local decision making but still remain under the control of the central government.) In the northeast of this region, peoples of the Altaic linguistic group, the Uigurs and Kazakhs, are of the Muslim faith. Traditionally, Uigur people are agriculturalists, but nowadays most farm or work in state-run craft cooperatives, textile facto-

ries, or carpet mills. Uigur women are silk makers, and there seems to be a link between the designs they make and the Chinese Buddhist, T'ang-dynasty paintings. Uigur men wear a long, loose tunic with a

scarf folded in a triangle, as a sash. For women, a similar loose robe is topped with a tight-fitting short vest, often quilted or fur-lined, with frogged buttonloops. One can still see men sporting silver-hilted daggers tucked in their belts under their coats. Both sexes wear fur-lined coats in the cold.

Women's dress fabrics are brilliantly patterned, and they like to wear thick, brightly colored stockings underneath. Unmarried women dress their hair with a center parting and braid their hair in a number of styles. Married women always wear two long braids, and favor large, hoop earrings.

Skullcaps are worn by both sexes, but the women wrap bright scarves, some still hand-embroidered, over them or wear round fur hats, as do the men. Other scarves might have a glitter of gold or silver thread woven in them. Daughters dress even more colorfully than their mothers, and use kohl to draw a line connecting the eyebrows in the

ABOVE RIGHT: **This Tadzhik family lives in Xinjiang, southeast China, across the border from Tadzhikistan, in the Pamir Mountains. They are most likely Shiite Muslims, the predominant faith of the Tadzhiks. The woman wears the typical round hat, or kola, under a white scarf. This hat is found widely across Central Asia, with all kinds of regional variations.**

LEFT: **These women in Kashgar market, Xinjiang Province, are embroidering beads on little hats, or kolas. The woman to the left is wearing a beautiful ikat-patterned skirt. Colors in Central Asian decoration tend to be vivid and primary: yellows, reds, and blues, with green as a common color in the background.**

camel herders, many have scaled down their wanderings to the herding of sheep and goats in summer, and live in settled communities during the winter months. They wear clothing cut as described above, but also wear their own distinctive pointed beige caps, trisected by black felt lines: these are called *kalpaks*.

NORTHEAST CHINA

China's northeastern zone is home to the Manchu, once conquerors of all China but now virtually assimilated, with little trace of their distinctive culture. (The impact of Manchu dress has already been described above.) Only two small subgroups, the Oroqen and the Ewenki, resisted change and until the past two or three decades still lived a nomadic life, in birch-bark and hide tents. They have now settled in villages on the northern rim of Heilongjiang Province, bordering on the C.I.S., in a hard, cold climate that has only 100 days annually that are free from frost.

Men wear hide jackets, trousers, and fur-lined boots and hats. Their coats (some of wolfskin) are exquisite: they are cut in the crossover shape, and have black hide appliquéd patches that form a round yoke effect. They are edged with rich gold stitching in symmetrical designs that reflect their closeness to nature and the hunt. Oroqen women wear similar robes decorated with appliqué and embroidery, with wide sashes and fur-trimmed cuffs. The women consider

the repetition of embroidery motifs an expression of wifely duty, and although silk or synthetic floss has replaced grass as their thread, they still use the antlers of roe deer to carve curling designs on their birch-bark sewing boxes.

SOUTHWEST CHINA

This area contains the ethnic groups that have been written about under Thailand – the Miao (also known as Hmong and Meo) and Yao peoples (see pages 126–128). The Miao, Yao, and Tung peoples, in fact, are scattered across five southern provinces: Hunan, Kwangsi, Guandong, Guizhou, and Yunnan. The province of Yunnan alone

middle, following the distinctive looks of Fatima, daughter of Muhammad.

The neighboring Kazakh people wear clothing appropriate to their herding tasks: thick sheepskin coats and heavy boots. The men are distinguished by their long mustaches. The Kazakh women's gowns are also colorful, like those of the Uigur, but they like to add three rows of trimming to the lower edge and wear knee-length dark coats over them. Kazakhs live in *yurts*, thick felt tents, even when they become sedentary. These are always full of colored rugs.

Kyrgyz horsemen also live in the northwest borders of Xinjiang. Traditionally Bactrian

*ABOVE LEFT: **This Dai minority woman of Yunnan Province wears a rich indigo-dyed jacket, trimmed with six different types of braid, and a homespun wrap skirt, in common with many other southern Chinese minorities.***

*ABOVE RIGHT: **A Uigur woman and child of Xianjiang. Although they are poor, they still keep to the old customs, such as the voile headscarf covering the woman's head. Uigur women are renowned craft workers, making silk textiles and carpets.***

*LEFT: **Women of the Bai minority stroll in a market street in Yunnan Province wearing indigo-dyed, knee-length tunics over trousers. The men are wearing the widespread Han-style worksuit. The older women to the right wear sleeveless tops of velvet over their tunics.***

RIGHT: *Schoolgirls of the Shui minority of Guizhou Province parade in their best finery: cross-fronted black velvet tops, braided, with appliqué embroidery on wide apron panels, over long trousers of indigo homespun cotton. Their round turbans are encrusted with silver chains and silver beads. Long silver chains form neck chains that also serve as apron strings.*

BELOW: *Some of these pilgrims in Tibet are wearing typical northern* chupas, *or robes. The man has his outer one belted at the waist, with the top half wrapped cloak-fashion over his shoulders. Underneath he wears a very fine robe lined in blue silk. He wears a recent arrival – a Chinese cap. The other women pictured are also wearing cheaper Chinese ready-made clothing.*

contains nearly half of the 55 minority groups identified in China. The Yi women of Yunnan wear a simple, long-sleeved tunic dyed with indigo and embroidered all the way down the front section. They are also noteworthy for an unusual headdress – a rolled and folded piece of cloth that is kept in place by tying two side braids over the top. In general the men wear black Chinese trousers and buttoned jackets with mandarin collars, or ready-made shirts.

In the Stone Forest area of Yunnan, the Sani people, who are a subgroup of the Yi minority, wear a distinctive blue-black and white long-sleeved tunic, formerly hand-embroidered on collar and cuffs, but now normally finished by machine. In the rugged mountains of south Yunnan there is a small tribe called the Jinuo, who wear a variation of hill-peoples' dress.

In contrast to the mountainous habitat of the north, south Yunnan is a tropical zone and is the home of the Dai people of Xishuangbanna Autonomous Region. In this area the dress is similar to that of Southeast Asia. The Dai wear sarongs, long-sleeved fitted blouses, and sandals. Market-bought towels are adopted as headwraps. The Dai men practiced tattooing, but both their customs and their traditional Buddhist faith were discouraged by China's Red Guard movement, and are on the wane.

A pleasant custom among the Bai, another southern group who are hill rice farmers, is for a man and woman to hang up their

clothes together on a bedpost as a symbol of their marital harmony. The women wear tunics of red corduroy or linen over white cotton shirts (these days machine-embroidered), and embroidered cloth headdresses, folded and tied on with black ribbon. Unmarried women add a long wool fringe to these, married women add a shorter one.

TIBET

Before the Chinese conquest in 1959, this high plateau region was the home of the Dalai Lamas, considered incarnations of the patron deity of Tibet, the Avalokiteshvara. The current Dalai Lama now lives in exile in north India, where many Tibetan refu-

gees are also settled. Up until the 1950s, it was possible to see virtually the same dress in the streets of Tibet that had been worn for several hundred years. The population was divided into the priests, one-sixth of all adult males; the nomadic people tending

their herds outside the holy cities; peasant farmers; and a ruling elite that centered on the capital around Lhasa. Now, however, Tibet has a majority population of Chinese, and traditional Tibetan dress and culture are being suppressed.

Only in remote Tibet does traditional nomadic costume persist. Nomads wear the long, loose crossover coat or robe, or *chupa*, of the type worn by Kashmiri men (see north India page 144), with a bagging pouch at the front. Everyday wear for nomadic Tibetans is a homespun brown or off-white wool *chupa* worn over a full-length Manchu-style under-tunic. Mountain shepherds wear a shorter, wrapover quilted robe over a mid-thigh tunic. Loose trousers and a weather-proof black wool cloak, and a tight-fitting sheepskin hat, with flaps upturned or covering the ears, are also worn. Leather fur-lined boots keep out the cold.

Nomad women wear *chupas* too, with a variety of different fur hats or bonnet-shaped hats, and treasure their coral, turquoise, or silver bead necklaces. Certain groups of more sedentary peasants also wear a *chupa*, but it is made of more elaborate and fine textiles. For example, a wealthy Lhasa woman's robe might be made out of silk or fine wool, and would be covered with a strip-woven cloth apron, which is joined to make a pattern out of the irregular conjunction of the striped weave. This apron style is more traditionally worn in the central and eastern parts of Tibet.

Taiwan, Hainan, and Hong Kong

ABOVE: *Women of the Ami tribe, a hill people of the island of Taiwan, are well known for their beautiful embroidery, or* rukai. *The front panels of their tunics are exquisitely decorated in rich colors. The girl on the right is wearing a robe that is decorated with appliquéd arabesques.*

RIGHT: *A Hong Kong wedding procession in which the bride's carriage is preceded by musicians wearing short red kimonos and trousers. Red is a symbol of luck, prosperity, or health in many eastern countries.*

ABOVE: *The Hakka minority people of Hong Kong wear typical Cantonese "coolie hats." The woman's is decorated with a thin cotton ruched frill; both wear tight caps underneath the straw brims. An alternative domed hat with a turned-down brim is called a* tanka. *It is worn by the fishing-village people living throughout the region.*

Taiwan and Hainan are the largest islands off China's south coast, and they have retained some local variations in dress, such as the costume of the Kaoshans, the generic name applied to Taiwan's hill farmers. They have traditionally employed cotton, hemp, and palm-fiber cloth from which to make their clothing. Women wear short trousers under their wrap skirts, and lightweight vests over thin, collarless blouses. Men wear trousers with bibs over their store-bought workshirts.

Between Hainan and Taiwan lies the island of Hong Kong. The largest ethnic group of the Chinese hinterland province of Guangdong (and in Hong Kong itself) is the Cantonese, who call themselves *Punti* or

"local people." Another large group is the Hakka, who were originally from Shandong and Henan to the north. The official dress of the Chinese Republic since 1912, for both men and women, was the *cheongsam* (a long, high-collared robe), worn with the *ma kwa* (a mandarin-collared jacket) and a round satin hat. The *cheongsam* survived as a style in Hong Kong long after the mainland gave it up, becoming a tighter-fitting female garment, with a pronounced side slit. It is still worn today by some women, although western-style dress is much more prevalent on the island.

The traditional *kwa* jacket, in red with silver or gold embroidery and frogged buttoning, is no longer worn by Hong Kong

people, but remains popular with tourists, as does the Cantonese "coolie hat," a flat circle of woven straw with a hole in the center called a *leung mo.*

In eastern Hong Kong, the Han work suit still predominates as normal everyday wear. There are remnants of the old traditional dress, as in the use of lacework sandalwood fans (most fans are now made of Mongolian oak, but are still very fine). Today, the field-workers can still be seen wearing their wide-brimmed, conical-domed straw hats, tied under the chin.

Sometimes raincoats woven from straw are still seen in rural areas – farmers wear them for political rallies as a sign of their enduring traditional values.

Korea

A glance at any Korean painting of the late Choson dynasty (18th to early 20th century) shows that Korean clothing today has changed little since, and, as in Japan, the continuance of the traditional ways is carefully conserved in the Republic of South Korea by a system of living national treasures. The old costumes are now worn only for special occasions, but in the past decade, there has been a marked increase of interest in this aspect of Korean heritage, as a rich evocation of the past and a tangible connection with all the old values.

Both Korea and Japan are long, thin land-masses with a pronounced variation their in climate from north to south. North Korea has always been more influenced culturally by Central Asia, while South Korea lies on trade routes with China, Japan, and points farther south. Korean sailors exported many

*BELOW: **A group of older Korean men wear traditional** chogon, **or jackets, with white** paji **trousers, the most common color of national dress. The style of clothing in Korea has remained unchanged from about the first century BC. Trousers usually indicate a horse culture, linking Koreans with the people of the Asian steppes.***

aspects of their culture to Japan, most particularly their militaristic philosophy.

In general, as in Japan, South Koreans are returning to traditional ways after a long period of assimilating western ideas and manners. The cultural dress of the Choson period is being reevaluated.

Also similar to Japan is the acute attention Koreans give to the precise wearing of dress – the amount of cuff and collar revealed, the folding of bows and sashes, the exact angle for a hat or haircomb. It is significant that the colors and patterns being chosen now

are much more in keeping with the older Korean aesthetic. For example, there is a preference for white and other neutral colors, with subtle pastels, an emphasis on curved lines with a minimizing of the upper torso and an enlargement in volume of the lower body half. This classic triangular silhouette is also achieved by using light, crisp fabrics.

The normal components of *hanbok*, or Korean costume, are the skirt, or *ch'ima*, and the *chogon*, or jacket, for women, with the same cut of jacket for men, worn over *paji* trousers. This system of clothing has remained unaltered from about the first century BC. As has been mentioned elsewhere, the wearing of trousers is usually indicative of an equestrian culture and reveals Korea's historic links with all the other peoples of the Asian steppes.

In addition to those garments mentioned, a vest, or *chokki*, and a long overcoat, or *turumagi*, are also worn by men, with leather or silk shoes and a black horsehair hat with a raised bun shape at the back of the crown. Older men used to wear a fine stiffened black straw with a straight brim and small cylindrical crown, as a symbol of their age and their status.

Traditionally, Korean costume follows a system of use by age: children and young people wear bright colors, culminating in the vivid reds, greens, and yellows of the silk wedding robes. The groom wears a hat for the first time on his wedding day, and thereafter, the couple will wear white or other neutrals until they reach old age, for which white alone has always been the customary color. (A bride wears a delicate crown, or *chokturi*, beaded and decorated with flowers and tiny pendants.)

Whereas once western clothing would have been worn for a wedding or for special occasions such as New Year or the Full Moon Feast, it is more common for the traditional attire to be carefully adopted these days. Young men also wear a silken cord, called a *sejodae*, worn around the chest under the armpits, on ceremonial occasions.

It is very characteristic of how Korean costume is made that the cut and such details as the ribbon-trim jacket fastenings do not vary at all; only small changes in the combination of colors used, or possibly in the

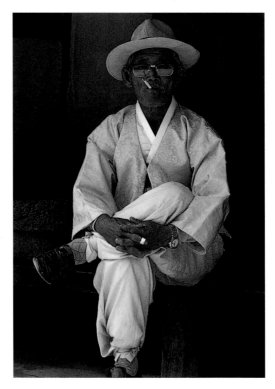

length of a jacket, are considered acceptable.

Traditional Korean fabrics are silk, cotton, ramie, and hemp. There is a particular lightweight silk gauze, called *sa*, which is virtually transparent; the finest quality is called *kapsa*. A striped silk version is called *hangra* and is also woven of cotton or fine ramie. Opaque silks (*tan*), or satin (*kongdan*) and damask (*mobondam*), are also popular, and these are always very subtly patterned and never as ornate or opulent as some Chinese brocaded silks.

The successful addition to an ensemble of numerous accessories is much admired in Korea: hair ornaments (*norigae*), sashes or sash pendants, and small pouch bags are popular. Some of these little drawstring bags are made in sections, using the "five directional colors" peculiar to Korea (although they are based on an ancient Chinese system of cosmology): blue represents east, white is west, red south, black north, and yellow the center.

A most attractive feature of Korean costume is *pojagi*, or wrapping cloths, which have always held significance: their name derives from the word *pok*, meaning "happiness," and signifies the joy that may be wrapped in the cloth – presents, precious objects, and secrets. The meaning and the practice are subtle.

It is also up-to-date: in *Korean Costume*, the writer Yi Song-mi records that recently Korean housewives have protested at the over-use of plastic bags for supermarket foodstuffs by carrying their own *pojagi* for groceries instead. At the other extreme, wedding gifts will be given to the bride and groom in elaborately folded *pojagi*, which are specially made for the occasion.

Japan

As expert orientalist Alan Kennedy has said in *Costumes Japonais*, the traditional arts have done better than survive in Japan. Unlike in other industrialized countries, here they have flourished. But he has also pointed out that the conditions for such a flowering have not always existed in Japan. The country went through a prolonged period of westernization, which led to an attitude of shame toward some aspects of the old culture. The speed of change had a lot to do with it: Japan progressed from being a feudal culture, through industrialization, to a militaristic, neo-imperialistic state in less than 50 years; but all that came to an end after World War II.

In general, even with the adoption of western-style clothing, the Japanese wear a uniform for everything – for every stage of life, every job and hobby. Traditional clothing is now also well on its way to being rein-

BELOW: Women wearing a sumptuous display of kimono costume seen at the Aoi Matsuri Festival in Kyoto, Japan. Aoi is the Japanese word for hollyhock; the flower festival traditionally ensures protection from storms and earthquakes.

corporated into the everyday dress of the Japanese as "the proper thing to wear."

Japan has learned that it is important not only to preserve national works of art but also to ensure the endurance of the skills that make such artifacts possible. In the 1950s, a new catalog of treasures – a list of people who were expert in certain crafts – was created to conserve certain textile manufacturing techniques, such as indigo dyeing and wax-resist work. Pieces of clothing made by such masters are considered to be as valuable as paintings or sculptures.

RIGHT: *Traditional clothing this century uses the generic term "kimono," although the general term used to be* kosode, *which signifies "little sleeves." This style of kimono, which was originally a simple undergarment, was favored by the samurai because it harked back to their humbler origins and was more suited to their equestrian life. These young men at a festival in Kyoto show how the medieval style of dress of the warrior caste differs from the modern kimono shapes.*

LEFT AND BELOW MIDDLE: *A bridal couple show the precision that is the essential character of kimono dress – the preparation, wearing, and state of mind that goes with the attire has virtually a philosophy to it. Young Japanese now go to evening classes to study the art of kimono, including the numerous styles of tying of the* obi *sash (see below middle). The groom's costume is a white under-kimono, with a black* haori *or short kimono, and* haori *cords. The* hakama, *a long pleated skirt of silk, is worn below. The bride wears a* uchikake, *or quilted robe, often white, but sometimes red, with motifs symbolic of happiness.*

Kosode, the entire form of traditional dressing, is based on a costume style that has its origins in the 13th century. Not only costume, but other aspects of Japanese culture are in an exciting and delicate balance between conservation and renaissance: Noh theater (which is closely linked to *kosode*) is enormously popular and gaining a wider audience worldwide. The same holds true of Japanese spiritual practices. Walter Fairservis has written, in *Costumes of the East*: "China, Korea and Japan had old animistic faiths that tended to institutionalize in response to Buddhism's spread, and by so doing, survived into the 20th century."

Museums and societies preserve rare original garments, but there is also a thriving craft economy in the exact replication of these pieces for exhibitions and shows. There is a separate tradition of manufacture for costumes in Noh theater. Now that schools teach the art of kimono, there is a subsidiary manufacturing industry for all the accessories that accompany it.

The only truly casual "living" piece of clothing worn by the Japanese today is the *yukata*, cut like a kimono, which is worn at home or supplied as a matter of course in hotel rooms along with towels and linens. Another informal style coming back into

favor is a piece of farmers' clothing, the baggy cotton trousers called *monpe*. These are still widely worn in the countryside, but have been looked down upon by townspeople until very recently, when smart boutiques began selling remakes of authentic styles. It is also worth noting that the wearing of traditional kimono by children and young people for visiting shrines or festival days, such as Coming of Age day at 20, is on

the increase. Two million young adults attended such ceremonies in formal costume in 1994.

The kimono tradition is an aristocratic one. The poorer people have always worn clothing of another kind. Japan has a long tradition of using unusual fibers for making

clothes: until the late Edo period (1615–1868), only the wealthy could afford silk and the poor were driven to weave fabrics from anything they could find. *Fuji*, or wisteria-fiber coats, are still found, and rice straw was used for hats, rain, and snow coats – these are still worn today by farmers. Hemp, or *asa*, weaving is still practiced, but more as an art than a craft today. Lengths dyed with indigo can be seen "setting" in cold streams by the sea in country areas such as Okinawa.

The most intriguing designs are found on Ainu clothing. The Ainu are Japan's indigenous people, now concentrated mainly on Hokkaido. Ainu means "human." Their chain-stitch embroidery on simple square kimonos is unlike other Japanese designs, and all the motifs are symbolic. There has been a surge of interest in Ainu culture since the Year of the Indigenous People, which occurred in 1993.

It is noteworthy that the influence of Japanese traditional dress has not only become a main part of Japan's cultural life but has made a massive impact on the style of clothing worldwide. Designers such as Issey Miyake and Yohji Yamamoto have translated the kimono style into western clothing design, which has had a profound effect on the international consciousness. There are also certain attractive components of this development: Japanese clothing is non-figure revealing, therefore liberating; unisex and therefore egalitarian. It can be made in traditional fabrics as well as sophisticated, synthetic textile inventions, which makes it aesthetically exciting and original. Perhaps more important than any other factor for the 21st century: its finished look is completely ageless.

Rising to prominence in the 13th century, the kimono dress form is a crossover open robe, cut without any shaping or buttonholing, and held in place by the *obi*, or sash. The kimono is perfectly adapted to a country of great humidity, and where the prevailing domestic custom is to sit on the floor or to kneel, rather than use chairs. Court ladies used to wear *junihitoe*, or 12 unlined robes, one over the other, so that the glimpse of an under-collar, or the folding back of one sleeve, or the exact width of a series of glimpsed hem edges, all combined to create a complicated, meticulous beauty. In this classic medieval period, the *obi* was relatively simple; it became wider and more significant in the Edo period. The colors of all 12 robes would be visible: the ensemble was called the *kasane no irome*, and importance was always given to the correctness of color and pattern for the event or time of year.

The kimono fashion was supported by the rise of Noh theater, a form of entertainment

exclusively for court patronage. In Noh theater, costumes are elaborate, symbolic, and – as with most flowerings of Japanese culture – of a refined, hermetic sensibility. To this day there is a separate art of Noh costume making, using brocades and colors that create heightened theatrical effects. The cut is more angular, the fabrics stiffer in Noh costumes, which are in effect just fossilized versions of the dress from the

Muromachi period (1336–1573), but they are more stylized. Each type has its own name: men wear *kariginu* when playing gods, *happi* for demon gods, *choken* for effeminate roles. *Maiginu* is for a dance robe, *karaori* for a woman's outer stage garment. There is a comic form of theater called Kyogen, which has its own costume styles and rules, including the *kataginu* robes, which have particularly large motifs, such as gourds, arrows, or birds.

For traditional clothing in this century, *kosode* as a generic term has been replaced by the word *kimono*, which means "piece of clothing." *Kosode* signifies "little sleeve," and refers to the ancient style of kimono, in which the long vertical side seam of the kimono would be stitched up to leave only a small gap for the hand at the top. This was worn only by the aristocracy in medieval times as an undergarment, with another kimono form, called *hirosode*, or simply *osode*, meaning "wide sleeves," allowing a glimpse of the *kosode* at the wrists. But with the rise of the samurai, the *kosode* became more popular, as it harked back to the warriors' humble origins and was more suited to an equestrian, military life. Two or three might be worn together – unlined for summer and quilted or lined for winter.

Three types still evoke the samurai era. *Furisode*, or "floating sleeve," is now worn only by young women on ceremonial occasions. The *uchikake* is worn as a robe over a

ABOVE MIDDLE: **An indigenous Caucasian people of Hokkaido, the Ainu, are famous for their distinctive robes, originally made of plant fiber, animal skin, or even fish skin from the Amur River. Their patterns are usually in white on blue, green, or black backgrounds. Appliqué work or elaborate chain-stitch is used in motifs that have an ancient occult symbolism. The clothing of chiefs, shamans, and brides and grooms have particular patterning, but otherwise a group will wear identifying, unifying patterns.**

LEFT: **The undergarments of the kimono are almost as complicated as the top layers. To achieve the correct smooth drape both men and women will tie on small pads to even out bumps, and use stiffened, padded undercollars to support the necklines of their robes. The split-toed socks, or** tabi, **and the white-thonged sandals, or** zori, **are worn by both sexes.**

kimono, without a sash tie. (This makes the patterning of the fabric bolder and more continuous, as the middle section is not interrupted by the sash line.) This type, along with others, often has a quilted neck-line to help it to hang better and to give a finer framing to the neck, which is considered a very appealing part of the anatomy in Japan. A third type, *koshimaki*, was a summer garment of the samurai, a single layer of textile in a muted color, but decorated with tiny embroidery motifs. In illustrations this form is often shown hanging off the shoulders, anchored only by the *obi*.

As Alan Kennedy has explained in *Costumes Japonais*, every style has its own name, and its manufacture relates to social and economic change – the influence of China, for example, a period of recession, or a lack of certain materials at some time.

The patterning of each type of kimono also is categorized: for instance, *dan gamari*, for alternating blocks of similar motifs; or *katami gawari*, in which the right and left halves of the kimono bear a different design; or *sode gawari*, in which each sleeve is differently patterned. Close rapport with nature is seen in the precisely observed, highly refined motifs such as a blizzard of blown blossoms, flowing water patterns, or scattered maple leaves on pine bark. It is easy to see how much the kimono embodies the culture and history of Japan, and why it is studied today with such appreciation by a younger generation eager to find its roots.

The elements of correct Japanese attire today are perhaps best described through the bridal attire. A man will wear a white under-kimono, with a black kimono or five-crested *haori* (short kimono coat) with *haori* cords on top. This all fits over a *hakama*, or long pleated skirt of white Sendai silk, and is worn with white *tabi* (split-toed socks) and *zori*, or sandals, with white toe thongs. A bride wears an *uchikake*, or quilted robe, often with a pattern of cranes, waves, and pines, as symbols of happiness, with an under-kimono and an elaborately tied *obi*.

Female underclothes are just as complex: there is a *hadajuban*, or thin camisole, with short sleeves, and a *susoyoke*, a wraparound slip of a light fabric, and a third under-kimono, usually of a light, white fabric. Both sexes will make use of long-stringed rolls,

pads, and towels (or for men, a padded vest), to even out any defects of the body line, and to create a smooth "foundation" on which the kimono will hang perfectly. Particularly useful is the *date-eri* or under-collar in a contrasting or matching color to the outer kimono, worn in place of a full under-kimono.

The five-crested *haori* is another aspect of the tradition lying behind this formal attire. The crests refer to the little circular motifs printed or woven into the *haori* cloth, representing a person's clan ancestry. Japanese heraldry is older than European and comprises 400 basic family crests, with over 20,000 sublineages. In terms of design, these little circles are exquisitely varied.

Space permits only a brief mention of the diversity of textiles used in kimono design. The simple shape, as mentioned before, allows freedom for a vast range of visual effects, with pattern, texture, and color. In *The Book of the Kimono*, Norio Yamanaka writes of a highly rarefied woman's kimono, called *kasuri*, or *ikat*, which is made of handspun, or *tsumugi*, silk. Reputedly only middle-aged women are employed in its manufacture, as the saliva they spit on their fingers contains the right level of hormones to create a perfect thread! *Kasuri* originated in India and was brought to the Okinawa region in the 16th century.

Yuzen is a starch-resist dye technique using rice paste, soybean juice as a mordant, and a cypress steam box for the fixing process. This type of textile is very often decorated with gold-leaf work. *Komori* is a technique of paper-stenciling on fabric – intricate, fine designs, often applied to a figured satin *mon rinzu* or crepe *chirimen* or the spun silk *tsumugi*. *Jofu* is another variety found, a fine hand-woven linen textile.

Needless to say, the history of the sash, or *obi*, is a subject for a book in itself; there are numerous accessories made to go with the sash, such as the under-cords, *obi-jime*, the *obi ita*, or stay, and the *obi makura*, or pad. The bows have great significance: certain shapes are only worn by unmarried or married women, some are put on for town wear, others in different colors are worn for certain seasons of the year. An attractive custom is the tying of the sash to resemble flowers, for wearing in the month of their bloom.

Blue Miao boy from southwest China in distinctive blue and silver clothing.

Kazakh

KYRGYZSTAN *Kyrgyz* XINJIANG UYGUR

Xibe *Uigur*

Nomadic Tibetan

TIBET

•Lhasa

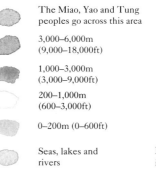

White Miao girl from South China in elaborate gold and white costume.

Key

The Miao, Yao and Tung peoples go across this area

3,000–6,000m (9,000–18,000ft)

1,000–3,000m (3,000–9,000ft)

200–1,000m (600–3,000ft)

0–200m (0–600ft)

Seas, lakes and rivers

Note: peoples are shown in italics eg: *Miao*

Far East Map

Korean child from Seoul in traditional first birthday headgear.

The Far East presents some interesting contrasts. Many countries have turned to western clothing, leaving only their remote minority tribes to continue old dress forms. This is apparent in China, where minorities are also allowed more dress freedom than before. A mix of western dress and traditional clothing is widespread in such places as Taiwan and Hong Kong. Recently there has been a revival of costume and culture in Korea and Japan.

Ewenki

Oroquen

HEILONGJIANG
Manchu

Ainu
HOKKAIDO

Hulanbeier   •Ulan Bator

MONGOLIA

Han

CHINA

NORTH KOREA

•Seoul

JAPAN

REPUBLIC OF SOUTH KOREA

•Kyoto

NGHAI

SHANDONG

HENAN

YELLOW SEA

Lancang

Yangtze

EAST CHINA SEA

PACIFIC OCEAN

HUNAN

GUIZHOW
Shui

Miao
Yao
Tung

Bai Yi
Sani
Blang

YUNNAN

KWANGSI

GUANDONG
Cantonese
Hakka

Ami
Hwalien
TAIWAN
Kaoshan

•Okinawa

Jinuo

SHUANGBANNA
Dai

HONG KONG

HAINAN

A man in ancient samurai warrior uniform at Gion Matsuri festival, Japan.

Hwalien tribeswoman from Taiwan in festival dress.

173

HEAD COVERINGS

TOP ROW, LEFT TO RIGHT:

Girl of Kunming, China, wearing stiffened ribbon appliqué hat with braid bows at the back.

Dai minority woman of south Yunnan, China, in market-bought terry cloth, now used as a headwrap material with a straw hat.

Japanese child in traditional floral headdress and red-and-gold kimono.

Decorated Black Miao minority headdress for a young unmarried girl of Xingren, southwest Guizhou, China.

Dai minority woman of Jinghong, Yunnan, China, with a silver chain wrap headdress over a red cotton headband.

MIDDLE ROW, LEFT TO RIGHT:

Blang minority woman in a black turban with tasseled ends, from Yunnan Province, China.

Hani minority woman of China carrying basket with a headstrap, over a headdress covered in silver beading and trade bead tassels.

Samurai costume at the Aoi Matsuri festival, in Kyoto, Japan.

An old man, follower of Confucius, in a stiffened straw, wide-brimmed hat, a symbol of his age and status, in South Korea.

A farm worker from Rishiri Island, Hokkaido, wearing a traditional headwrap and some indigo clothing.

BOTTOM ROW, LEFT TO RIGHT:

Eastern Mongolian huntsman wearing a typical karakul fur hat.

Japanese bridal headdress in white-embroidered, stiffened satin.

Horse rider at the Aoi Matsuri festival in Kyoto, Japan, wearing a stiffened horsehair hat.

A Miao minority girl from southwest Guizhou, China, wearing heavy silver collars and a tall felted hat.

Child wearing a fringed bonnet in red at a Gion Matsuri festival in Japan.

175

OCEANIA

This chapter surveys the dress of the Pacific Islands, including Polynesia and Micronesia, Melanesia, and Australia and New Zealand.

Polynesia's name – from the Greek words for "many islands" – describes it perfectly: it consists of a string of volcanic reef atolls and islands in the middle of the Pacific Ocean, from Hawaii (the most recent addition to the United States) in the north, down to American Samoa and Western Samoa, the Cook Islands, French Polynesia, the Society Islands (including Tahiti), the Marquesas and Tubuai Islands and Tonga. Once, "Polynesia" referred to the entire region; now it stands for some of the islands mostly south of the equator, alongside Melanesia, whose indigenous people are darker skinned and Papuan in origin. Melanesia (or "black islands") comprises New Guinea and the islands close to Australia.

Micronesia, which means "small islands," defines the area above the equator and comprises over 600 islands in the western Pacific, some volcanic, which are more fertile, and some coral, which are less so.

Since 1962, with the independence of Western Samoa from New Zealand, the movement of Pacific islands toward the dismantling of colonial powers has gathered pace, with Fiji, Tonga, Tuvalu, Vanuatu, and Western Samoa severing their connections with Britain, Australia, and New Zealand. American Samoa is also self-governing. Decolonization is a major issue in the French territories of Tahiti-Polynesia, New Caledonia, Wallis, and Futuna. Easter Island remains a colony of Chile.

The population of the Pacific's Islands is divided between Melanesians (80 percent),

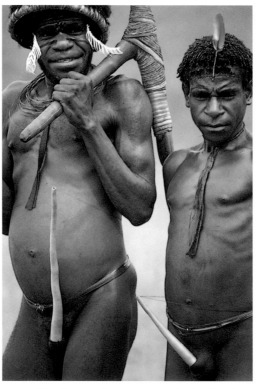

ABOVE: West Papuan Dani men wear little other than their penis covers and bone or teeth ornaments.

OPPOSITE: Fijians, like other Polynesian peoples, have a tradition of using plant fibers for dance costumes; the rustling sounds are intrinsic to the dance movements.

Polynesians (7 percent), Asians (6 percent), Micronesians (5 percent) and Europeans (2 percent). The indigenous population's traditional clothing was simple: loincloths for men and grass skirts for women; and these are still worn in many of the less developed rural communities. In general, however, a great deal of westernized clothing is worn. Pandanus leaves supplied the fibers for the original skirts, which are still worn in some parts for dances and special occasions. The leaves are also woven on small belt looms to make accessories such as belts and bags. In

Micronesia the fibers of the hibiscus plant have long been used to make the women's "grass" skirts. Nowadays, women wear long, loose, puffed-sleeved dresses (called *puletasi* on Samoa, *nikautang* in Micronesia). These styles are based on the clothing introduced by the early missionaries. Appliquéd skirts are also worn.

Plant fibers are still used for making hats, sleeping mats, and larger bags for carrying and storage. The practice of tattooing and body painting is now found only among some tribal elders. On Samoa, men wear the attractive *lavalava*, or wraparound sarong, found commonly all over Polynesia, and *leis*, the floral necklaces, offered to the gods in ancient times, but with which visitors and tourists are greeted today. During traditional religious dances, six kinds of *lei* were used, employing different materials: mountain ferns (*palapalai* and *pala'a*), red berries (*pukeawe*), mountain tree blossom (*lehua*), a tiny flower (*a'ali'i*), and a scented vine (*maile*). There are many different styles of *lei*, which encompass twining and stitching, as well as a tradition of combining flowers, leaves, and feathers.

Today, most of Micronesia and Polynesia is populated by immigrants from all over the world. For example, the northern Mariana Islands are home to Spanish, Filipino, Korean, and American immigrants, as well as the native Chamorros. This has resulted in a Spanish Roman Catholic culture overlaid with an American lifestyle. In Fiji, the Indian population, some descended from indentured laborers, others independent immigrants, maintains its Hindu, Muslim, and Sikh traditions in both lifestyle and dress, and now outnumbers native Fijians.

The Pacific Islands

This area is a good source of costumes made from natural fibers, such as bark and grass. Natural coloring agents are also used, such as black pigment from burned candlenuts and red from clay. Banana leaf stencils are also used to create patterns.

Dance festivals are important to these islanders; and today Fijians, Cook Islanders, and Paakehaa New Zealanders often join with the Maori of New Zealand, who are ethnically of the same Polynesian heritage, to stage them. There are 40 tribes in New Zealand in all, forming 10 percent of the small 3.1 million population.

HAWAII

In the north Pacific lies Hawaii, comprising a whole chain of islands extending some 1,600 miles (2,580 kilometers) diagonally on the Tropic of Cancer, from Hawaii Island, the largest, up to Niihau, to the northwest. Hawaii became the 50th state in 1959. There are fewer than 9,000 pure Hawaiians, most of whom live in subsistence-farming enclaves, such as Kalapan, on Hawaii Island,

and Hana, on Maui Island. The rest of the population is of Puerto Rican, Korean, Russian, Spanish, and Filipino descent. Hawaii has been in danger of losing its indigenous culture completely. In 1982, for instance, 4.3 million tourists came to visit the island, a total that overwhelms the native population. However, in recent years there has been a renaissance of interest in Hawaiian culture.

The traditional robes of the Hawaii chiefs were feathered cloaks and headdresses of yellow feathers. *Tapa* (otherwise called *kapa*), or bark cloth, was used to make clothing, and the manufacture of this was a virtually lost art until modern craftswomen began researching it – mainly in other South Pacific islands where women still practiced

*ABOVE MIDDLE: **Musicians of Moorea, Tahiti,** carrying traditional stringed instruments. The males wear the wrapped sarong that is found all over Oceania's islands. The woman's dress is a westernized adaptation with a fitted bodice. Originally she would have worn only a lei, or garland of flowers or leaves, like the men and a fiber skirt. There is a complex lore of lei making, using flowers, leaves, and feathers in numerous combinations; for religious dances six distinct types would be specified.*

*LEFT: **Hand-printed or hand-blocked fabrics** are found all over the islands of Oceania, in patterns that suggest the cultural affinities of the islanders with the craft traditions of Southeast Asia. Fabrics are used for a variety of body wraps such as sarongs, or for loose, flowing robes, called puletasi on Samoa and nikautang in Micronesia, for example. These cover-all dress shapes were introduced by European missionaries originally. This young girl wearing this style of dress in Fiji rows a traditional boat, or pirogue.*

RIGHT: Many indigenous Papuan tribes live in Stone Age conditions in west Papua and Papua New Guinea's jungle highlands. The Asmats specialize in elaborate carved totems, ritually used featherwork, and body painting, as seen here. One of their customs is to cut off a finger as a memorial to a dead relative, without losing much dexterity.

LEFT: Many Papuan ritual activities are forbidden by government edict. Warfare was always a "controlled" conflict between groups, with less loss of life than the weaponry and warpaint would suggest. These customs have lost purpose, but the dance and paint stays, as seen here at a cultural show in Simbu Province, Papua New Guinea.

traditional methods. *Tapa* is made from paper mulberry bark, which is softened in sea water, scraped, pounded, felted, sun-bleached, fermented, and pounded again, to produce a workable, felted textile that varies in quality from a tough material similar to corduroy to one as light as fine gauze. *Tapa* designs were transferred to the loose women's robes, or *muu muu*, and are the source designs for the popular Hawaiian shirts (originally plain dyed workshirts also introduced by missionaries).

Jewelry is very varied in Hawaii: jade from the Union of Myanmar (Burma) and Taiwan is popular, as is enameled jewelry, made fashionable in the 19th century by ladies of the royal court who liked their names inscribed in gold on black enamel-work. Necklaces of pink, white, or black (from Maui) coral are prevalent. In a sense, tourism provoked "Hawaiiana," and that in turn has created a successful arts-and-craft activity, satisfying both authentic and commercial motivations.

Nowadays, Hawaiian culture is officially part of the education system and *kupuna*, or elders, visit classrooms to talk about their ancestors and to relate myths and stories. Hula schools, which teach the dance and chanting that enshrine the culture (the original people had no written language), are very popular. Many Hawaiian families have left the cities and gone back to the land as a result of this new awareness.

TONGA AND FIJI

On both of these islands *tapa* is made. Tongan *tapa* is decorated by holding a relief pattern under the cloth, four bark-sheets thick, and overpainting the lines, in a manner similar to taking a brass rubbing.

Tongan handiwork is considered among the finest in all Polynesia. Fijian *tapa* (*masi kesa*) is distinctive for its geometric, flowing designs, created with stencils of green pandanus and banana leaves. Red coloring is obtained from clay, and black pigment from burned candlenuts. Candlenut is a product of the kukui tree, and is so named because its oil was used for lamps. The nuts are also polished to a high brown-black sheen and are very popular accessories.

TAHITI

On the French island of Tahiti, the *pareu*, or wrap skirt or robe, is hand-blocked or hand-

BELOW: These ladies' robes demonstrate the simple strength of floral patterning characteristic of Tahiti. They suggest one source of inspiration for the late collages of Henri Matisse, who lived there for a while.

painted in vivid colors. An adaptation that has become traditional is the making of *tifaifai*, a technique of two-layer patchwork taught by early missionaries to replace the islanders' "primitive" dress. This quilted fabric, used for bed covers and cushions, to cloak newlyweds, and as a burial shroud, is highly valued. Tahitian women have their own "trademark" designs. The artist Henri Matisse was said to have been inspired by the Tahitian patchwork techniques, adapting them for use in his "gouaches decoupées."

NEW GUINEA

In the southwest Pacific lies the island of New Guinea, which gained its independence from Australia in 1975. Irian Jaya is in the west part of New Guinea and is a province of Indonesia, Papua New Guinea is in the east. West and east Papua peoples live at a subsistence level in the mountain areas as pig farmers and sorghum eaters. There are approximately 800,000 Papuans and 240 language groups. The west Papuan groups best known to outsiders are the Danis and the Asmats. The Dani women weave knotted nets. These are part clothing, part bag, and are used to carry pigs or gathered food. Dani and Asmat men wear little other than penis gourds and an occasional grass skirt. The Dani males also wear a "necktie" of cowrie shells as a throat protector – as this is considered the entry point of the body for diseases and evil spirits.

Nose ornaments or headbands trimmed with kus-kus fur, feathers, and cowrie shells may be sported by the men for ceremonies. The influence of missionaries and other foreigners has resulted in many of the young men adopting shirts and shorts, with the girls wearing cotton T-shirts or dresses.

New Zealand and Australia

RIGHT: *Australia's original inhabitants, the Aborigines, had little use for clothing; Captain Cook noted that they left gifts of cloth on the beach. Their culture is largely oral, and they still stage "corroborees," to sing and dance their history, celebrate the hunt or battle, or for initiations (authentic events are held in secret at night around fires, stirring clouds of red earth with the feet). For Aborigines white is the color in which the dead return, so it is used for painted body symbols.*

BELOW MIDDLE: **The** *original immigrants to the many islands of Oceania covered great distances in boats, taking few possessions. This is reflected in their non-material culture, and explains the historic importance of sea trade and warfare. Rowing songs and tales of heroes feature in festivals, at which Maori men wear their fiber costumes, made of grasses and reeds, and paint their faces to imitate symbolic tribal face tattoos, as is seen here.*

The cultures of the New Zealand Maoris and the Australian Aborigines have been neglected in the past, but now with interest in their traditions growing, it is being revived through dance displays and festivals.

There are over 1,000 ceremonial Maori gathering places, or *marae*, in New Zealand, belonging to descendants of some distinguished ancestor, where the people gather to speak their language, eat their food, and keep up the ritual tellings of lineage.

In general, Maoris today wear western-style clothing, except for special ceremonies and events such as church festivals. Women wear headbands, with or without feathers, sacred neck pendants called *tiki*, shark-teeth ear pendants, bodices in *taaniko* patterns, flax skirts, and red or black underskirts. *Taaniko* is a type of finger weaving using a native flax plant (looms were unknown to Maoris). The colors used are red, white, and black.

The men also wear a headband, with or without feathers, a bandolier patterned in *taaniko*, a kilt worn over a pair of shorts, and perhaps à cloak. Since tattooing is no longer the usual custom, the faces of the men are painted with traditional patterning. The bodice and bandolier are modern innova-

tions – the bodice top was introduced for modesty's sake by missionaries, and the bandolier is a copy of 19th-century British military gear.

The kilt, grass skirt, or *piupiu* is made of dried strands of flax attached to a waistband. Parts of the strands are scraped, so that they dry out. When dipped in a dye of *whiinau* bark, the scraped parts take color and the unscraped parts remain golden, producing a stark geometric pattern. The grass skirts or kilts make a wonderful rustling noise, intrinsic to the Maori dance movements.

In Australia, Aboriginal culture is largely oral, although elements of their myths and totemistic past are glimpsed in their rock carvings and bark paintings. Their art and culture have undergone a revival, and street theater or "corroborees" now enact stories of Aboriginal history. The "Dreamtime" bark paintings are translated into T-shirt designs.

Key

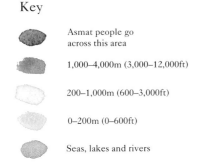

Asmat people go across this area

1,000–4,000m (3,000–12,000ft)

200–1,000m (600–3,000ft)

0–200m (0–600ft)

Seas, lakes and rivers

Note: peoples are shown in italics eg: *Aborigines*

The indigenous people of this region arrived thousands of years ago, in numerous waves of migrations from Asia. There are Melanesian, Polynesian, Micronesian, Euronesian, Eurasian, and other ethnic groups, including Indonesian, Indian, Chinese, and Vietnamese. The earliest settlers also spread from island to island, over the centuries. This pattern of migration tends toward cultures that are largely oral in tradition, and inhabitants who live as seafarers and traders. Forms of dress reflect the lack of technology and show available materials. It is here that grass skirts, feather capes, and shell and beadwork predominate.

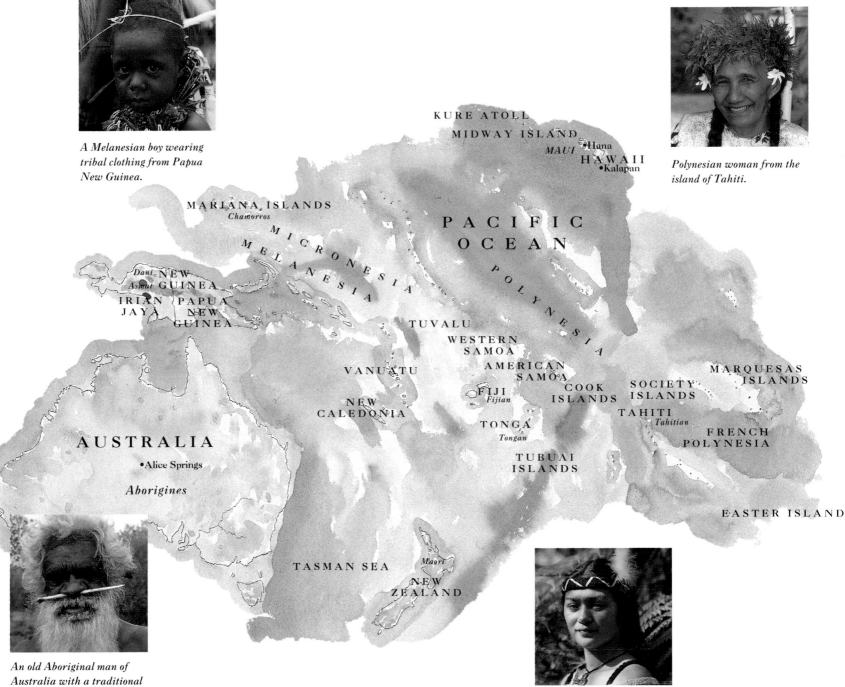

A Melanesian boy wearing tribal clothing from Papua New Guinea.

Polynesian woman from the island of Tahiti.

An old Aboriginal man of Australia with a traditional bone nose ornament.

Maori girl, a native inhabitant of New Zealand.

KURE ATOLL

MIDWAY ISLAND

MAUI •Hana

HAWAII

•Kalapan

MARIANA ISLANDS
Chamorros

PACIFIC OCEAN

MICRONESIA

MELANESIA

POLYNESIA

Dani NEW
Asmat GUINEA

IRIAN JAYA | PAPUA NEW GUINEA

TUVALU

WESTERN SAMOA

AMERICAN SAMOA

VANUATU

FIJI
Fijian

COOK ISLANDS

SOCIETY ISLANDS

MARQUESAS ISLANDS

NEW CALEDONIA

TONGA
Tongan

TAHITI
Tahitian

FRENCH POLYNESIA

AUSTRALIA

•Alice Springs

Aborigines

TUBUAI ISLANDS

EASTER ISLAND

TASMAN SEA

Maori

NEW ZEALAND

FIBER SKIRTS

TOP ROW, LEFT TO RIGHT:

Hula dancer in palm-leaf skirt, Hawaii.

Palm-fiber strip in vegetable-dyed skirt worn by male dancer, Hawaii.

A dyed grass skirt worn by child in Madang Province for a "sing-sing" in Papua New Guinea.

A musician in a dyed grass skirt from Viti Levu Island, Fiji.

A Maori male dancer from New Zealand in a dyed flax piupiu, or kilt.

MIDDLE ROW, LEFT TO RIGHT:

Palm-fiber cloth skirt trimmed with feathers worn by dancer from American Samoa.

Printed sarong and grass skirt worn by hula dancer in Hawaii.

Tongan dancer in block-printed bark-cloth (tapa) wrap dress.

Maori woman in piupiu dyed flax skirt or kilt at a Whakarewarewa meeting house, New Zealand.

Male dancer in grass skirt at Goroka show, Papua New Guinea highlands.

BOTTOM ROW, LEFT TO RIGHT:

Printed bark cloth or tapa wrap dress, worn by dancer from Tapu Island, Tonga.

Woman in grass skirt and bark-cloth rain cape from Papua New Guinea highlands.

Child in traditional painted bark-cloth fabric skirt and cloak on Fiji Island.

Long grass skirt worn by Tanna Island girl on Vanuatu.

Strip palm-leaf skirt worn by Yap Island dancer in Micronesia.

185

Glossary

Achkan An Indian man's long white or beige jacket that flares at knee-level; with stand-up collar and slim sleeves.

Appliqué or applied work The technique of embellishing a fabric or article of clothing with other pieces of fabric, sewn on with concealed or decorative stitches; also used to create designs with braid, ribbon, and other trimmings.

Batik The Indonesian word for a resist-dyeing technique, usually with wax used as the resist. It is widely found in Southeast Asia, India, and Africa.

Baju A shirt or blouse outfit and **sarong** from Southeast Asia.

Broadcloth A densely woven woolen cloth, so named because of the relatively wide loom on which it was originally produced. The term now also refers to some other closely woven fabrics – e.g., cotton broadcloth.

Burga A face veil used in Saudi Arabia.

Burqa (sometimes spelled **Burga**) A long black all-covering outer garment worn by Muslim women in Afghanistan, Pakistan, and the Middle East.

Calzoncillos Baggy trousers for men, made in various styles. They were introduced into Latin America by the Spanish .

Chador Muslim women's head-covering shawl in Iran, or a shawl for both sexes in India. The term also refers to regulation Muslim dress for women.

Chalwar Loose, draped, pleated, or gathered trousers that are fitted tight at the ankle. These trousers are worn by women (usually of the Muslim faith) living in India and also in countries of the Middle East.

Chapan Loose coat or **robe** worn by both sexes in Central Asia.

Chemise Basic long-sleeved shirt, cut from straight pieces of cloth, for under- or outerwear. It was formerly widely worn in Europe by both sexes.

Cheongsam A Mandarin-collared, tight-fitting dress with side slits that crosses over in the front. It originates in Hong Kong and was formerly a looser **robe** for both sexes.

Chirpa A pre-Columbian loincloth or stole worn by men in Uruguay and Chile.

Choli A tight bodice worn with full skirt, or **ghagra,** by women of north India.

Couching An embroidery technique in which a thick thread (sometimes gold) is laid on the surface of a fabric and anchored with tiny stitches in (usually) a finer thread.

Cutwork A form of embroidery in which holes are cut in the fabric and the edges finished with buttonhole or overcast stitch.

Damask A type of fabric (traditionally silk or linen) produced by contrasting areas of satin and twill weave. The design is reversible: on one side the pattern appears in twill, on the other in satin.

Dhoti Full-draped, trouser-like wrapping length of cloth worn by men in India.

Djellabah Hooded, full-length open robe worn by both sexes in the Middle East.

Dolman Loose robe worn widely in Central Asia.

Fez A Turkish round felt hat, or *tarboosh*, usually red, with a soft tassel on the center crown.

Fibula An antique buckle or brooch consisting of a metal circle with a pin shape, which is pushed through cloth and rests across it.

Fichu A small triangular shawl, usually in a fine fabric such as muslin or lace.

Fustanella A man's skirt with a mass of **gore** pleats worn in the mountains of Greece.

Gandoura A wide, often open-sided man's **robe** worn in West Africa.

Ghagra A very full, tightly gathered or pleated woman's skirt with much varied decoration worn in north India.

Godet A triangular insert that adds width to the lower edge of a skirt, the hip area of a jacket, or the underarm panel of a **robe**.

Gore A triangular or tapering section of a flared skirt.

Gusset A triangular or diamond-shaped insert placed in underarm seams or in trouser crotches for ease of movement.

Haik An all-encompassing white **robe** that originates in Saudi Arabia.

Hanbok An authentic Korean costume.

Hardanger A form of geometric openwork embroidery that originated in Norway.

Huipil An indigenous Indian tunic garment made from several narrow loom widths and found in Central America.

Ikat A Malaysian term for dyeing warp or weft yarns in bundles before weaving, to produce blurred, randomly colored, but repeating patterns of great complexity and beauty.

Jaspé ikat A Guatemalan cloth with dark patterns.

Kaftan A tunic-shaped garment with wide sleeves worn by both sexes, found both in Africa and in the Middle East.

Kain A **sarong** worn by both sexes in Indonesia.

Kameez A flared **tunic** top with long, slim sleeves, worn with baggy trousers, or **salwar,** by Muslim women of the Punjab area and elsewhere in India.

Kasuri ikat An indigo **ikat** cloth from Japan.

Kebaya A shaped blouse of variable cut and length, which is worn with a **sarong** or **kain** by women in Indonesia.

Keffiyeh A checkered cloth used as a head cover by Arab men. The black-and-white weave is particularly associated with Palestinians.

Kente cloth A fine grade of West African cloth made by Asante and other African women.

Ketoh A hide bowguard used to protect the wrist in archery by North American Indians.

Kimono A tradition of national dress worn in Japan, as well as the name of its principal garment. Literally meaning "piece of clothing," kimono involves layering of straight-cut, wide-sleeved, open robes.

Kola A round embroidered cap for both sexes which is worn throughout India and Asia.

Kurta A men's muslin tunic shirt from North India.

Kosode Old style of **kimono** dressing in Japan.

Lungi A loincloth or brief wrap skirt which is worn by Hindu males in India.

Manta A Spanish term for an indigenous simple cloak. Also the name used for Guatemalan white cloth woven on a broad loom, and the short poncho of the Chilean *huaso*, or cowboy, in Latin America.

Molas Reverse **appliqué** panels made by Cuna Indians in the San Blas islands, Panama. Layers of contrasting cloth are cut to reveal outlines of colors beneath, in patterned gradations. The raw edges are then finished, sometimes with decorative stitching.

Obi A Japanese **kimono** sash.

Opanky A sandal with a broad sole that wraps around the bottom of the foot, covering the toes. It is then tied around the feet and legs with long leather straps.

Ohrna A woman's scarf or stole from India.

Parka A hide over-**tunic** with closed front and hood, worn in the Arctic regions.

Peplum A curved or bias-cut section of a jacket or dress attached at the waist to create fullness over the hips.

Plangi A resist tie-dycing process. The material is tied tightly so that the dye does not penetrate that area. Pebbles or rice are often placed inside the tied material to create a pattern.

Quechquemitl Indigenous Central American woman's top garment made of one long strip of narrow weave cloth folded in various ways for straight seaming, to give a shawl like effect.

Quillwork North American decorative technique using cut feather quills. These are applied to fabric, or stitched together, for vests or decorative panels.

Quilting Most commonly, a technique of producing a warm, padded textile by placing a layer of soft, fleecy, thermal-retentive material between two pieces of cloth and stitching them together in a decorative fashion.

Rebozo A shawl of Spanish origin, worn in Latin America.

Robe This term is used in this book to mean an open crossover garment, as in a bathrobe, and also a closed-fronted, full-length garment worn by men and women in different regions.

Salwar Long trousers cut with a band at the ankle so that fullness falls in folds. Worn by Muslim women in the Punjab with **kameez**.

Sarong A wrap skirt of variable length and modes of drape which is widely worn by both sexes in Southeast Asia and the Pacific Islands.

Serape A term of Spanish origin for a rectangular cloak that is worn in Latin America.

Smock A full-bodied, full-sleeved work over-garment with decorative stitching over gathered fullness. It is worn throughout Europe.

Tagora An Indian loincloth of Central America.

Taaniko Maori finger flax weaving in New Zealand.

Tapa A cloth made from mulberry bark in the Pacific Islands.

Thawb or **thob** An alternative term used for a **robe** or **kaftan** in Middle Eastern countries.

Tracht A term that literally means "that which is worn." It refers to dress derived from historical costume in Austria and Germany.

Trade beads A means of trade or exchange.

Tradecloth A printed fabric that was supplied to colonies. It is now a generic term for a type of fabric, often locally manufactured as well as imported, in traditional patterns.

Tunic This term is used technically in this book for a shape made by folding a length of fabric at the shoulders and cutting a center opening for the head. It is used generally for any loose, long garment. It also describes a classical garment made by tying, pinning, or stitching two pieces of cloth at the shoulders.

Twining A form of fine basketry work found in North America and in the Pacific Islands which is used for making nets, bags, and simple clothing.

Twill A weaving method that produces a diagonal ribbed effect by passing weft threads over two or more warp threads in a stepped pattern.

Wampum Strings of beads of shell made by Native Americans. Also became the term for North American **trade beads**.

Bibliography

Altermann, Gail, *Ethnic Dress*, Costume Society of America, 1989.

Achjadi, Judi, *Indonesian Women's Costumes*, Djambatan, Jakarta, 1976.

Banateanu, Tancred, *Din Tezaurul Portului Traditional*, Editura Sport-Turism, Bucharest, 1977.

Beckwith, Carol, and Fisher, Angela, *African Ark*, Collins, London 1990.

Beckwith, Carol, *Nomads of Niger*, Collins, London 1984

Bishop, Robert, and Safanda, Elizabeth, *Amish Quilts*, Laurence King, London 1991.

Biswas, A, *Indian Costumes*, Ministry of Information and Broadcasting, New Delhi, 1985.

Bonavia, David, *China Unknown*, Hodder and Stoughton, London 1985.

Barshaw, Angela, *World Costumes*, Adam and Charles Black, London 1977.

China House Gallery, *Richly Woven Traditions*, China Institute in America, New York, 1987.

Cordry, Donald, and Dorothy, *Mexican Indian Costumes*, University of Texas Press, Austin and London, 1968.

Czarnecka, Irena, *Folk Art in Poland*, Polonia, Warsaw, 1957.

Elliot, Aubrey, *Tribal Dress*, Struik Publishing Group, Capetown, South Africa, 1986.

Fairservis, Walter, *Costumes of the East*, Chatham Press, Riverside, Connecticut, 1979.

Feest, Christian, *Native Arts of North America*, Thames and Hudson, London 1980.

Fisher, Angela, *Africa Adorned*, Collins, London 1984.

Flynn, Dorris, *Costumes of India*, Tircolour Books, London 1985.

Folk Art Committee, *Ukrainian Folk Costume*, World Federation of Ukrainian Women's Organizations, Toronto and Philadelphia, 1992.

Highwater, Jamake, *Arts of the Indian Americas*, Harper and Row, New York, 1983.

Garret, Valery, *Traditional Chinese Clothing in Hong Kong and China*, OUP, London 1987.

Gosudarstvennyi, E, *The Art of Costume in Russia*, Aurora Publications, Leningrad, 1983.

Hibi, Sadao, *Japanese Detail*, Thames and Hudson, London 1989.

Hosbon, Sarah, *Family Web: A Story of India*, J, Murray, London 1978.

Homan, Peter, Schefold, R Dekker, V de Jonge, N, *Indonesia in Focus*, Kegan Paul, London 1991.

Jacobson, Margaret, *Namibia's Nomads*, New Holland, London, 1990.

Kalashnikova, N M, *National Costumes of the Soviet People*, Planeta, Moscow, 1990.

Karasik, Carol, *The Turquoise Trail*, H. Abrams, New York, 1993.

Kennedy, Alan, *Costumes Japonais*, Biro, Paris, 1990.

Kwasnik, Elisabeth, I, (ed.) *Bulgaria, Tradition and Beauty*, National Museum and Galleries on Merseyside, Liverpool, 1990.

Lamb, Venice, *West African Weaving*, Duckworth, London, 1975.

Mather, Christine, and Woods, Sharon, *Sante Fé Style*, Rizzoli, New York, 1986.

Lewis, Paul, and Elaine, *Peoples of the Golden Triangle*, Thames and Hudson, London 1984.

Mead, Stanley, *The Art of Taaniko Weaving*, Reed Books, London 1968.

Mejia de Rojas, Idalma, *Change in Colotenango*, Museo de Ixchel, Guatemala, 1989.

Minor, Marz, and Nono, *The American Indian Craft Book*, University of Nebraska Press, Lincoln and London, 1972.

Mrazek, Rudolf, et al, *Bali: The Split Gate to Heaven*, Orbis, London 1983.

Museo Etnologico de Barcelona, *Tejidos de Guatemala*, Ajuntamento de Barcelona, 1989.

Olschak, Blanche, *Bhutan*, George Allen and Unwin, London, 1971.

Paine, Sheila, *Embroidered Textiles*, Thames and Hudson, London, 1990.

Rachow, Ernest, *El Traje Musulman*, Instituto de Estudios Africanos, Madrid, 1953.

Ribaric, Jelka, Radus, *The Folk Costumes of Croatia*, Ethnographic Museum and Spektar, Zagreb, 1975.

Ricciardi, Mirella, *Vanishing Africa*, Collins, London 1974.

Ross, Heather Colyer, *Art of Arabian Costume*, Arabesque, Fribourg, 1981.

Roosevelt, AC, and Smith, JG, *The Ancestors: Native Artisans of the Americas*, Museum of the American Indian, New York, 1979.

Sayer, Chloë, *Mexican Costume*, British Museum Publications, 1985.

Scarce, Jennifer, *Middle Eastern Costume*, Royal Museum of Scotland, Edinburgh, 1981.

Scarce, Jennifer, *Costumes of the Near and Middle East*, Allen and Unwin, London, 1986.

Sichel, Marion, *South America*, B.T. Batsford, London 1986.

Stewart, Ian Charles, *Indonesians: Portraits from an Archipelago*, Paramount/Concept, Singapore, 1984.

Stone, Caroline, *The Embroideries of North Africa*, Longmans, Essex, 1985.

Snowden, James, *The Folk Dress of Europe*, Mills and Boon, London 1979.

Song-Mi, Yi, *Korean Costumes*, IBM Gallery of Science and Art, New York, 1992.

Third World Guide 93/4, Instituto del Tercer, Mundo, Columbia, 1994

Tilke, Max, *Costume Pattern and Designs*, Rizzoli, New York, 1990.

Weir, Sheila, *Palestinian Costume*, British Museum Publications, London 1989.

Wilcox, Ruth Turner, *The Dictionary of Costume*, BT Batsford, London 1970.

Wood, Margaret, *Native American Fashion*, Van Nostrand Reinhold, New York, 1981.

World Directory of Minorities, compiled by The Minority Rights Group, Longmans, London, 1991.

Yamanaka, Norio, *The Book of Kimono*, Kodansha International, Tokyo and New York, 1982.

Index

Acknowledgments

I am most grateful to my longstanding friend, Caroline MacDonald-Haig, who wrote the European sections of this book and who was a wonderful support editorially; Angela Jeffs for all her notes on Japan; Chenube Roy for researches in South Africa, including meeting Aubrey Elliot; Pip Rau for her expert knowledge on Afghanistan and Central Asia; Neal Street East, Covent Garden for the loan of special costumes and several valuable books and Madeline Ginsburg for her general encouragement.
I would also like to thank The Royal Geographical Society who kindly allowed me to use their library.
Caroline MacDonald-Haig also wishes to thank Franka, Flora Turner, Ken Ward, Gill Adam, Rosemary Gibb, Michael Duharnis, The Ukrainian Bookshop, London W2, Father Alexander Natzen, Aglika Markova, Olga Ratycz, Irene Garland, Jane Gordon-Dean, Zbyszek Szydlo and Sarah Posey.
My thanks also go to Judith More of Mitchell Beazley for making the book possible, Chris Morley, Emma Shackleton, Larraine Shamwana and Geoff Fennell, for all their efforts with the text and the design, and a particular acknowledgment is due to my editor Mary Lambert for all her hard work, tact and patience with a demanding project and author.